FINDING HOME IN THE FOURTH
DIMENSION

ALSO BY CAROLE LUNDE

The Divine Design
How to Spiritually Interpret Your Life

You Are in The Bible
Metaphysical Bible Interpretation for Your Life

Stories from Martha's House
The Biblical Gathering Place for Friends and Strangers

Deborah, Judge, Prophetess, and Seer
The Woman Born to Become God's Military Leader

The Great Highway of Life
Navigating the Bible Through Metaphysics

FINDING HOME IN THE FOURTH DIMENSION

CAROLE M. LUNDE

FINDING HOME IN THE FOURTH DIMENSION

iUniverse books may be ordered through booksellers or by contacting:

iUniverse
1663 Liberty Drive
Bloomington, IN 47403
www.iuniverse.com
1-800-Authors (1-800-288-4677)

ISBN: 978-1-5320-3981-2 (sc)
ISBN: 978-1-5320-3982-9 (e)

Print information available on the last page.

iUniverse rev. date: 12/22/2017

Dedication

Finding Home in The Fourth Dimension is dedicated to Rev. John Weaver Hess, Unity Minister, teacher, and dear friend. Weaver ran the counseling office at Unity School of Christianity in 1983 and 1984 when I was a ministerial student there. He was affectionately known as Weaver by the students.

He told me that I was "living in the fourth dimension a majority of the time, while most people lived in the third dimension, touching the fourth only occasionally." It took many years for me to understand and grow into what he said.

Weaver attended San Francisco Theological Seminary and began his ministerial career. In 1962 he founded Grace Presbyterian Church in Sacramento, California. From 1981 to 1987 he served as faculty and was ordained a Unity minister at Unity School of Christianity. He peacefully passed on into his next expression in living in 2015.

Thank you, my friend, and God speed on your way.

Acknowledgement

I would like to thank my friend and editor, Steve Sanders, who faithfully reads and edits my work. He was always encouraging me to continue through the many times I felt unsure of how to proceed and what should come next in this book. Bless you, Steve, for being such a caring friend.

Introduction

A person's life story is a journey and at the same time a saga that has a message to be shared with others. I wanted to tell the story of a relatable psychological and spiritual development. Becky's journey is inspired by a true story.

As with all of us, the past molded my responses to the present world. It meant decades of struggle for me to learn to be in command of the kingdom of my own being, my feelings, and responses. My hope is my readers will find some similarities with their own experiences and perhaps some insights. Also I hope that you, dear reader, will enjoy the story.

Writing this gave me an opportunity to view my life from another perspective. Reliving some of the trauma while writing it was unavoidable, but it gave me a way to continue to neutralize some of the negative memories and treasure the good ones. The characters brought up hidden emotions I didn't know were still there. As I created the characters, they taught me to look again at my responses to life with courage, love, and gentle humor.

I thank Becky, her family and all her friends for giving me gifts I could not have found within myself without their love. I gave them life though only on paper, and they returned the favor by imprinting themselves on my heart.

The Apostle Paul said, "…forgetting what lies behind and straining forward to what lies ahead I press on toward the goal for the prize of the upward call of God…" *Philippians 3:13* Spirituality is our goal.

A friend introduced me to spiritual teachings years ago, and declared that she would never try to live them. She only liked to read and argue about them. In ministerial school I was curious as to why so many people read the books about Truth Principles but did not comprehend that they needed to live them. The teachings are a precious roadmap and to live them is the only way to teach. In living them day by day, we learn how to ultimately live the spiritual life.

As I wrote in the dedication, a teacher said to me, "You have to realize that most people live in the third dimension and touch the fourth occasionally. You live in the fourth dimension all the time and touch the third occasionally." This was a mystery to me that another saw in me what I did not see or even understand at that time. I was humbled. I did not know how this happened or when. Now that I look back upon my journey there were many guides such as this friend who pointed out that I was on a path and I did not yet realize the true nature of it. They shined a light in a direction and slowly I began to realize what this path was about.

In Spirit there is no ego pride or thought of unworthiness. Pride and fear are nonexistent in the fourth dimension. There is only "well done good and faithful servant. Now step up higher." As written in the Book of Revelation, St John the Divine stepped up higher and said he was in the spirit. In this state he was taken high above the battles directly to the New Jerusalem.

I certainly didn't start out in the New Jerusalem. I started taking classes first in Science of Mind and then in Unity. I read books and more books. There were books in my kitchen, my living room, the bathroom, the car, and my place of work. Truly a wonderland was opening to me that I was thrilled to explore. It lifted me from a dim three-dimensional existence where I thought I was a victim of circumstances, to become the hero of my life.

In the three-dimensional level, being the hero of my life meant battling through circumstances with wit, resources and fortitude. I was a single mother, holding down two or three jobs, raising two sons, finishing my college degrees, and deciding upon a career. The question would keep coming to me, "Is this all there is?" I wanted to be a counselor and I counseled at the university for a few semesters. It was good to help people with their problems, but in that setting, I couldn't talk to them about their deeper question which was spirituality.

A great example today is the Dalai Lama who knows no fear, only love, joy, and peace. In living in this fourth dimension he has terrified the entire Chinese government. They want to control or eliminate him. But how do you control someone who has no fear? How do you instill hate for someone who has only love? How to you squelch joy and peace with the powerlessness of darkness? You can light one small candle and no matter how large the room of darkness, it cannot put out the light. The light always puts out darkness.

It is easy to slip into the quandary of "How do I do this?" The key is that we don't do it. We recognize our Original Nature and Truth comes forth from within. In the physical world the wisdom is, the harder we work the more we will accomplish and gain. The more doors of psychological wisdom that we knock on and classes of gurus that we attend, the more discouraging it becomes. We try to walk their path, thinking we either don't already have one or we need the to find it through them. When we strive to reach it, when we are busy trying to get there, we create shadows of doubt and confusion. Our path is already within us, a path of light, a realm without shadow, darkness, difficulty, or strife. In the spiritual world we don't work hard, but simply let go of strife and allow it to come forth.

This book is about finding home in a world that obscures the spiritual nature and the hides the way to it.

Contents

One

Touching the "save" selection on the menu, Professor Rebecca Lawrence Richardson Temple, Ph.D. pushed back from her computer. She swung her chair around and put her feet up on a box she hadn't yet unpacked. Her office never looked like she had moved into it completely, even though she had been there for nine years.

The class she was designing needed a bit more research and she gazed over the books that surrounded her on all four walls. Over the bookcases were framed certificates and awards. A large ornately framed copy of "The Road to Emmaus" and a wall hanging, "O Jerusalem," both depicting Jesus in scenes described in the Gospels, hung on one wall. Tacked on the bulletin board, on another wall near the door, were pictures of family, favorite jokes, Post It notes, and a calendar.

Soon Becky was not seeing what was around her, but what was looming up inside. Her earliest memory began to unfold in her mind. She was five years old, sitting on the floor of the kitchen in her childhood home, begging her mother to let her see the family album again.

"I'll let you look at it if you promise not to cry," said her mother.

Becky nodded and reached for the tattered album, bound with a black woven cord that tied the pages and the covers loosely together. Slowly she turned the photograph-filled pages until she came to the one that always brought on her tears. There they were, her father and mother, sister and brother, all smiling. But she, Becky, wasn't there. Mother had explained to her that she hadn't been born yet. It didn't seem to help. She was missing, left out of the happiness signaled by the smiles. Her sadness was overwhelming. Puzzled, Mother eased the album out of Becky's hands and put it back into the drawer. She pulled Becky up from the floor and sent her outside to play.

This was Becky's first memory of a strong emotional reaction to something. It presented itself in her mind over and over, as if it were a doorway. She couldn't determine if it represented a doorway through which she had arrived, or a doorway she was looking for that held the solution to a mystery. What mystery could that be? Why did it have such an impact on her as a young child?

A collection of cartoons and quips were festooned under one push pin. Her favorite was on top. It was one of those large square cartoons showing a couple of beings hatching out of a small space vehicle and looking around in amazement. "How did we get here?" At the bottom in very small print it said, "Wrong turn at Arcturus!"

That is what life had felt like to Becky so far, a wrong turn somewhere. Here she was near midlife and that feeling was still with her. Her brothers, sister, and cousins seemed to have made the right turns or the right decisions. Their lives followed the pattern of the American norm for happiness and success. They were educated, married, had children, steady careers, and retired comfortably. Becky's higher education had a thirteen-year interlude. She completed two years of college right after high school, and went back fifteen years later to finish her bachelors and advanced degrees. Her three marriages were unsatisfactory and therefore short. Her career consisted of a nonsensical zigzag of clerical jobs, sprinkled in among her marriages, all going nowhere. She raised her two children alone and counted herself most fortunate that, somehow, they turned out well despite her wanderings and misadventures.

Matt was gone. Matt Gregorsen was the love of Becky's life. Becky was the love of Matt's life as well, but timing and circumstances had eventually driven them apart. Thirty years later his life was snuffed out by a disease that arrived suddenly like an alien destroyer taking him painfully and quickly. Matt was the background music for Becky's life. Somewhere in the distance was that melody that she could hear and dance to in her dreaming. Now the music was more like a distant echo. The music of that relationship, that dream, was fading away despite her best efforts to keep it going.

They met by accident in Glenwood Park. Was it an accident? She saw him walking toward her on her usual path in the wooded area. Becky didn't believe in love at first sight, but whatever happened at that moment certainly fit the description of it. At first sight of him she couldn't breathe and her knees went weak. They stopped to chat for a while and discovered they had mutual friends. They set off on the path together and on a journey of joy, pain, and mystery that would not end even with their eventual parting, and not even with his death.

This had been as mysterious to Becky as her childhood reaction to the pictures of her family that shouted her absence. She and Matt were bound together forever and yet, except for correspondence and an occasional lunch together when she was in town, absent from each other's lives for over thirty years.

Matt was gentle, a rebel, hilariously funny, and lost in his own world of unanswered questions. His family's chosen religious affiliation placed many restrictive demands upon his childhood. Matt's anger and resistance to his parents' religion grew over the years. He told Becky, when they met, that he had just lived the first relatively happy year of his life. Becky was shocked to hear this. It was her first window into his troubled past and his valiant struggle to overcome it on his own.

The age of self-help psychology was dawning. Becky had entered college for the second time after fifteen years to finish her degrees. She was still searching for a major or focus of study that would satisfy her interests and the requirements of graduation. She was delighted to find a new department at Hamilton University that featured this area. Going back to school Becky had discovered a piece of "being here" and why she felt so "not here" throughout her life. But eventually school would end, and then what?

Becky had brought a reluctant Matt to some of the self-awareness groups that she and her class mates were conducting. It became an amazing experience for him. He discovered that people actually liked him. His group mates looked up to him and wanted to be with him to chat and share. Matt had been reclusive for so long that he had forgotten, if he ever knew, what it was like to be accepted and even revered.

The telephone rang and Becky jumped, kicking over the box under her feet. It was Georgina with the latest campus news. Georgina knew everybody and everything that was happening in the important places. Becky was sure that Georgina remembered everyone she had ever met including every detail of their lives. It was fascinating to see her move through a crowd smiling, laughing, and chatting, and come away with a whole new group of close friends. Becky was more reluctant to jump right in. She had trouble envisioning herself in the picture, any picture. Becky was a loner and enjoyed being alone with her work, her music, and her books. Put Becky in front of a microphone with a class of students and she was in her element. Give her a class to teach and she was energized. Small talk and opening new conversations one-on-one exhausted her.

South Bennington College was a midsize college in the small-town setting provided at Johnston Crossing. It was just right for Becky. She was professor of Psychology of Religion which enabled her to explore with students two fields that she was most interested in. Their lively discussions brought these two studies together as a basis for understanding the interaction of religion and psychology.

Georgina was professor of vocal music studies and often coached Becky in her singing. Becky was a late bloomer when it came to singing. It had become an avocation as Becky continued to train her voice, which was surprisingly beautiful and powerful. Becky and Georgina spent many evenings together at the opera and area theaters enjoying the music, critiquing the performances and gathering new ideas to try.

"What's up Georgi? Any heads rolling today? Do we still have jobs?'

"No bloodletting today, Beck. But there is a rumor afoot that two great, brilliant, handsome guys are being hired, and we'll need to check them out!"

"Right. Two aging divas setting upon the young and tender new hires. That should chase them off. What's really up?"

"These guys are real, Beck. Well maybe not great, brilliant and handsome, but interesting. One teaches Kabbalah and Religious Mysticism, and the other New World Religions. You've got company. You can psych them out along with their religions."

"Holy cow, Georgi! How did this happen? We haven't had any new blood here since you and I were hired back in the dark ages. Did the college get a grant or an endowment or something?"

"Research. It is a research grant sponsored by the Morgan and Dunn Foundation, whoever they are. It is supposed to be a four-year grant. And if all goes well, funding could become permanent."

"I didn't think we had anyone here forward thinking enough to apply for something like that. It took me years to get the powers-that-be to move away from old Freudian thinking into a psychology that was new and at least usable."

"Bulletin! Welcoming tea tomorrow at three o'clock in the president's suite. What are you wearing?"

"Let me catch my breath. Clothes… What have I got that is suitable to wear to meet two guys who could be dragons or trolls."

"What if they aren't dragons and trolls as you say? What if they are the right and perfect ones for you or me?"

"Matt was my right and perfect soul mate. I'm not looking for another. Nothing measures up to the feeling I had for him right from the start."

"How about coming down to earth for a bit, Beck? You don't need to continue this self-imposed exile forever, you know."

"I did that once, Georgi. After Matt and I broke up, I went for a teddy bear of a guy who would be my hospital while I licked my wounds. Of course I didn't characterize it that way when I met Allan. I was going for love regardless of our differences in education and career. He was a factory worker and I was getting my master's degree. It didn't make any difference to me, but eventually it did to him. Even after he took a few college courses and did really well, he couldn't get past it. He began lying and cheating on me. Not fun. No more."

"Well, let's just look. Window shoppers don't buy anything, right?"

"Right. Leave your credit card home. See you there."

Window shopping is what Becky thought she did best when it came to life. She was on the outside looking through the window at the party going on inside. She wasn't really there. She wasn't in the picture. Thank God for Georgi who pulled her along socially and fronted for her in the gatherings.

Children are to be seen and not heard. In Becky's case it was better not to be seen at all. If she wasn't within her father's sight, he wouldn't be irritated with her. She never knew exactly what irritated him, but she knew he would rather she was not around. Becky would stay out of sight. He would listen to his opera on weekends, and no one dared let a pin drop. He escaped into the music and didn't want to be brought back to reality, having the highlight of his experience spoiled by a noisy kid. Lord help anyone who said something when the singer was hitting that diva note. It was definitely better not to be there at all. Becky did her best to be absent as much as possible wherever she was.

Her childhood friend Sandy lived across the small street that ran between their backyards. Sandy was always dressed right, her white bucks (oxfords) were always polished pure white. If Becky and Sandy went for ice cream cones together, it would be Becky who got ice cream drips on her clothes and shoes. Sandy managed every drop without spilling one. And Sandy's father was always nice to her. Becky wondered why her own father could not speak to her as kindly. Lots of other fathers were nice to their kids. Why not hers?

Becky wondered if that was why she married men who could not do her any emotional damage. They were weak or inept, and Becky would be their rescuer. They were not bad people, but not particularly esteemed by others, so Becky would be their protector. They were not very interesting, so Becky would turn to other interests. The marriages died of lack of interest and neglect. She was attracted to more interesting men, but couldn't trust that they would keep her heart safe. She had to protect herself. Don't "be there" for them and get hurt.

Georgina and Becky arrived at the tea determined to look and be cool. They stayed at the edge of the room looking over the top of heads to spot the guests of honor. Georgina was leaning so far forward on tip toes that she nearly tipped over the h'ordeurve tray carried by a student who was serving them. After profusely apologizing to the student Georgina whispered to Becky, "There is a short sort of rotund guy with lots of black wavy hair and a taller slimmer one with thinning blonde hair talking to the president. I wonder which one is in which department!"

The president touched his glass with a spoon for attention. He introduced short dark-haired Chaim Levin as the Kabbalah teacher and the tall one, John Edward Sherman, as the New World Religion person. Their qualifications were long and impressive, and everyone applauded vigorously. Becky always dreaded the awkward introductions, the socially shallow and polite inquiries about each other's work. Couldn't she just run into them in the cafeteria and drop into an informal chat or something? But no, now comes the reception line with the president introducing each of the staff to the newcomers.

It was like being in the first grade at five years old. Becky had been only five when she entered first grade. All the kids seemed to know what to do, where to go and what to say. The teacher seated Becky in a separate row from Sandy, and Becky was lost. She didn't know anyone else and a strange girl, very tall, blocked Becky's view of Sandy. The teacher told Becky to pay attention to the front of the room and the black board. Tears came. Hot embarrassing tears. She wanted to hide, but where.

Becky was known as a cry baby that first year. Especially when the school nurse came to give them shots. The students lined up in the hall and went into the school kitchen one at a time to face the terror of the needle. Becky was so frightened that she became hysterical and had to be taken home. Many painful years later mother would say she should have kept Becky home until she was six and things would have been better.

The next day the classes at South Bennington were filled with buzzing about the new teachers. Mostly it was the girls who whispered and giggled everywhere in the halls and corners of the classrooms. At lunch Georgina and Becky decided it would be a good idea to post a "Welcome" message on their bulletin boards for the new teachers, outlining their bios and qualifications. That seemed to quell the speculation among the students, and it also brought the new teachers into their rooms after classes for that informal chat Becky had dreaded at the tea.

Thank heaven Chaim said his name before Becky pronounced it with a "ch" making him sound like a doorbell. She couldn't quite get the same beginning sound he did, but he didn't seem to mind. Hebrew was not her forte. Neither was Kabbalah, but she would read more about it when she got home.

Yes, that was her way of getting around the embarrassment of not knowing. She was chronologically and physically a year younger than her junior high classmates. They spoke of bodily functions about which she knew nothing. The girls suspected she didn't know, so they kept poking fun. Becky was too ashamed to ask the girls or her mother. She would simply look it up later or bluff her way along until the information became available. Everyone else was in the know, and again she was not included.

In junior high Becky met her friend, Karla. Karla was at the top of the heap scholastically. Her parents had consented to allow her to skip a grade. Becky and Karla had something in common. They were both younger than their classmates. At first Karla, who was transferred in from another school and had no close friends, was skeptical of Becky who seemed to dog her steps. For better or worse, and for all their challenges together and apart, it seemed to be written in the stars that their friendship quickly grew.

Chaim was warm and personable. He was unpretentious about himself, his credentials which were considerable, and his deep involvement in the mysteries of life. Becky became more at ease in his presence knowing that she could ask him things without feeling judged. She didn't have to run away to secretly read so she could appear intelligent and informed. He didn't make her feel stupid and clumsy. He made her feel welcome in his world, even though she couldn't actually be in his world. But she was happy to look through the window that he provided. She was happy to be a student. It was the closest she could come to being in the picture.

Becky was waiting for Georgina in the school cafeteria. Chaim came over to her table, full tray in hand, and Becky invited him to sit down. Georgina would be along any minute, but it was nice to have a few minutes to chat with him alone.

"How are you settling in?" Becky began. She remembered how awkward and alone she had felt years ago moving to a new place.

"Well," said Chaim, "it has been interesting. It seems that I have arrived ahead of my funding, ahead of my books, and ahead of the preparation of my office space. Other than that, it is great! I am doing well. Some of the students have volunteered to clean up the office area and draw a map for me to the kosher food store in Springfield."

"How fortunate that Springfield has such a place! I thought everything would be early American pilgrim fare. We're so patriotic in New England."

"Where there are Jews there is kosher, and we are everywhere. Just kidding. I was surprised too. I thought I would have to do my grocery shopping by mail order."

"Your bio mentioned that you lived in Safed, Israel, for several years. What is it like? Why did you decide to live there?"

"Safed, as Americans pronounce it, is a city high in the mountains in northern Israel where the Kabbalah was written. The name has several pronunciations, most of which are unintelligible. I went there to find the roots of Kabalah and savor the atmosphere of the place. Actually the old city is largely rubble because of the earthquakes. Most of the buildings have fallen down and they've given up rebuilding it, just to have it fall down again. The old part is an artist colony now. I really enjoyed the rarified air, its remoteness, and the mystical feeling that the ancient Rabbis are still there in spirit."

"I hope to travel to Israel someday. I'll definitely put Safed on my list of places to spend some time."

Georgina came in with her usual flourish, greeting and calling out to those she knew. Becky smiled up at her, pulled out a chair for her, and settled back to eat her own lunch. She knew Georgina would pick up the conversation right away and carry it on through lunch. Becky was always hesitant to ask questions, feeling like she might be prying, but Georgina had no such compunctions. She gathered information as comfortably as an interviewer. Her interviewees never seemed to mind. In fact it always intensified the connections she made. Becky watched in amazement, but still content to just observe.

John Sherman was sitting alone in a far corner of the dining room. He seemed to be deeply absorbed in a book. Becky wasn't sure if he appeared unavailable because he didn't want company or if was the reading was urgent. Either way, it had the same effect. No one had approached him.

Becky resolved that she would drop by his table to say "hello" after she turned in her tray. Taking a deep breath as she turned from the tray window that went into the kitchen, she started for his table but he had gone.

"What's the matter, Beck? You stopped so suddenly."

"I was going to greet John Sherman and ask him how he was doing, but he disappeared. Slipped out while I was returning my tray."

"I stopped in his classroom just before lunch and he was pretty busy or preoccupied," said Georgina frowning a bit. "He didn't exactly brush me off, but offered a brief 'hi' only glancing up. So I left. Maybe it's not a good time or else he isn't very sociable. You never know with these research types."

Maybe he was like Donald Jackson in Becky's high school class. Donald lived two doors up from Becky from first grade through high school. Becky and Donald played together as little kids and he seemed full of energy and curiosity. Some of his curiosity led to hanging dead frogs by their back legs on his mother's wash line to dry them out. Lord knows what for. As years went by Donald became more and more withdrawn. He didn't graduate because of failing grades. Becky went to a dance with him once and he simply abandoned her there. Her mother said she should dance with other fellows too. So she did and he simply left. Someone else walked her home. Men who acted withdrawn and antisocial always bothered Becky after that. Who knew what they were thinking? Twenty-five years later he sent shock waves through their class reunion when he committed suicide, leaving a wife and two young daughters.

Becky and Georgina headed for their classrooms, agreeing to meet after classes for Becky's voice lesson. After hearing about Georgina's experience with John, Becky was almost relieved that John left the cafeteria before she got to him. Was he like Donald? Time would tell. She vowed to let him make the first move next time. She wasn't going to risk rejection or whatever it was Georgina got for her kindly effort.

Voice coaching was something that Georgina loved to do, especially with Becky who had a lot of potential. Most of Georgina's students were college students or younger. Their voices and commitment were not highly developed as yet. It was stimulating for her to work with Becky who called herself a late-blooming diva.

Becky had come to love something she was sure she would always hate. Opera. Since her father was unpleasant about anyone interrupting his listening time, she had associated this music with her childhood feelings about him. She remembered stomping out of the house when she left for college, glad she would never have to tiptoe around or hear that music again.

"What are your plans for your singing, Beck?" You are making this huge investment in your voice and music. What are you going to do with it? Have you thought of a goal?"

"You mean like the Met? Just kidding. I really don't know. I love to sing, and it is a little late for a career in singing. I mean, kids are getting degrees in vocal music and auditions are for those who have won contests and all. You can't even enter a contest if you are over thirty years old. I have thought of music therapy in senior facilities. I read that even patients with Alzheimer's respond to powerful operatic voices. I just figure that something will open up when the time is right. Or it won't. I'm just happy singing for now."

As a teenager Becky had never thought about a career singing. It just didn't come up. She had taken piano lessons for several years prior to junior high. The church choir was the only place she sang and was a good alto. The end to even that singing career came when she was asked to sing a duet with a tenor for the Easter service. It was a classical aria. Becky had no training and with the wrong kind of singing technique, she had managed to put scar tissue on her vocal cords. She thought it was just a little laryngitis from the strain and it would go away. It didn't go away.

For the next twenty-five years she could not string two notes together. Her singing sounded like a dotted line and was slightly painful. So she didn't attempt to sing. Neither did she check with a doctor. She thought talking was good enough. After twenty-five years went by her voice began to return. Her lower register had a smooth line, and little by little the upper register began to function as well. It was a gift from God as far as Becky was concerned, and she vowed she would never sing untrained again. She called a voice teacher and began training. The voice teacher told her vocal cords, given enough time, would heal themselves. But career singers didn't have a quarter of a century to wait, so they sought medical help. Becky was glad she never sought a medical remedy and just left it to heal on its own.

Her plan was to train for a few years and learn good technique. But her voice kept developing far beyond her initial expectations. Just as she had never dreamed she would love opera, she didn't expect she would sound like an opera singer one day. It was a surprise and a joy. How could she make plans or set goals not knowing all of this would happen?

Becky had insisted upon paying Georgina like any other student. She wanted to keep the lessons on a professional basis and not presume upon their friendship. That arrangement also helped her honor her own investment by practicing and progressing.

The stress of the day ebbed away as Becky sang out her heart and soul. She loved the physical act of singing, the emotional expression, and the joy of hearing her own voice as it sailed away to another place. That other place was home, belonging, and peace. Becky saw only glimpses and felt only touches of that magical marvelous place. It wasn't a location on the roadmap. It was her own voice calling back to her to fill her heart. It helped her to return. But to where? It helped her belong, but to who or what?

Two

"Hi, Mom."

"Nathan, where are you? Yes, I know. I can't ask that. How are you and what's up?" Becky stretched out her leg and kicked at her office door to close it.

Nathan was Becky's son who had chosen a career in the CIA, much to Becky's horror. The Central Intelligence Agency of all things. Why not the FBI or something in this country at least? His life was never his own, but he seemed to love the work. Becky knew absolutely nothing about his work except what she read in international spy novels. He always gave her a disgusted "Mother!" with his eyes rolled up when she mentioned them.

"I'll be home sometime next week. Not sure which day. Don't worry, I still have my key and will find you when I get in if you aren't at home. I know where you hang out. Unless of course you have a boyfriend by now."

It was Becky's turn to roll her eyes. "No, no boyfriend. Just me. If I get one I'll have you investigate him for me. I wouldn't want to get tangled up in one of your top-secret cases or blow your cover!"

"Not a chance! I'll have 'em all checked out before they ever get to you. I gotta go. See you soon. Love ya!"

"I love you too. Bye."

Those terse conversations always left Becky feeling like she had somehow failed to communicate something real or special. Other mothers probably gushed out something loving or some relevant news. Becky and Nathan just managed a few jokes, but that is how they always seemed to communicate best. Anything more seemed unnecessary and embarrassed them both.

Lissa was three years older than Nathan, married and traveling the world as well. The difference was Becky usually knew where Lissa traveled. Her office bulletin board was full of postcards from everywhere in the world. "Having a wonderful time. You should come with us next time!"

Didn't the poet, Gibran, say something about our children being our arrows, going far beyond us? Well that was certainly true. Lissa and Nathan seemed to have gone far beyond Becky into a world unknown to her.

Nathan would be home soon. Becky's small townhouse was full, and it was easiest to unfold the living room futon couch when he came. His leave time was usually no more than three days and then he was gone again.

Her dining room served as a music studio or an office with her computer on the table and piles of papers on the floor. Becky ate her meals on a tray in the living room in front of the computer or TV. Formal sit-down meals at home were a thing of the past.

Her second bedroom was a library, lined with book shelves. Becky always disliked public libraries. Libraries were just too neat and quiet. They put her to sleep. So she bought reference books from library sales and did her research at home in her pajamas where she could have music, food, and make a mess in general.

Her parents maintained the family homestead and Becky's room was always made up and ready for her. But Becky had moved from place to place, going to school, getting married, getting divorced, and finding professional positions. Being able to buy houses was not in the realm of possibility. She lived on a shoe string, pay check to pay check. Large apartments that had guestrooms were out of her reach. Becky parked her kids in makeshift bedrooms filled with other things.

Nathan didn't mind the accommodations at all. He was happy to bunk anywhere. Military training made Nathan portable, able to travel light, and be glad when the bed was comfortable. Lissa, however, preferred to stay at a motel when visiting her mother. Since she was usually in the middle of a business trip, it was no problem. But Becky still felt that she had somehow failed them. She saw herself falling short compared to her brothers, sister, and cousins who had accomplished the American dream seemingly without a hitch.

But did she ever want the American dream? Homes, mortgages, life insurance, boats, vacations at resorts? It looked acceptable and stifling at the same time. It was another of those windows that Becky looked through, but never found herself on the inside. She had finally trained her mind to stay away from nagging comparisons when she was in their company. Becky was determined not to let anything spoil her enjoyment of the people she loved.

"Hey, Georgina! Nathan is coming next week!"

"Great! It is always fun to have him here. I have tickets to a show he might like. We'll drag him out of his life of intrigue into some everyday fun!"

"I don't know which day he'll be here or for how long as usual. We could plan so much more if we knew. But like his mother, he doesn't live the standard American dream."

"You two like it that way, and you know it! Neither of you do anything so called standard. Don't you know that you are the envy of those stuck in predictable lives? You look so romantic, flying free and unfettered. At least that's what people think." Georgina had drummed this into Becky's head for several years now.

"I have to admit that I love it, even though it scares me. Nathan loves it and he scares me. I couldn't stand losing him. Why I think he would be any safer in a different life style I don't know. I guess my relatives have all had safe lives, or lives that appear safer than mine anyway."

"So, is it the theater? I have complimentary seats for any performance whether we use them or not. New perk for coaching some of the actors and singers."

"Yes! We'll plan on it either way." Becky hoped with all her heart Nathan would be able to go. It would give them something to share outside of the impenetrable CIA wall.

The arrangements started in her mind immediately: File the piles of papers, put the scattered sheet music away, move the coffee table over against the bookcase, pull out the futon couch and shift it into bed position. Put an air mattress under the futon and pump it up with her cold spot hair dryer setting. Thank heaven she was strong and could move all that stuff. If she started as soon as she got home, all would be ready whenever Nathan arrived.

Chaim poked his head into Becky's room, "Just wanted to let you know I'll be gone for a few days. My father has been ill and seems to have taken a turn for the worse. He is in Los Angeles. I'm leaving shortly."

"Thanks for letting me know. Sorry about your father. Anything I can do? Are you settled in your place?"

"Could I give the movers your name and office number? I have some research stuff coming, and some file cabinets. If you could watch for them and sort of direct them where to put it all in my office, that would really help. Just have them put the file cabinets against the north wall and stack the boxes along the other walls so I can at least walk through. I can make it pretty later." Chaim had that engaging grin that made Becky feel warm and comfortable, as if he were family. Perhaps like a younger brother she never had.

"Sure. I'll do my best. When are they coming?"

"Tomorrow afternoon about two. They are pretty punctual. Mine will be the last stuff off their truck, so they will be eager to get rid of it."

"Perhaps you'll be back in time to meet my son, Nathan. He'll be here sometime next week. He is like a phantom. I never know when he will show up or for how long. He works for the CIA, but I don't know what he does." Becky felt a little stupid hardly knowing what her own son did on his job.

"I understand completely. My brother is in some sort of secret service in Israel, but comes to Washington a lot. Beyond that I know nothing. I'll let you know when I get in. Thanks hugely for the help! Bye."

"Bye…"

How interesting thought Becky. "I wish I could see what is in his research. The mystical always fascinates me."

The next day at one-thirty there was a call and at two o'clock sharp the movers showed up at her office door. Becky dropped what she was doing and guided them to Chaim's office. The students had done a good job of creating some semblance of order already. The movers began bringing in the file cabinets. Not one, not two, but ten! She looked at the labels on the drawers to determine some kind of order. Fortunately the labels were alphabetical.

Then the boxes were brought in on pallets. Four pallets of boxes stacked four high. Sixteen rather large boxes were pushed against the other walls, leaving room to walk between them. No wonder Chaim needed someone to oversee it all. Forget feng shui! The office suddenly resembled the Smithsonian archives after an earthquake. What could be in all of them? Becky was dying to know.

"Georgi, guess what? Chaim's research just arrived. Ten file cabinets partially full and sixteen large boxes of it! We may need to knock out the wall between his office and the storage room next to it. Come and take a peek."

"Be right there."

Becky and Georgina walked through the stacks of materials reading labels, but not being so rude as to open anything. Then quietly they stepped out of his office and locked the door.

"I guess when you get research funding, you have to have something offer, and he certainly seems to," whispered Georgina. "I wonder how many years of work that represents and what he is working on in particular. It looks like enough to set South Bennington on the map!"

"Maybe that is what South Bennington is counting on. We could use a boost of some kind. This is fascinating!"

Nathan arrived on Sunday at noon, a little earlier than he had thought, and Becky was thankful she was prepared. There was just enough time to have lunch and then go to the matinee with Georgina. The play was a comedy entitled "One Night at a Famous Hotel." They were still laughing at dinner that evening.

Nathan broke the news that he had become engaged. Becky was stunned. To whom? When? Where? She was clueless, happy and tearful all at the same time. It was too confusing! All her emotions seemed to crash into each other.

"Mother, we wanted you to be the first to know. We haven't even told Lissa. Her name is Juliette Farone. I met her while on a local assignment here in the states. I couldn't tell you at the time because my assignments are confidential. Even her parents couldn't know." Nathan was really concerned about Becky's possible reaction to hearing about it after the fact. She didn't know he was even seeing anyone.

Becky was still breathless. "It's O.K. I understand. Really I do. When can I meet her? Are you setting a date? Tell me more about her, if that isn't classified too. Just kidding. Do you have a picture?"

"Oh! Yeah." Nathan fumbled with his wallet, hands shaking a little. "It's only a snapshot. We'll get better at this, pictures and all. Our schedules make us crazy."

Juliette was tall and slim, dark hair and a dazzling smile. She was clinging to Nathan and he to her. They looked radiant. Becky felt a happiness well up in herself as well. She was always concerned for Nathan's happiness and hoped he would find someone who loved him as he deserved. She couldn't be happy unless her children were happy, especially Nathan. He seemed so capable and so vulnerable at the same time.

Georgina was already ordering the champagne for a toast. "When is the big day?"

"Well, we haven't gotten that far yet. We're taking things slow. There are a lot of adjustments to be made. I may not stay in the CIA. She is finishing a college degree that she started several years ago. We have to plan how we can fit our lives together and still work at jobs we enjoy."

"Well, let's toast to the success of those plans and many years of happiness!" Georgina could always jump on the train wherever it was going.

Becky was still wordless. Again she felt like she was outside looking in. She would never let Nathan know that. It wasn't his problem, it was hers. She had to include herself wherever possible and not hang back. It was hard to know what the first step should be, but she promised herself she would be alert for it. Oh, if she could only be as smooth as Georgina! If she could only chime right in. Why was it so hard?

The champagne helped Becky ease up and relax. Soon they were laughing and talking about all sorts of things. Nathan relaxed too and was having a good time. How she loved him. From the first moment she saw him after he was born, it was as if she knew him. He looked so familiar, almost like looking at herself. How strange that sounded. But it didn't feel strange. Nathan was as close to representing home to her as she ever felt. He was her very precious son. "Oh, please Juliette, love him. Love him," she silently prayed.

Nathan had to leave before Chaim returned from Los Angeles. He came into his office looking a bit worn and tired. His father had improved a little and became cranky and demanding. Chaim was torn between guilt at leaving his father and family to cope without him, and eagerness to get back to his work.

"Becky! Thanks for watching over my stuff! You did a great job. Everything is just where I imagined it should be. If you have any time, maybe you could help me open some boxes and get started."

Becky was thrilled. Like Chaim, she too was pulled in two directions, heartache at Nathan's leaving so soon and eagerness to see what was in those boxes. She had a sense that a new chapter was opening up for her. The answer to her lifelong struggle just might be there in Chaim's research hidden in one of these mysterious boxes. Could one be eager, thrilled and terrified all at the same time?

"Sure, I'd be happy to help. When shall we start?" Becky did her best not to sound over eager. She hoped Chaim couldn't see right through her.

"Give me a day to get myself together and I'll sound the shofar."

"You have a shofar?" Becky felt a chill run all through her from head to foot.

"Third box from the right. Shabbat shalom!" He picked up his duffle bag and headed out the door.

"Right. It is Friday. Shabbat," thought Becky. "At least I know that much." She made a mental note to stop at the bookstore and pick up some books on Jewish customs and holidays. She could at least start by getting the obvious things firmly in mind.

Becky had been younger than her high school class mates. She started school at five years old. The girls would hide magazines they were giggling over when she came by because she was too young to know about menstrual pads. They were discussing female things and taunted her, accusing her of not knowing what they were talking about. Becky would declare that she did too know, and flounce off to research on her own. Mother had asked her if she knew about "these things" and Becky was too fresh from the humiliation in school to admit she didn't know. So she said, "Of course I know!"

Even when the school nurse drew the blinds in the gym and showed slides to the girls of drawings of the menstrual cycle, Becky found it difficult to connect it to the human body. There were no anatomy books available to the public in those early years. Becky was sure she was the only freshman in college that still wasn't sure where babies came from and never had an occasion to know what a man looked like. Those were supposed to be blissful years of innocence, but to Becky they were painful years of hidden shame and ignorance.

Georgina came to Becky's classroom at the end of the last hour. "Georgi, do you know anything about Kabalah or Jewish rituals?"

"You know, a couple of great books have come out on the subject just recently. Probably Jewish rituals for gentile dummies or something. Let's stop by the bookstore and then find some dinner."

"Dummy is the word. I would really like to dig in deep this weekend and educate myself a bit. I don't want to feel like a complete fool when Chaim speaks of these things. Besides, I think there might be some teachings that I can use in my classes."

"Let me get my stuff and I'll meet you in the parking lot in a few minutes." Georgi sailed out the door. She loved to have a mission and they would exhaust the inventory of the local bookstore and beyond if necessary.

The bookstore's Jewish section turned out to be a treasure trove. There was nothing about being a gentile dummy which relieved Becky. She hated those titles, Computers for Dummies, French for Dummies, etc. It was a comfort and an insult at the same time.

There were books on the Jewish holidays, their meaning and rituals. There were explanations of kosher, how and why to keep foods kosher. There were tie backs to the ancient world. It was all there and Becky bought several books to cover all those subjects. She planned a quiet weekend and lots of reading. She had one class she planned to revamp to accommodate the new material. There was enough time to make it all fit in. She could even ask Chaim intelligent questions.

"Lord, Beck, you always buy a whole library! How do you manage to read all this stuff?"

"Well, I read in it, not necessarily all of it cover to cover. I don't need all the introductions and stuff they throw in. I like to get right to the good parts, take notes, high light, or whatever. I want to lift information out to put into my religion and ritual class that is just beginning."

"You want to teach some of this? What about leaving it up to Chaim?"

"I want the students to have a heads up, sort of an introduction, so they can sound a bit intelligent about his content when they go to his class. I'm not sure what he will be teaching, but it won't hurt to have some students who are a little savvy. We won't look back woodsy."

"You mean you, yourself, want to be a little more savvy. Does it really bother you that much not to be in the know?" Georgina was clearly concerned.

"Yes, I guess it really does. I spent too many years being in the dark. I was a year younger than my grade school and high school classmates and the teasing was awful. I guess I didn't want that awful feeling again, so I began a long time ago to surround myself with reference books to keep me up to date. My home library is about four hundred books. I try to keep it from growing any further by giving books away to the Friends of the Library organization to sell."

"I've seen your home library, but I didn't dream there were for hundred! Wow! I pretty much confine my books to music. If I need to know something else, I'll make an appointment with your library."

"Anytime, and you know it!" They had a good laugh, thinking up names for her collection like "Becky's Brain Books" and "Boot Up Your Brain at Becky's."

Georgina was always expressive of her appreciation of her friendship with Becky. Becky had broadened her areas of interest and helped her apply new ideas to her music. It was great that Becky could sing which made Georgina feel that she had something to share too, in being Becky's voice coach.

They went to dinner at their favorite haunt. It was a funky little restaurant with red checkered cloths and candles on the tables called Mom & Pop's. The owners often played operas over the speakers and sometimes their meal times became sing-a-longs. It was always great fun. They could also hide in a back booth and have those special conversations about anything and everything.

It seemed like an unlikely place to see John Sherman, but there he was. He always seemed to simply appear. They weren't sure they ever saw him actually come through a door. He acted so cool and reclusive, contrasted with this friendly, anything-goes restaurant. He was sitting by himself in the farthest corner as if desiring not to be seen.

"I wonder what new world his religious studies are about," pondered Becky. "I haven't heard word one about what he teaches or what his classes are about."

"I wonder if it is a friendly world where anyone can get in, or just him! Maybe we should ask him."

"Now?" Becky didn't want to give up their cozy dinner time to be magnanimous or curious. Her first brush off from him was enough.

"No, silly, not now. The right time will come along when it will seem appropriate instead of nosey." Georgina had that glint in her eyes that told Becky she would create a way if one didn't come up naturally. Georgina was not too shy to pry just a little. It would be interesting to see if Georgina's fire would thaw the icy Mr. Sherman. It would be fun and terrifying to watch.

Becky knew she could never just launch into someone else's business. She was planning to move closer to the world of Chaim Levin, but for professional reasons of course. Georgina didn't need a reason other than she was Georgina and there was a tempting barrier in front of her to leap over.

Deep in conversation, Becky and Georgina were suddenly aware that John Sherman had approached their booth. They weren't talking about him at that moment, but they stopped their conversation mid-sentence out of sheer surprise.

"I'm sorry to interrupt," began an awkward John Sherman, "but I fear I was a little abrupt when you stopped in at my office, Georgina. I'm never good at chance meetings and pleasantries. I just came over to apologize and promise to do better in the future."

Becky was flabbergasted, but Georgina came to the rescue. "Hi John! I thought you were just busy and I broke your concentration. No harm done. Do you have a moment to sit down and tell us briefly what your subject is about? We've been curious and interested. Beck here deals with religious psychology. Is there any correlation?"

John flushed a little and was obviously pleased to be asked out his work. "My order will take a few minutes. Let me see if I can at least make a start on it. I believe there is a new world order coming. By that I mean we are evolving in mind and spirit, and we need a new expanded understanding of God and our purpose for being here. I study the basic principles in current religions to see if I can discern the next step. You see, Teilhard de Chardin and Buckminster Fuller saw something more for humanity and were essentially scoffed at. Even Jesus Christ saw more if he actually said, 'In my Father's house are many mansions.' He was speaking of many dimensions of being right here within us. Oops, there is my dinner. Perhaps we can continue this conversation another time. Again, I apologize for my awkwardness." And he was gone as quickly as he had appeared. In fact, Becky wasn't sure she ever saw John Sherman walk through a doorway. He just seemed to appear and disappear.

"What a strange man, but some interesting ideas, eh Beck?" Georgina's curiosity was definitely on a rampage.

"Yes, he has very interesting ideas. I have been looking for some answers to questions I've had about what we are doing on this planet and what our experience is supposed to mean. Guess I'll need more books!"

"I knew it! Back to the bookstore, or can it wait until tomorrow?" Georgina was grinning that "gotcha" grin Becky knew well.

"Let's have our dinner and let this all simmer a bit," Becky said trying to stifle an all too revealing smile. She was more excited about this little bit of information that she wanted to let show. She had a book on her shelf she had picked up last year that might be part of what John Sherman was speaking of. In fact, now that she thought of it, she wasn't sure if perhaps John hadn't been the author! She would check it out tonight as soon as she got home.

Their conversation turned to other things and they went on with their evening. The music came on and they sang along with Luciano Pavarotti and Renee Fleming. Voices piped up from other tables and the kitchen as well. Becky wondered what John would think of this, but when she leaned a little way out of the booth to see, he was indeed already gone. His dinner must have been carry out. Why was she not surprised?

Three

Late September was usually cool and sunny, so the changing leaves looked spectacular. This weekend turned cold and rainy. It was a good time for Becky to curl up with hot chocolate and her new research books. There was a lot to do to modify her class syllabus and insert new material. But she had to know what she was talking about, and be prepared if there were questions. She went over the names in her class and was fairly sure no one was Jewish. That could be good or not. A knowledgeable Jewish student could be a big help. Not knowing that someone was Jewish could find herself being corrected unexpectedly. Becky would have to ask at the beginning of class.

Just as she suspected, there were a zillion holidays and rituals to know about. It seemed there was a remembrance for every event in the Torah, the first five books of Moses. How would she ever get a grasp on them all in one weekend, or one lifetime! Maybe her idea was too ambitious. But if she stayed with the big celebrations and didn't try to encompass everything, it could work. Becky began to list the sacred days familiar to her, Shabbat, Chanukah and others.

They used the lunisolar calendar to mark the dates of the events of the Jewish year, and dated the creation of the world to 5778 BC. She wondered how that came about. Did they count backward from the Common Era? Did God know about this calendar thing? Or was it simply to mark the events in some way that suited their culture?

Hours spun by as Becky copied passages and made notes. The job got larger and larger regardless of how she tried to pare it down. Judaism wasn't just a religion, it was a whole culture. It couldn't be described in something like the Nicene creed that she heard recited by devout church goers. Becky visited churches on Sunday mornings from time to time, but had not found them to be stimulating or enlightening. They just raised more questions in her mind.

Yet religion fascinated her. Becky grew up in a main stream Christian church that didn't demand the memorizing of creeds and observing of rituals. There were a few rituals like communion, but they were open to everyone and optional. When she asked questions, the answers were ambiguous such as, "We know a tree grows but we don't know how it grows." It sounded good at the time, but added nothing to her understanding.

As a child Becky enjoyed singing in the choir and going to church camp in the summer. At church camp she could meet kids from other churches and listen to them talking about their experiences. The mystical vesper service deep in the woods was her favorite. They would all line up two by two, light their candles at the eternal flame in the center of the campus, and march off into the darkness with one of the leaders guiding them. Soon they came to a clearing with wood benches arranged like an outdoor sanctuary and a stone altar up front. Cheese cloth covered a huge picture of Jesus, and when they were ready to begin, someone lit the cloth and it burned away in a blaze of light revealing the picture. It was fabulous! When the light died down, one of the leaders told them a wonderful story. To her child's mind it wasn't boring at all, like church services.

Then there was the talent show where the kids put on skits, played the piano, or danced to show off their talents. The skits were the best. They were always clever and funny.

Dinner time was fun too. Kids at one table would chant to the next table. "There ain't no bugs on us! There ain't no bugs on us! There may be bugs on the rest of your mugs, but there ain't no bugs on us!" It was shouted with great gusto and pounding rhythm. They prided themselves on making up the cleverest chant right on the spot.

Yes, religion fascinated Becky because of the psychological effect it had on people. The effect of the church camp inspired her for many months after with never-to-be forgotten experiences. The music in the choir was like no other music. Who sang hymns but the protestants? Sacred music touched the soul with its richness. The psychology of religion was an innovative field that Becky had begun to create during her pursuit of a Ph.D.

"Are you going to bury yourself all weekend in your books or can we go to a show?" Georgina's voice full of laughter was always welcome.

Becky looked at the clock. "Yes, what time? I can stop right now. I keep reminding myself that I don't have to plan the whole semester this weekend. A few days at a time will do."

"I had a few student make-ups this weekend and have been composing for a new musical between appointments. Already students are behind and it isn't even October. They have more excuses than I could ever think up! Meet you in a half hour at Mom & Pop's for dinner and then we can pick a movie."

"Good. Sounds like a plan. I'm going to walk. I need to work out the kinks. Will you drive to the theater?"

"Sure. See ya there."

The lights were dim in Mom & Pops and the Intermezzo from Cavaleria Rusticana was playing. People were talking softly and it all gave the place a classier atmosphere than it normally had. It was more like old Italy tonight.

"Georgi, how much more do you have to go on the music? That was a big chunk to volunteer to write the whole thing!"

"Yeah, well it was one of my mad, mad moments. I've always wanted to do it and something has to push me to get me moving on it. I figured this was as good a time as any."

"How do you start?"

"First, I wrote a short story. I didn't have any idea of setting it to music when I wrote it. It was just one of those story lines that kept bouncing around in my head until I set it down on paper to get it to quit bothering me. Then I could hear some songs and melodies that went with it and next thing you know, it is writing itself."

"Lovely! And do you write the words too?"

"Actually I'm having an English student do that. She wants to be a lyricist and was very interested when I suggested it to her. I've given her melodies and she gives me words. We sing them a bit and edit here and there. It has been working out quite well. I'm surprised. Pleasantly surprised."

"How did you know she wanted to be a lyricist?"

"A little birdie in the form of an English professor mentioned it. You could learn a lot in the teacher's lounge if you stopped in once in a while, Beck. And they don't allow smoking in there now, so the air isn't blue anymore. They've scrubbed the walls and changed the carpet, too. It is really quite pleasant."

"I've always hated that place. The smoke smell would be in my hair and clothes just walking by. And the gossip doesn't interest me. I don't chit chat well. I don't know how you do it. Sometimes I wish I could, but it just doesn't come. I draw a blank."

It made Becky think of John Sherman's awkwardness. She could relate big time. She half wondered if he came here to the restaurant often. Maybe he would come in for his carryout again and give them a few more clues to his mysterious studies.

"Let's go to see something gooey and romantic. There are a couple of decent choices listed in the paper." Georgina liked the romantic radio stations and romance novels. Her husband had died soon after a whirlwind courtship and a few years of a honeymoon-like marriage. It was idyllic and somehow the romantic offerings always attracted her. From time to time she would talk about Paolo. He was a musician, too, and quite a talented one. They met at a music conference in New York. It was love at first sight. He had one of those hidden heart conditions that had no symptoms and took him quickly. Becky wished that Matt could have gone quickly and painlessly like that. The agony of his illness and deterioration was tragic and unbearable for him and everyone around him.

"O.K. with me. I'm in for gooey tonight." Becky really didn't mind. She knew how these stories somewhat filled in the empty spaces for Georgina.

Monday classes started off with a jolt. The weekend rain had found the leaks in the building roof and was dripping in the halls and gymnasium. The students were cringing along the walls to get past the cold water and puddles. The janitorial people were placing waste baskets everywhere to catch the water and prevent more and bigger puddles.

Becky found her class most receptive to the new material. In fact they were so excited that they decided to form research teams on their own and bring their findings to class. Becky was blown away. How neat that she could study to keep up with them instead of having to shoulder the whole presentation herself.

Two students were of Jewish descent on one side of their family or other. They knew little of the traditions and were going to ask parents and relatives to join the research. There seemed to be no end to the ideas the students were coming up with.

"Hey, you don't have to do the grunt work, just direct it like an orchestra!" The orchestra idea from Georgina sparked an idea for Becky. She could divide the groups into areas of study so everyone didn't overlap. Becky could hardly wait to get to class Tuesday and map it out with the students.

By the end of the week word had gotten around the school that there was this big Jewish project going on. They naturally thought it was Chaim's idea, but he quickly dispelled the notion.

"Actually Becky started it. I am thrilled because it means I can get to the meat of my research faster. What a great idea!"

Becky was relieved that Chaim liked what she was doing. She hadn't though that she might be stepping on toes by jumping into his subject like that. She stepped into his office to apologize for not coordinating with him. She felt guilty and stupid.

"Don't worry about it another second. Really. I was concerned that I was getting off to a slow start because of my father and getting set up here. I thought the powers-that-be might think they made a mistake hiring me. You covered that for me beautifully and I thank you from the bottom of my heart. You took the pressure off me and probably saved my job!"

Georgina and Becky met for lunch in a far corner of the cafeteria. "I was grateful for his reaction," Becky whispered, "but I still felt guilty. How could I have grabbed the bit in my teeth and run with it like that without considering him? God forbid he should think I'm protecting my territory or something."

"Beck, it was your desire to be in the know that overshadowed everything, remember? You were honestly enthusiastic. You didn't get crazy, the kids did. Lighten up on yourself, girlfriend!"

"I guess in this case, all's well that ends well. Did Shakespeare say that?"

"Probably. Chaim is a really cool guy. He seems to go through a lot with a level head and an affable demeanor. He doesn't seem the type to be rattled or threatened. He's pretty sure of his territory and I guess sharing it makes it more fun for him. Relax. He likes you."

"We're going to start unloading his boxes tomorrow. You are welcome to help, of course. He is making plans where to put stuff and creating the space. I'm sure he will feel more on top of things with his work unpacked. I know I can't stand to live among boxes for too long. I still have a few that aren't unpacked, but it is stuff I don't need or it is convenient to have it in boxes right beside my computer."

"I'll be there. Wouldn't miss it. I love to go through other people's stuff and see what they are about. Give me a ring when you are ready. I'll be in my office." Georgina had that impish sparkle in her eyes again. Becky never knew what was going on in that mischievous mind of hers, but she could always trust it was nothing hurtful.

Becky grumbled to herself, "I remember when someone told me that computers would eliminate paper work. Hah! I've got more than ever. And I don't trust computers to be the sole possessor of my work. They crash, the programs decay, or I completely forget the DOS path. What kind of security is that? I would be wiped out if I didn't keep an actual paper trail."

Evening found Becky occupied with grading papers, sorting research information, and getting her class notes in order. With all the excitement of new people coming in and new departments being created, it was all too easy to let things slide in her own work. She wanted to be caught up, so she could help Chaim tomorrow and not feel guilty about neglecting her students.

There continued to be an upsurge in student interest since she introduced holidays and rituals of Jewish families. There was a deeper delving into the psychology of practicing rituals. Now they had actual details to talk about and in some cases, personal experience. Students started greeting each other with "Shalom" in the hall ways.

Becky hoped to have Chaim come to her class if he had time and perhaps perform one of the rituals with the students and discuss it with them. He could give them a better understanding of what it meant to him and why the Jews kept them alive for thousands of years.

There must be something in all this that answered a deeper spiritual need. She could still only guess at what it might be, even with all her studies. There was something missing for her, something she couldn't find in books, and she was determined to discover what it was.

The next afternoon Georgina, Becky, and Chaim bent over plans for his office that were laid out on the floor. It looked like a Chinese puzzle at first, but as he explained it all, the plans made sense. They each took a corner of the office and began to drag boxes and carry files appropriate to that corner. File drawers began to fill up and bare spots appeared on the floor where boxes had been.

The hours passed with lots of hard work and great conversation. Becky explained about her students just taking off with the material she provided to them and he laughed about them greeting each other in Hebrew in the halls.

"It all sounds wonderful, Becky. Ritual practice is not my focus and I am delighted that you are filling them in on it. It will give them a taste of the cultural atmosphere in which the Kabalah came about."

"I must admit I thought I had inadvertently stepped into your territory with my enthusiasm."

"Believe me, Becky, there is enough territory for all. Study of the Kabbalah is a mystical one. It requires mystical or spiritual interpretation which is a specialized skill. People have spent lifetimes learning and exploring it."

"Well, do the rituals come into play too?"

"They are reminders for the masses. They provide a spiritual experience without them actually having to know the ins and outs of spiritual interpretation and mystical study. The population of old was uneducated and needed a way to practice their religion. The Kabbalah underscores it all, as well as carrying the soul forward."

Becky was really mystified now. "Is it sort of like a mystery school teaching?"

"Yes, you could say that. It is also a lifestyle. It requires tremendous discipline and an aptitude for it. Not everyone wants to do it, or should do it. There are learned teachers who act as guides, who screen and inspire their students."

"How did you decide to do this? Isn't it an ancient thing rather than modern day?" Georgina's interest was peaked now.

"If you know now to interpret, Kabbalah is as relevant today as it was thousands of years ago. The modern world has carried the population into rampant materiality and they have lost touch with the underlying reality of their being."

Ye Gods, thought Becky, the reality of my being. "Is this reality not just the intellect and the psyche interacting to create personality as a response to the environment?"

"Ah, well, intellect is our rational nature and can turn either direction. It can be focused upon studying the outer or turned toward learning about the inner. But it is not our spiritual nature. It can only report on what it finds and try to make sense of its information. Psyche functions in the midst of mind at the center of thought and feeling. You could call it the soul. Personality is the resulting face we show to the world, but it is not truly who we are."

Georgina decided this was getting pretty deep and she was hungry. "What say we break for dinner? Mom and Pop's? We can come back and have at it again for a while. I do better on a full stomach."

Becky and Chaim nodded in agreement. "Just let me get a few more things arranged here so I don't lose my place," said Chaim.

Becky was as ready as Georgina to take a break. Her curiosity argued with her stomach. She wanted to hear more. But there was a lot to mentally digest with just the little he had said. She wanted to look up some things in her books while she processed it all. She remembered something she had run across last weekend that alluded to their conversation.

"Hi Mom, how are things going?" It was Lissa calling in as she usually did a couple of times a month.

"Hi Love, I'm fine. Things are going well. I'm gaining a new interest. You've probably heard of the Kabbalah?"

"Yeah, Mom. How did you connect with that? Sounds pretty deep."

"New professor here on a grant. I just helped him arrange his office and we got into a conversation about it. It may be the key to something deeper I've been looking for a long time. I'm not sure what just yet, but I feel like I'm on an exciting quest. Where are you? What's happening with you?"

"Well, we're heading out to South Africa next week. Mark has some clients there and wants to do some on-site work with them." Mark Davies worked with communication routers and networks. He was in great demand, not only for his expertise, but because his company was almost alone in the field.

"Sounds interesting. How long?"

"Maybe a month. I want to swing by before we go. Time is tight. Is Friday evening O.K.?"

"Yes, fine. Anything special?"

"I'll tell you when I get there. Gotta go. Love ya, Mom."

"Love you too, Lissa."

After Nathan's sudden news of his engagement, Becky was a bit apprehensive. Lissa and Mark had their challenges. At one time Lissa almost despaired for the survival of the marriage because Mark was so engrossed in his work. They had managed to work things out where they could travel together, and her work could continue during their journey. Mark had begun to train a group to assist him and was turning more of the every-day tasks over to them. Since they were going to South Africa for a month together, things must be all right between them.

Friday evening Lissa arrived in a flurry. She was breathless and radiant. "Mom, we're pregnant! We're going to have a baby in seven months."

They threw their arms around each other, danced around and laughed. "That's wonderful news. Was this planned? Did it just surprise you? What?"

"We planned it, Mom, as well as you can plan anything that happens spontaneously. We're taking some time for ourselves to explore a bit of South Africa and just be with each other. The doctor said it was O.K. to go since it is early and I'm healthy. Just so we don't spend a lot of time bouncing around in a Jeep or Hummer, or whatever they have there."

"Will you keep your job?"

"Oh yes. The company is willing to go to any lengths to keep me around. I'll be working from home later on and after the baby comes.

I have to keep up with the latest developments if I want to stay in the business."

"Can we grab some dinner somewhere. I'm famished. Is that quaint place Mom & Pop's open?"

"Sure is. Let's go celebrate!" Becky was walking on air. Nathan was engaged, Becky was pregnant, and herself on a fascinating new spiritual adventure.

"Mom, tell me about this new quest you are on. Is this a spiritual thing like Don Quixote?"

"Well some folks might think I'm jousting windmills I guess. But I've always suspected that there is more to religion and psychology than what I have yet discovered. So far everything is logical and makes sense, but what powers it all? Why did a branch of vertebrates decide to develop into a thinking being? Why did awareness push through from two dimensions and create a three-dimensional being? Does biology push us along, or are we drawn by something more?"

"Geez Mom, you really have launched into the upper stratospheres! You'll have to write to me and keep me up on it all."

"Have you had any experience with spirituality, Lissa? Does something nag at you or have you been in touch with someone who is into this?"

"Well I met the Dali Lama once. It was an other-worldly feeling being in his presence. I couldn't quite fathom what I was experiencing but it was definitely something expanding, freeing, and exhilarating. The feeling faded away after a few days, but the memory of it is sharp and clear. It makes you want to be there again and again."

"What did he say?"

"Oh, we were in a group and he just blessed us. Said something about our being more than we believe we are and have powers beyond what we now know. I don't remember too much of it. It sounded great. I'll have to get a book about him."

Becky smiled. Just like her mother, get a book about it. "That's great. You study the Dali Lama's teachings and I'll try to fathom the Kabbalah teachings. We'll see what we can come up with."

It was a fun evening. The best that Becky remembered with Lissa. Lissa was more solid, more mature, and more open. She was focused on their conversation and not flitting all over the place. It was a good change.

Becky rang up Georgina over the weekend to tell her all about Lissa and their conversation. Georgina invited Becky over to her place to hang out, sing a little music and explore her new music compositions.

It was always good to be with Georgina. She was comfortable to hear whatever Becky was dealing with, and they could always dissolve any concerns into music and laughter.

"I've got news, Beck. John Sherman wants to get together with us. He didn't say much more than that. Maybe he had heard all the whoopla in the halls and wants to be in on the fun. Maybe he feels left out. Who knows? I told him I would talk to you and get back to him with a time and place."

"Really? Well that is a change. He is reaching out. What he was talking about in Mom & Pop's was fascinating. I wonder if he will share more of his studies or his thinking."

"Maybe he just wants us to help arrange his office. We did such a good job on Chaim's. We may be the primary office arrangers of South Bennington."

"Does it include a raise in pay?"

"Probably. Those muscle jobs usually pay pretty well. I think my house cleaning service makes more than I do."

"Any day after classes would be fine. You're office or mine?" Now Becky had that mischievous look in her eye.

"Very funny. I'll let you know."

Four

Becky was deep into her research when someone appeared at her office door. There was a polite "ahem" that roused her from her notes.

"May I help you?" He wasn't a student or anyone she recognized.

"Could you tell me where I might find Professor John Sherman?"

"Yes. His office is three doors down on the left. I believe his name is on the door, but I'm not sure. He is new here."

"I know. I'm his son, Jim."

"Oh! Nice to meet you, Jim. I am Becky Temple. If he isn't in his office, his classroom is upstairs at the end of the same hall. I'm sure he will be glad to see you."

"Well, I'm not too sure about that. I'm just kind of showing up. Thanks. Nice to meet you too."

Georgina came in just as Jim was heading down the hall. "Who was that?"

"That was John Sherman's son, Jim. Mystery professor has a mystery son! He said he just 'showed up' and wasn't sure his father would be happy to see him."

"Oh? How interesting! Well he looked like a nice enough guy. Is that all he said?"

"Yeah, pretty much. I gave him directions to John's office and classroom. Is his name on his door yet?"

"I haven't looked. Hey, I just wondered if you have access to any Jewish or Israeli music. It might be fun to explore it a bit."

"Well, Lissa sent me a tape of Israeli music last year when she was there. I'm not sure what kind it is. I haven't listened to it. They have everything from rock to folk to religious. Their teens are as hip as ours when it comes to music. I'll look for it when I get home."

"Sorry to interrupt again. My father's office is locked and he's not in his classroom. Would you mind giving him this book? I picked it up at a weekend seminar."

"Oh sure!" piped up Georgina. "Are you sure you don't want to wait for him, or inquire at the college office? Maybe he told the secretary where he is today. Do you have his home address?"

"Actually, I have to catch a bus pretty soon. I need to be in Baltimore this evening. Thanks for all your help."

Becky and Georgina waved goodbye at Jim's departing back. They stared at each other for a minute and then at the book, "The New Order of Being" by Lawrence Shelling.

"Well, let's have a look, Beck. Maybe it will unravel some of the mystery. We might get a clue about what John wants to meet with us about."

"I told you, he probably wants us to help arrange his office too." They both laughed.

Sitting down Georgina began to read aloud. Becky reached for a legal pad to take notes. They felt a little sneaky, as if they were partaking of some forbidden fruit.

"There are DNA codes behind our present one that are waiting for humanity to advance in consciousness, so they can emerge and carry us into the next level of being. We reach that deeper level through a deeper understanding of our spiritual nature, through thinking and living according to higher understanding."

"Wow!" exclaimed Becky, writing as fast as she could. "Maybe we should just order a copy for ourselves. I would like to know more and have some time to digest the ideas."

"Here is the publisher on the back cover. Take that down, and we'll keep on going for a while longer. Let's see what else is here. Where did this research come from and how valid is it? I've never heard of the author or the publisher, and believe me I've sleuthed 'em all looking for a place that will take my work."

Georgina was flipping through the pages quickly, looking for chapter titles and other clues they could pick up quickly.

They called for Chinese take-out so they could continue with the book at Becky's. Their entire evening was spent in intense reading and discussing. It was late when Georgina went home.

Becky stayed up to go through her notes and put them in her word program. Her head was spinning with ideas crashing into each other. She woke at the crack of dawn, still curled up on her couch and the computer still running.

Classes the next day were a nightmare. Tests were looming on the horizon, students were restless, and the first papers of the quarter were due shortly. It always seemed to come all at once, even though Becky tried to keep things reasonably spaced out. It seemed that all the loftiness of teaching and exploring ideas came crashing down to earth at grade time for both her and the students.

She brought a floppy of her notes to school so Georgina could print copies for them. It seemed that Becky had completed the task of editing them sometime before she fell asleep on the couch. She hoped they made sense.

Georgina brought a copy along with the disk back into Becky's office. "Sorry I couldn't get to this sooner. My classes were nuts."

"This is fine. My classes were the same. Did you look them over? Did they make any sense?"

"Oh yes, they are really good. I've been looking in catalogues for other books on the same subject. There are quite a few, actually. I was surprised. I guess that is what happens when you keep your nose in your own subject too long."

Becky delivered the book to John's office and found him deep in thought. "Your son was here yesterday and left this for you. We asked if he could wait but he said he had a bus to catch."

"Oh! Thanks. Let's see. Where was I? Oh yes, I had an appointment. Guess I missed him. He was probably going to Baltimore to check on his project. He's an engineer and is building a system for some company or other."

"I'm afraid I took the liberty of looking through the book. I hope that's O.K. It looks very interesting. Does it have anything to do with your work?" Becky was a little uncomfortable with her sudden urge to confess.

"No problem. No problem at all. I'm glad you found it interesting. Some people find this sort of thing heretical."

"Then you already know what the book is about?"

"Oh yes. Lawrence is a friend and colleague. We've collaborated on many projects. Jim agreed to pick up the book for me. I was hoping he would also be interested in reading it."

"He said he was at the seminar." Becky was uncertain if she should respond.

"Well he picked it up at the seminar Lawrence was giving, but I doubt if he attended." John's expression darkened a bit.

Becky was feeling even a little more uncomfortable not knowing how much to say. It seemed that everything she assumed was turning out to be wrong. "Well it was nice to meet him, anyway. I've got to get back."

She was glad to escape, but escape what? She hated to feel stupid, but she just couldn't seem to get on track with him. Was it her fault? She couldn't shake the guilt as if she were responsible somehow.

"Georgina, it was the weirdest thing. I took John's book to him and it was a strange conversation, if you could even call it a conversation.

"What happened?"

"Felt like everything I said was wrong. I mentioned that I had looked through the book. That didn't seem to bother him, but he was so…so cavalier about his son. The kid is an engineer overseeing the building of something in Baltimore. He didn't even know what that was. He said the kid probably didn't attend the seminar, just picked up the book. Go figure!"

"What did you say that was wrong?"

"Well nothing in particular, I guess. I just couldn't get on track with his thinking. I thought he would be more concerned that he missed Jim. He wasn't. I thought the book would be something new. It wasn't. It was written by a friend of his. I couldn't wait to decently make an exit!"

Georgina shook her head. "Hey, this isn't your problem. It is his. We do our best to be welcoming and friendly, and if it doesn't work, it doesn't work. Shall we grab a beer and shake off the willies?"

"Mom and Pop's it is! I have some papers to gather up. Meet you there."

The crowd hadn't arrived at Mom and Pop's yet. Becky and Georgina headed for their favorite booth in the back where they could observe, but not be easily seen. It was the perfect spot for their "sorting out stuff" sessions.

Midway into their conversation there was a cheery "May I join you or is this a personal and private session?"

"Chaim!" said Becky pleasantly surprised. "Have a seat. Personal and private stuff can wait. You've been busy! Haven't seen you roaming the halls or haunting the cafeteria. How's your Dad?"

"His usual irascible self, complaining and making everybody miserable. Glad I'm here. Really I don't want to interrupt."

"Nonsense! We're delighted to be interrupted. So what's happening with you?" Georgina always ready to pick things up out of the serious to the exciting.

"Well, I'm wondering if you might be interested in an evening class for an hour once a week to let me present my work to the faculty and sort of get integrated a bit? I don't want to be considered a mole constantly burrowing around in my office and file boxes, hiding from the known world."

"Yes, you bet! What evening? When do you start? Can we do anything to help?" Becky was amazed that Georgina was into this, so bubbly.

"I would love to attend. I've been trying to read up a bit on my own, but a class would be so much more fun. Anyway, I'm not sure what I'm reading is on track with what you do."

"What are you reading, Becky?"

"Well I picked up this embarrassingly large stack of books on Jewish life, rituals and celebrations. Just trying to get my feet wet. My students are doing the same on their own! I've been amazed at their interest."

"Great! You will have a good background on the ancient Jewish people."

"You sound like I'm sort of out in left field. Am I?" Becky felt the little flush of uncertainty that she hated.

"No, not at all. You are one of the non-Jewish people who actually starts at the beginning. Most people jump into the middle and have their feet firmly planted in midair. People want to understand the essence of the mystery before they know the origins and progression of thought, and it leaves them sort of floating without an anchor. It also causes them to either lose interest or go way off the deep end."

"Do you mean they get radical like the extremist groups? Religion seems to do that to some people." Georgina was genuine concerned.

"Yeah, they become extremist in that they forget they need to live on the earth. Someone said they get so heavenly that they are no earthly good. People get into the mystical and think that can relinquish responsibility for their morals, families, and obligations and just float around."

"So it's not the violent stuff?"

"No, this is not religious fundamentalism. It is spirituality. Seeing the interweaving of the divine in everyday events. Actually sensing the Divine within ourselves as creations of God."

Becky was a little puzzled now. "What about those people in mental institutions that think they are Jesus Christ or John the Baptist? The messianic complex?"

"There's a difference between thinking you are someone else, and sensing a greater dimension in yourself than you are currently aware of. You are still you."

"What good does this do us, to sense this greater dimension? I hate to always be thinking about what's in it for me, but what do I use it for?" Georgina wanted to get to the nitty-gritty.

"You discover that you have the power to be at cause in your life. God is First Cause and you, being a creation of God, cause or choose your experiences and what you will learn from them."

"Whoa, do you mean that I cause everything that happens to me? What about when the other guy cuts in front of me and causes an accident? Is that me?"

"Ultimately yes, Georgi, but not the same as choosing what's for supper. It has to do with setting the direction of our lives with how we think. Our predominant thinking sets us on a path that brings into play certain experiences matching the kind of thinking we do. Most people are not conscious of this until they learn more about it."

"So, how might I be thinking if I am involved in an accident?"

"It has to do with believing that accidents are inevitable, and that you can be a victim at any time. It has to do with believing that others are always endangering us in some way. The newspapers and magazines are full of it. Novels are predicated on the victim and hero theme. It is practically imprinted on our genes because humanity as a whole has believed it all throughout history."

Lights came on for Georgina. "Yes, my students have much more difficulty singing if they don't believe they can sing, or if they think they don't sound good enough. Is it something like that?"

"Definitely. The human mind is a powerful instrument. Predominant thinking such as 'I'm not good enough' has a huge influence on performance. But positive thinking is just part of it. Positive thinking is definitely beneficial. But people who then decide to think positively all the time, soon discover that the mind rebels and they fall into moroseness and disillusionment. More work is needed."

"O.K., since I'm the one who starts at the beginning, what are the roots of this that we need to know. Why does the mind rebel? Why can't we control it?"

"Training needs to be based in spiritual principles. In the beginning God created, and God saw that it was good. God didn't waffle and wonder if it was really good. God is the Creative Principle, which is the positive. The manifestation, or physical dimension is the opposite, and when the two meet there is a burst of energy and something new is created. When we decide to be God and be positive all the time, the negative part of creation asserts itself with a vengeance. Have you heard that for every action there is an equal and opposite reaction? Same thing."

"Oh, one hand clapping makes no sound, but two coming together from opposite directions cause a burst of energy that becomes a sound!"

"Good stuff, Beck! Well done! You've just blown the cover on my first three classes." Chaim was applauding and the whole restaurant clientele turned to look at them. Then they decided to applaud as well. Becky stood and took a bow. The three of them collapsed on the table shaking with laughter.

"This is the key I've been looking for in my psychology of religion pursuits." Becky was seeing all sorts of possibilities all at once. "It has been the missing link to connect mind and spirit. I love it!"

Chaim shifted in his chair toward Becky. "What exactly is your field about? What is your focus?"

"I've been aware of the psychological effect that religion has on people, good and bad, and exploring the how and why of that effect. I looked into Freudian studies and there was much of the Catholic influence about women and their place, and how religion kept them subservient. Then I began studying Yung, and his theory of individuation intrigued me. I've been trying to create a study that serves as a bridge that I can bring into my classroom to assist students in making the mental jump. I think it is the religion part that has been holding me back. Spirituality isn't the same thing, is it?"

"No. In fact religion was created to sideline the heretics, those who believed in the individual spiritual path, the search for the divine within each person. Religion was needed to control the masses, so rituals and prescribed credos became their tools of oppression. It was easy because the masses couldn't read and write, so they depended upon the church to tell them what to believe. Interesting that your Jesus was one who advocated the individual spiritual path. Interesting that Jesus' words 'the kingdom of heaven is within you' are not emphasized in the Christian church. And the apostle Paul is written to have said, 'Christ in you, your hope of glory.' Still Christianity, in my opinion, remains blind through choice to the true teaching. They insist upon some traditional teachings formulated by the church to keep everyone thinking they are a worm of the dust."

"Wow," exclaimed Georgina. "I never thought of it that way. I guess I've been just as blind as everyone else."

"You were taught to be blind. We are taught by our culture what to see and what not to see. The miracle is now you see!" Chaim was in his element. "Someone who wants to control you will not teach you that divinity is within you, that heaven is in the midst of you, or that the power of God is within you. They will tell you that it is up above and you can reach it only through them. They put on impressive robes, take on a holy air, and make themselves the intermediary and thus the controller."

"You are speaking of all priests then?" Becky was scandalized. "They give themselves the power over others. They are not ordained by God on high? It was the same bogus idea as divine right of kings after all. What a racket!"

"All priests and actually anyone who sets themselves up as the exclusive connection to God. They let others believe they have some special dispensation and wisdom, even though they may be dumb as a box of rocks. Men enter the priesthood for many unsavory reasons: to hide their homosexuality, to avoid rejection, or because they need the rigid structure to make them feel safe.

"In ancient times priests had to be of the tribe of Levi. Some who could not prove they were of the tribe of Levi, then claimed to be of the order of Melchizadek. Later on they had to come from a prominent family that could purchase their priesthood for them. It is a rare and wonderful person that comes into the priesthood because of the pure calling of Spirit. By that I mean the pure motive to follow the highest teachings and live them faithfully without needing to exercise power over others. I think that is almost a lost art in the priesthood. Now, however, we have many people attempting to understand and follow an individual spiritual pathway in their own lives. I think that gets back to the teachings of Jesus."

"So you have studied the Gospels and are interested in Jesus? I thought being Jewish you wouldn't be interested in Jesus. Don't Jews regard Jesus as a work of fiction? They certainly don't think he is their messiah." Becky wasn't sure she was treading on safe ground and looked doubtfully at Chaim.

"Yes, I study the life and teachings of Jesus. I read much of the scholarly work that is written about him. There's a reason why the Christians became so prevalent beyond becoming the state religion of Rome. There is a reason also that his teachings seem to come in second to the apostle Paul. I believe Jesus was trying to update Judaism. I don't believe he was trying to establish a new religion."

"Update it how?"

"Well, the treatment of women for example. He spoke to them in public and he taught them. Women were not to be acknowledged in public and they were not to be educated. Two ridiculous taboos. He told the story of the Good Samaritan to expose the evil of caste levels. Jews didn't speak to Samaritans. Priests didn't stop to help the common people. 'Love your neighbor as yourself" was unheard of. Love, if you can call it that, was reserved for one's own family or tribe. It was really possession more than love. It was survival to protect one's own and everyone else be damned. Neighbors were for alliances and business transactions, but not love."

Georgina was frowning, deep in thought. Chaim looked at her quizzically. "You O.K. Georgi? You look a bit troubled."

"Oh, I'm fine. Everything you say makes sense. So much so that my mind runs in a zillion directions with many possibilities. I'm wondering if anything I've been taught was the truth."

"Most of what we are taught is tradition created by the early church fathers. They weren't interested in truth. They were interested in structure, and in keeping themselves and their religion safe from question or attack. They needed money for the church coffers to keep from starving. They threw threats of punishment into their translations and teachings, so people would give more money out of guilt and fear. It didn't matter if the people were starving and sacrificing their wellbeing. They were expendable."

"It seems as if love really doesn't enter into much of anything religious. They preach love of God and all that, but there is no loving action behind their words. Even the obligatory charities were for show so that people would give more to the church. A welfare system. I guess this is what has been holding me back when I study the psychological effects of religion. The negative affects, which are myriad, are symptomatic of the lack of practicing real love and caring."

Chaim shifted in his chair. "Giving to our charities is often obligatory. Companies require their executives to give a percentage of their salaries to the corporation's favorite charities. The real love and caring is displayed by those on the front lines assisting people, and even they are hamstrung by rules and lack of adequate funding."

Becky looked around. "Have you noticed our audience has left and the owners would probably like to close up?" Sure enough, the pies were out of the display case and the salt shakers were refilled. Chairs were upside down on the tables and the cleaning crew was ready to mop.

"How did we not notice them closing up?" Georgina was shocked.

"I guess we were blind?" Chaim was laughing.

They picked up their belongings and with apologies to the staff, made a brisk exit, the staff assuring them it was no problem.

On their way out to the parking lot, Becky reminded Chaim that he hadn't set an evening for his classes.

"So far, Becky, the office has given me Monday evenings at 7:30 in Frederick Hall room 210. I don't know if anyone else is interested in attending, but we'll have a good time even if it is just us."

"Right you are about the good time. But I wonder why Frederick Hall. It is at the other end of the campus. Sort of weird. Kind of far for the students at night I would think." Georgi was genuinely concerned.

"Well," piped up Becky, "let's advertise meeting at Mom & Pop's at 7:00 for coffee and all going over together. It is closer to the dorms. That might make the students happier and create a closeness among them. After all, some of this is tough stuff for them to deal with and friendly company to walk with might ease the tension."

"Great," said Georgi, 'I'll make posters and put them up. Are we starting this very Monday evening?"

"Yes. This Monday. Too short notice?"

"Nah, we can do it. We'll pass out fliers in our classes too."

"You two are incredible! I've never felt like part of a team before. Thanks."

"And thanks to you too. See you tomorrow." Georgi and Becky sounded like a duet. They laughed as they headed for their cars.

Five

Monday evening class started off with a bang. Thirty students gathered at Mom & Pop's for a pre-class gathering. Chaim, Becky, and Georgina were thrilled. The staff at the restaurant was amazed. Georgina had called them to let them know there might be as many as fifteen coming in for coffee and a snack. Students were piled into booths six deep and crowded around tables. It was a gala start to the journey they were about to take together. A few names were mentioned of people who would be coming later.

Chaim had already enlisted Becky and Georgina to help him hand out papers and handle audio/visuals. Georgina offered to make a dash to the copy machine to increase their handout supply and Becky would go to Frederick Hall to be sure there were enough seats.

"I really feel guilty asking you two to do all the running."

"Not a problem," sang out Georgina as she headed out the door.

"Chaim, you need to be here with your students. Don't worry about a thing. We just have to shift into a higher gear. I'm calling maintenance to be sure Frederick Hall is ready. They said they would have thirty-five chairs in the room. I'll go check to make sure. I'll drive over. See you at seven-thirty." And Becky dashed away.

Not only had Nick, the maintenance man, brought more chairs, he set them up and stayed around to be sure all went well. Becky thanked him profusely, telling him how many were at Mom & Pop's, and more were coming as well. He was amazed too. South Bennington hadn't seen such enthusiasm since the last presidential candidate made a whistle stop a decade ago. This was a pretty sleepy little town and had a sleepy little college to match. He was definitely going to be in on the fun.

"Do you suppose I might sit in on the class, Professor Temple? I've always been interested in this sort of thing. Never had a chance to study much, but I would like to do a bit of it if nobody minds."

"We would love to have you stay for the class. It won't be just faculty and students. There are more than a few folks from Johnston Crossing and beyond coming too."

Just then the first of the crowd began to file into the room and wend their way through the chairs for a good seat.

"Grab a seat, Nick. It's going to fill up fast." Becky was heading for the front of the room herself, reserving a couple of seats for herself and Georgina. Chaim's high teaching stool was in place and boxes of handouts lined the wall behind it. Becky noted that his books were stacked neatly on the head table and all seemed to be in order.

People were packed in wall to wall. As Chaim walked to the front he looked around to see if they seemed to mind being stuffed in. Everyone seemed to be happy just to have a seat, and had smiles of anticipation on their faces. When the room became quiet, he sang a Jewish prayer and greeted them with "Shalom."

Chaim began by having Becky and Georgina hand out a sheet of paper to each one with questions and a place to write a brief answer. They were questions about their basic beliefs, what tradition had taught them, what they thought of it all. As he repeated the questions students were invited to share their answers with the class. There was a little hesitation at first, but it soon got rolling and there was a lively discussion. Chaim interjected provocative ideas as they went along, and the interest was intense. The hour turned into two and Chaim had to finally call the halt.

Readings had been copied and were handed out. Chaim said they might be able use a theater-style class room on the first floor next week, especially if more people came. Everyone promised to come back. As they all left, Chaim sunk into a chair. He was spent. Nick offered to store everything in a storage closet and bring it out next week. He gave Chaim an extra key to the closet just in case he needed something out of it, and set about carting boxes and books down the hall.

"To the Pub for an ale, mates!" called out Georgina. "Jacks? My treat."

Becky and Chaim jolted upward out of their chairs and followed her. Jack's Pub sounded really good to them, too.

They pulled into the parking lot, driving separately. The place was full to overflowing. Georgina leaned out her car window and called out to Chaim and Becky, "I think the whole class is here. Shall we go over to Northwick to the Patrician Bar and Grill?"

They parked two cars on campus and rode with Georgina. Perhaps they would gather with the students at the pub after class some other evening, but this evening had been hectic. It was twenty-five miles, but the peace and quiet would be most welcome.

"How many classes were you planning on having, Chaim?" Becky was beginning to relax, her mind had stopped spinning from the discussions.

"I'm not sure. I thought it might be just six weeks, but maybe there's enough interest to last the whole semester. We'll have to play it by ear. The school may have plans for those classrooms later on."

"We might get a better idea of the true interest when we see who comes back next week and the week after. If the attendance doesn't seriously drop off by the fourth week, it could keep going on for a semester or more."

Georgina pulled into the Patrician's parking lot, which had only a few cars in it. "Yea, we may have the place nearly to ourselves." The place wasn't crowded at all and they found a booth away from the other patrons so they wouldn't disturb anyone else when their discussion took on a fervor, as it often did. The food from the other tables smelled good and they realized how hungry they were.

"I'll just spring for the beers," said Georgina aware that a question was hanging in the air since she had offered to treat. "Let's eat."

"We're going to get your dinner. You drove." Chaim looked at Becky and she nodded. "Oops, I didn't mean to obligate you, Becky."

"No problem. I was about to suggest it myself. How do you plan to narrow the focus, or do you?"

"The first class is always a bit scattered, but the reading material will help with that and then I have a syllabus I'll hand out at the end of the next class. It is still fairly open to encourage discussion. Most people already know what is missing. The just haven't articulated it for themselves. Often they say, "I knew that, but I guess I just didn't take time to think about it."

Georgina was puzzled. "How do they already know if you haven't told them? I don't quite get it."

"You have a mind, emotions, a body, thoughts and experiences. What part of you knows you have all that?"

"What part of me knows? Do you mean like a higher self of some sort?"

"Yes, exactly. Some call it the observer self, some call it higher mind or the spiritual nature. That part of us always knows the truth and if we are sensitive to it, it tells us when something we think or say is not the truth about us."

"Oh, could it be the little twinge of discomfort that we try to suppress when we're trying to fit into a box or a creed or a religion? If that's the case my higher nature has been sounding alarm bells all my life." Becky was amazed at how potentially pervasive this was in just her own experience.

"So, you've progressed from nudges to alarm bells? Time to listen!"

"No kidding. I've put myself down for so many years thinking I was a coward, completely clueless, or a fool who was way off the track of life. It was as if I were dropped off on the wrong planet so my mindset was incompatible. Everyone else seemed sure of whatever they thought they knew, and I would doubt myself."

"That's a good description of what happens to us until we begin to search for ourselves."

Georgina had been quietly taking it all in. "Have you ever been ridiculed or ostracized for going on that search? For questioning the status quo?"

"I hope to tell you! I've been the addled one, the one whose father didn't apply the strap to my butt enough. The rabbis would send me out of class in exasperation. They would call on my family to see what I was being taught at home. My father was always roaring livid at me.

"You disgrace the whole family! Think of your poor father and what you do to your mother! How will she hold her head up? Think of your ancestors! What will we tell your aunt Hannah? Your uncle Jacob? Who will want to be around us? They will be ashamed of us! Get out of my sight! Get out!" Chaim really got into the drama and folks were beginning to glance toward their booth.

"Geez, I thought my family was bad," moaned Georgina in a lowered voice. "I thought it was just the Italians that got overly excited like that."

"Did he mean get out forever?"

"No, just get out of his sight so he could calm down and try to think of what to do with me. It was always best to disappear for a while after his outbursts. There was no talking to him when he was like that, which was most of the time come to think of it."

"Back to roots again. Where did you start? How did you decide and then take the first steps?" Becky was ready to take notes for her own next steps.

"I suppose everyone comes to it a little differently. It is like pressure builds up until the psyche can take no more. The structure that the intellectual mind sets up to make sense of things breaks down at some point, and you either lose it or you step out into the unknown looking for something that does make sense."

"Did you go outside of Judaism?"

"Yes, at first. The things I found in other writings and spiritual teachings then led me back to Jewish mysticism. Many of those teachings have their roots in Jewish mysticism."

"How could you tell if what you were reading was real? Or the truth? Or just the figment of someone's imagination?"

"Imagination is actually a powerful pathway to the truth. It takes us out of the box, so to speak, and gives us freedom to move through ideas and images until that higher self within us says, 'Hold it. This is part of it.' Someone else's imagination may give you a clue or a key to something very important for your life."

Becky had seen this operate the other way in some people. "Looking at the religious art such as Dante's Inferno and some of the other portrayals of hell has really spun the population into fear and dread. How were they to know?"

"If you are in fear and dread, Becky, that it isn't truth. Our Creator is a creative principle. Creativity is the expansion of life, not the withering of it. The negativity in those paintings and much of the religious writing breeds fear and withers the life force within the person. Don't you feel sort of like shrinking instead of expanding and trusting, when you look at those images and read about hell?"

"You mean hellfire and brimstone are not real?" Georgina was back in the game. "Even the Greeks had myths about the underworld and Hades, the God of the underworld who kidnapped Persephone. It seems that humanity has always feared and believed in some dire punishment."

"Hellfire and brimstone are born out of our own ignorance of who we are. Not knowing we have divinity and divine potential within us, it is easy to believe we are hapless victims of something, everything. We make up angry gods, dire punishments, and ways to appease the angry gods to regain our equilibrium so we can go on with life."

"A vicious circle. The operas are full of them. Whether it is the gods, or the fates, or the evil of humanity, the characters are always victims of it. Mired in it. Of course people's lives back then were so full of pain and agony that it was always mirrored in their myths and then their music. A comic opera is rare. There are a few of them, but even they were tinged with tragedy."

"Amazing isn't it Georgi," mused Becky, "that some of the most beautiful and heart rending music comes out of that pain? It makes me think of the thorn bird that impales itself on a thorn in order to sing its most beautiful song while dying."

"I wonder if it is just that we haven't learned to put the energy into joy that we put into agony. Many of the most glorious arias are about joy. It is just that the looming tragedy colors the background to the aria, and impending doom keeps the picture dark." Georgina was thinking about her own family undercurrents. Always the threat to watch out for and don't get too happy because something bad is just around the corner."

"We have learned to put joy on a background of pain instead of the other way around. Happy, healthy, and empowered is the person who can maintain that sense of the joy of living regardless of what happens. It isn't easy, but it is worth training ourselves to do." Chaim was thinking of his father and all the pain that he lived with choosing to not give joy a chance.

The food was served and the conversation was temporarily on hold. Under the lighter banter and laughter, each had a chance to digest the thoughts as well as the food.

Becky entered her townhouse to the ringing of the telephone. It was her high school and life- long friend, Karla. "Hey, how are you? What's happening?"

"Great! Just great! You?"

"Super. All goes well. I'm excited by some new stuff that is really sparking my thinking and ideas here."

"Something exciting is happening at South Bennington? Amazing. New pizza shop?"

"No, they don't believe in pizza here. Just kidding. We have two new professors who are here on big grants and bringing revolutionary ideas to sleepy Johnston Crossing. One of them is giving an evening class to sort of introduce himself and his work. It's called "What Religion Left Out.""

"Wow! What's his turf?"

"Kabbalah!"

"No kidding! How did that happen?"

"Think it was time to wake South Bennington up or watch it die. New ideas and especially new money. Maybe now they won't be shocked at the little bit of cage rattling I do. They didn't want to know anything about the psychological effect of religion. It was sacrilege when I brought it here. Even had a few veiled threats from the more conservative clerics."

"I remember. Hey, I have a deal that might be interesting. I've got a new radio show weekly and maybe you would like to call in. The station will pay for the call. We could talk about what you're up to now."

"I'm not sure I know enough to talk about much yet, but we could start easy. Do you interview people and take calls on the air?"

"Yeah, I have missed the academics if you can imagine that, and thought I would take this offer to have intellectual discussions and whatnot. It's on at ten Monday through Friday. I have some folks lined up and will be starting the first of January."

"Oh good! By then maybe I'll have my feet under me a little better. Yes, I'd love to be a call-in guest. Is there any format? Do others call in to ask questions, or curse us because they don't agree, or think we are heretics?"

"All of the above. There will be staff to screen the calls and I let them know how crazy it should be allowed to get. How is this Kabbalah professor affecting your thinking? What's he about?"

"He's Jewish of course. We've been discussing everything from ancient mysteries, to the divinity within the individual, sort of like Jung's individuation. Talking about how humanity has developed in the wrong directions, bringing anguish and pain into their whole society for eons. We just had the first class tonight and it was a blockbuster. It was supposed to be for faculty, but it attracted students and town folks as well. Georgina and I helped him advertise it a little. Doesn't take too much here. The town has one bulletin board."

They burst into laughter. "How was the response?"

"We were jam packed into a thirty-five-seat classroom. If they all come back, we may try for one of the theater style classrooms. We'll see how it shakes out."

"Did folks like it? Was it what they were expecting?"

"I think they got way more than they expected. The room was so tense you could cut it. They all promised to come back. Georgina, Chaim, and I were wiped out. Oh, yes, his name is Chaim, leave off the "C.""

"Right. I knew that from Chanukah. Well, neat. Sounds like great stuff. How about sharing with me some of the references he uses and all that?"

"I will. We need to get together one of these days. Some face to face time, you know? We'll need to collaborate, plot, and plan where we can see the whites of each other's eyes, or some such thing."

"You bet. Well, I've got to ring off. Appointments tomorrow with producers, lawyers and all that. Good to hear your voice. Love ya!"

"Hey, thanks for calling. Love you too."

Becky made some coffee and sat down to ponder the events of the evening and watch the late news. She liked to know what was going on in the world, knowing that her son and daughter were out there somewhere.

It would be interesting if Nathan changed jobs and she could know more about what he was doing. She wanted to be able to chat with him about anything at all without him having to say, "Sorry, Mom, I can't talk about that." And how was Lissa feeling with her new pregnancy. A grandchild! Becky hadn't ever thought of herself as a grandmother. She felt young and wanted to keep it that way. What was it like to be old? She couldn't imagine.

Becky floated through her classes the rest of the week. The Monday night discussions lifted her spirits and opened her perspectives. She was feeling the background of joy that Chaim had mentioned. Had she seen her life against a background of pain? She didn't think so. It was more like a background of blah. Life was supposed to resemble a blank page that you wrote your experiences on. Maybe, like her stationery, the background of her life could be yellow, light blue, and pink, with flowers, fleecy clouds and sunshine.

Georgina had planned an end of the semester recital for her students. Becky hadn't participated in the past. Now she thought she would like to sing in it. Georgina was overjoyed. She had been hinting for a long time that Becky should have some short-term goals for her music. That's how hobbies turned into careers, she told her. Becky had scoffed at the idea of a singing career. Who would want to hear her, much less hire her? There was that blah uninspiring background stuff cropping up again. She chose the music, two arias, highlighted the words in yellow, and began to work on them in earnest.

"I meant to come to Chaim's first class, but my son, Jim, needed my assistance. How did it go?" John Sherman was at Becky's office door.

Becky couldn't be sure if John was just patronizing to get information, or if he was sincere. She tried to keep the prickliness out of her voice.

"It was amazing. More student body and town folks showed up than faculty, but the discussions were lively, and the place was packed. Sorry you couldn't be there. Can you be there next Monday? We were meeting in Frederick Hall on the second floor, but I understand we have the theater room on the first floor this coming week. From the little you've told me about your work, it sounds like there might be a lot of compatibility with Chaim's. Maybe you would like to explore that with him and share too, if it would work out in his schedule." Becky suddenly felt a slight panic. Was she overstepping, suggesting that John share in Chaim's class? Well, she had only suggested, not said for sure, that it would be possible, but it was too late to take it back. Why did he always make her so nervous?

"Well, I wouldn't want to impose. And I'm not really ready to meet the town folks. That sounds pretty scary. From what I've seen of this town, they haven't moved much beyond the Declaration of Independence. History hangs heavy here."

Becky was relieved that he refused and she certainly wouldn't bring it up again. "You could be right." And she left it there. He moved on down the hall and disappeared into his office.

"Georgina, I did it again. I let that man's odd aloofness throw me off balance. It is frustrating. I need to find a book on self-esteem or something."

"Nah, you have a zillion of them. I've seen them in your library. Wasn't your father something like that? Not involved in your life, I mean?"

"Yes, big time. I was always stumbling and saying the wrong thing around him too. And he never let it go by. He had to tell me I wasn't as smart as I thought I was or that I should be quiet around teachers. Did wonders for my self-image."

"Can you think of others who acted like him or John that you had the same reaction too?"

"Yeah. I had a boss, tall guy, severe looking, handlebar mustache. Didn't walk, he stalked across the room. I was scared to death of him. I was in my late twenties. I decided that I had to get hold of my reaction and change it. After all, he wasn't my father and he wasn't even successful in his relationships. People in the city who knew him thoroughly disliked him. He was caustic and demanding with them as well as all of us at the company. It took me eight years, but I finally mastered it and became quite a good manager. I began to see myself standing shoulder to shoulder with him instead of beaten down in front of him."

"Maybe you should picture this guy when you see John. Get back some of that moxie. You worked hard for it. Use it."

"Moxie, huh? You are a trip, Georgina! I'm sure you are right. I'll try it."

Georgina and Becky spent the weekend helping Chaim pull the next class together and working on Becky's arias. Chaim even came to one of their practice sessions and was amazed to hear Becky. He was amazed at the wonderful team that Georgina and Becky made. It was a fun weekend full of hard work and lots of laughs. Becky didn't mention her conversation with John to Chaim. She hoped she wouldn't ever have to. She stuffed it into the back of her mind and dove into the work to be done.

Nick came to Becky's office Monday morning to tell her that he would set things up this evening and that she needn't worry about it. He would also get down to Mom & Pop's for coffee with the other students. He was so pleased to regard himself as a student. Nick had been in the doldrums for a long time since his wife became ill after the difficult birth of their daughter, Laura. It frightened him that he might lose them. He was beginning to have a sparkle in his eyes and hope in his voice. It wasn't just being a student, it was the subject matter. He, too, was seeing a whole new world unfolding for himself.

Again the class was full. The theater afforded them a little more room, and with the semi-circular seating, they could more easily see who was talking during the discussion times. A few more of the faculty showed up, but not John Sherman.

Becky was a little surprised and a little put off about that. She now knew she was right about his interests and Chaim's fitting together. Was he threatened? Shy? Put off by her sudden suggestion? He didn't say what Jim needed. Was it something with Jim's work? She forced it out of her mind. She didn't want to miss a word of the class material.

Chaim was asking her to comment on the current idea under discussion. She rose to the occasion with a good response and was pulled out of herself into the whirling energy of the class. She felt esteemed and honored. It was a great feeling.

Six

A note was tucked under Becky's office door to come to the front office immediately. Becky couldn't imagine what it could be about. It sounded like an emergency. Jenny, the administrative assistant, met her half way down the hall. "John Sherman's class meets in twenty minutes, Becky. His son fell from a scaffolding yesterday and he has gone to Baltimore. Could you possibly meet with his class and pass out this test for him? It is open book essay, so you don't need to stay in the classroom. Just look in on them. They are supposed to write through the whole class time."

Several emotions ran through Becky at the same time. Guilt for her thoughts when she didn't see him in Chaim's class, shame for thinking he didn't care about his son, and momentary concern about her own plans for the morning. "Sure, I think can do that. Yes, of course."

Jenny handed her the copies of the test with thanks for rescuing them all. Becky walked slowly back into her room, closing the door behind her and glancing over the questions. What John had talked about at Mom & Pop's several weeks back was flooding back into her mind. The book was "A New Order of Being" by Shelling that Jim had brought from a seminar. Georgina was reading their copy of the book and Becky wished she had it to refer to just now.

The class filed in and looked a little startled to see Becky there. "Dr. Sherman is in Baltimore with his son. It seems that Jim fell from a scaffolding. I don't know the extent of his injuries. Anyway, here is the essay test you are to take this morning. I understand this is to be open book and you arc to write throughout thc hour."

She expected a reaction from the students, but they reached for the test and seemed eager to get down to business. Was John Sherman so stand-offish with his class that they felt no connection, no curiosity about him? She wanted to ask what they thought of the class material. She knew there were all levels of conservatism as well as very liberal points of view among the students. She wanted to know how their beliefs were affected by this material. But there would be no appropriate opening. All was quiet and pencils were flying across the paper.

She looked over the questions again. "Explain the part of you that knows you have a mind, thoughts, emotions, experiences, and yet is not any one of those things. Where does it reside? How does it get its information? What does it know that you weren't aware of? Is it good, bad or neutral? Does it evolve or is it static?"

Becky wondered how she would answer these questions herself. She began to jot some ideas down. She had intended to return to her office to finish some grading, but when she looked up again, the hour was almost ended. She had written many pages and still had ideas to explore.

The students came forward and placed their essays on John's desk and left noiselessly. She understood that. She smiled but wasn't in a place in her mind to chat either. It was as if she hadn't even been present in the room for that hour. She wondered to what realm she had traveled. She needed to spend some time with her writings to discern the value of what she had discovered somewhere in the realms of her mind or spirit. She wanted to get to her office and review the notes she had taken from Shelling's book and others.

She leafed through some notes looking for where had she seen the term non-local mind. Did she have a mind that had no location, at least not in the visible world? The brain was commonly said to be the house of the intellect, but was it the container or the function? Was there more to the field of mind than just the brain? If so, how far did it extend and what was it for? Back in her office, papers sat ungraded as she pondered and wrote down more questions that came to her. Possibilities swirled in her thoughts as she attempted to answer them.

Her classes that day became a fertile field of student minds to help her explore her ideas a little further. She wanted to be careful to restrict the discussions to her own subject area. The subject matter was gripping and fascinating, but she didn't want to trespass on John's territory.

"Becky are you staying all night?" Georgina was at her office door.

"Oh, what time is it? I guess I've been really engrossed here."

"I see. Have anything to do with subbing in John's class this morning?"

"Yes, plenty! How did you know I subbed in his class? Is he back yet? I didn't hear who took his other classes."

"I took them. I saw the test too. Ye gods, arguments broke out at the beginning of one class about the inerrancy of the Bible and how this material wasn't aligned with God's word."

"My class was completely silent. What did you do?"

"I told them to write it all down. That's what the test was for, and they could discuss it with Dr. Sherman when he returned. By the way, he is back. I guess Jim checked out O.K. No serious injuries. The company sent him to the hospital probably to protect themselves from a liability suit."

With a sigh Georgina flopped into a chair and put her feet up. "What are you working on? What's got you glued to the seat?"

"Well, actually, trying to answer these questions myself. And I keep coming up with more questions. There seems to be no end to it."

"Good work! You found the right answer. There isn't an end to it. It goes on and on." John Sherman was standing at the door looking somewhat pleased.

"John, come in and sit down." Georgina pulled a chair out of the corner for him to join them. "All's well with Jim?"

"Yes, he's home. Is there any feedback from the classes? Any reaction. By the way thanks for pinch-hitting for me."

"Oh, sure," said Becky. "The first hour class was absolutely silent. No reactions. No comments. I wondered at times if they were still breathing."

"The third class was a bit more verbal. Arguments broke out and I told them to write it all down for you. No way was I going to get into the middle of that." Georgina was adamant.

"Oh yes, they are the conservative ones. They all seemed to land in the same class. I've thought about either splitting them up and sprinkling them evenly around, or isolating them so the others can progress. However, the school administration doesn't want me to do either, so I'll have to think of something else." John seemed unusually communicative

Becky set her notes aside. "There were arguments in my classes when I first introduced a psychological component to the effect of religion on people's lives. I thought for a while they would run me out of town. Once parents and townsfolk understood that the school knew what I was presenting and actually approved it, things quieted down."

John seemed puzzled at that. "I wonder what hold the college has over the parents or local churches? It seems unusual to be able to quiet the conservative side. They take their freedom of speech pretty seriously, and their so called God-given right to attack everyone else's beliefs."

"I think the issue was money. They were told to pay up or shut up. This college desperately needs funding for a lot of work on the buildings and equipment. The contributors to the capitol campaigns were largely the liberal set. I guess that settled it. So conservatives, support the curriculum or take your kids out!" Georgina reached for the coffee pot and offered to pour some for John and Becky.

Becky looked at Georgina quizzically. "Where did you find all that out?"

"It was published in the Alumni Magazine and I just happened to know who a lot of the donors are from other publications in the library archives."

"I didn't know you spent time in the archives. How did you know what to look for?" Becky was really curious now.

"I was looking up some music information from way back, and saw the label on a file drawer. Pulled open the drawer and there it was. I read through it. You can never know too much about what drives this place if you want to survive."

"Georgi, you're a regular Mata Hari!" John was grinning now. "I've been hesitant to speak to people around here, not knowing who was on which side or where the hatchets are buried. Now I can just ask you."

"Is that why you are quiet?" Slightly rankled, Georgina was ready to dig deeper here too.

"Am I quiet? Well, maybe. I guess I save all my talking for my classroom where I can spin out my ideas without fear of reprisal." John grew serious.

"You've had reprisals? Here? What kind? When?"

"Not here. Not yet anyway. I received a lot of negative publicity on one trip. It was sort of like the truth squad that followed the Apostle Paul around shouting that a liar was coming, and then following up with the same thing after Paul left. I wasn't exactly let down over the city wall in a basket, but I did pack and leave earlier than intended at one place. I was giving a series of seminars, and one person seemed really disturbed and followed me from place to place. She carried a placard and picketed in front of the conference place. It got the attention of the press and she was quite vocal. Some of the people who spoke with her called the hotel where I was staying and threatened me. I have no idea what was said. The threats were veiled and not very clear, I'm told."

Georgina passed the cream and sugar around. "Will we be in the dark ages forever on this one? I hate having my beliefs attacked with suspicion and condescension. People have assumed down through the ages that God is on the side of violence and hatred. I don't get it!"

"Personal power, Georgi." John seemed comfortable with shortening her name. "When folks feel powerless they victimize someone else. They fear they will become victims themselves. They believe power comes from having power over everyone and everything that happens. It gives them a false sense of security. It has been the problem with humankind since Adam blamed Eve for the forbidden fruit. Adam blamed Eve. Eve learned quickly and blamed the snake. Blame someone. Make everyone else wrong so you can be right."

"Well, Eve didn't exactly shove it down Adam's throat now, did she?" Georgi narrowed her eyes.

"No, but you notice it got stuck in his throat and it has been called Adams apple ever since." John tilted his chin up to reveal his.

"I guess he was so eager, he forgot to chew it." Becky had an impish grin on her face and they all had a good laugh. It was great to see John loosen up and enjoy himself a bit.

Becky's phone rang at two in the morning. She knew who it probably was. Her father called at that hour when he was drinking. "When are you going to come here and help us out? Your mother can't do everything you know. I know you have to work, but we need help and you need to get yourself down here."

Becky swallowed hard keep her anger at bay. "Dad, you have lots of help. I can't leave my classes and I don't know what I could there do anyway. You and Mom have nurses and housekeepers all helping you."

"You're our daughter and you should be helping us out. What's the matter with you. You owe us something, you know."

"Dad, it is two a.m. and I have to get up early. Give Mom my love." Becky quietly hung up the phone and turned the ringer off. She hated to do that in case Nathan or Lissa called, but there was no other way. He would just keep calling all night until he passed out.

If Becky ever wondered where her guilt came from, it was answered every time this happened. When he was sober, he was so solicitous of everyone else's needs and desires. Two drinks and he was off to nasty land, picking on her mother and making unreasonable demands of everyone. He had to have his own way, even when he was wrong. How had her mother put up with it all these years?

Becky was ten years old. "Finish eating that apple and get to bed, do you hear me? Eat it! Eat it!" He kept shouting and Becky was chewing as fast as she could. She finally backed into the downstairs bathroom and shut the door. Out of sight, out of mind seemed to work. She could hear her mother saying, "Bob, I said she could have it. She's eating it as fast as she can for heaven's sake!"

And her dad saying, "God dammit, Arlene!"

"Don't you damn me, Bob. Don't use those words on me."

"Well I didn't damn you, but it just makes me mad. She's got to learn to get up to bed on time." He slammed his drink glass slammed down on the end table.

Young Becky stopped listening, eased out the bathroom door, tiptoed through the dark dining room and quietly up the stairs. Mother came up later to kiss her and whisper that she loved her.

When Becky realized that her mother had willingly married him, even chosen him, Becky was secretly and guiltily mad at her mother for that. Why couldn't she have chosen someone who would be nice? These thoughts always made Becky feel torn with anger, love, shame and guilt.

Now Becky realized that her mother considered her marriage vows sacred and would not abandon them, so she had to put up with emotional abuse. Fortunately there was no physical abuse.

Becky had no such compunctions. She wasn't going to spend her life putting up with a bad partner. She had seen the results of that. She would rather be alone. There was a difference between being alone and lonely, and she had always been lonely in her marriages. Being alone meant she was in charge and could decide what she wanted to do with no reprisals, no recriminations.

Becky managed to fall madly in love with strong emotionally unavailable men and then to marry the weak ones. It made for a crazy quilt of relationships and she was no longer willing to trust her judgment to make a permanent liaison with a man. It was just easier to avoid the emotional turmoil altogether. She had wonderful men friends and loved them dearly, but not intimately. She believed in not spoiling a friendship by turning it into a disastrous romance or marriage.

Georgina was on the phone Saturday morning with plans for the recital, rehearsal schedules, and music ideas. "Have breakfast with me, Beck, and see what you think. I'm planning a motif this time to frame the student music recital, so the stage and atmosphere won't be so spare. I'd like to make a kind of musical of it, instead of the usual string of unrelated performances."

The Breakfast Nook was in the back of a farm house on the edge of town. Grandma Jones kept the place open for breakfast only. She started very early to accommodate the surrounding farmers. They would line their barn boots up on her back porch before entering. You could tell it was a farmer's restaurant by the mud-spattered farm trucks in the driveway, mud all the way to the roofs of most of them.

Becky and Georgina arrived as the farmers were finishing up and paying. The lingering smell of bacon, eggs and pancakes was delicious, and Grandma didn't mind if they chatted on a bit after they ate while she cleaned up the kitchen. She liked to hear their conversation, refreshing after all the talk about cows and hogs.

"I want to create an opera set that is similar to Cavalleria Rusticana with its church and scenery in the background and outdoor café in the front. Students can sit in the café instead of the front row of the audience or back stage. We can use the Intermezzo for the opening and at the end. Maybe the students can sing part of a chorus from it at the end. I know

Nick will help us build a set. Nothing too complicated. Mostly painting a backdrop and setting up café chairs and tables."

"I love it! I've painted scenery before. I'll be glad to help. There are old café-style cafeteria chairs in the storage barn. We could see what shape they are in and maybe paint them. There are probably tables too. If not, we should be able to borrow some round tables or buy some cheap plastic ones and cover them with checkered cloths. There's a flea market in Millersburg that might have ale glasses or something for atmosphere."

Georgina jumped up. "Let's go to Millersburg. I'm in the mood to escape and go shop. There could be all sorts of interesting stuff. Let's go have some fun!"

They paid their checks and headed for Millersburg. Becky was relieved to shake off the memories of last night's phone call and Georgina was excited about her staging plans. Becky had a sport utility van with room to haul whatever they might find, so they took that. Grandma had told Georgina to pull her car over to the side of the house and leave it. It was a cold crisp day, sunshine bright and promising. Becky settled behind the wheel as Georgina parked her car. There was nothing like setting off on an adventure with a good friend and no particular responsibilities for a day.

Millersburg had several antique and second-hand shops. Becky liked to look for second hand dolls, preferably from the sixties when they made large beautiful baby dolls. The store owner brought one out from the back of the store and said, "For some reason when I looked at you, this doll came to my mind. She just came in with a box of toys and junk. Five dollars and she's yours." It was a doll exactly like one of her childhood dolls. Becky didn't know how this woman knew she would be interested and decided to chalk it up to divine providence. Maybe God was watching out for her after all.

Five-year old Becky knocked on the door of the house where she and her family had moved from just a little less than a year ago. She told the new owner, "I think my mother left my doll here. She was in the pantry on a shelf."

"Well, we've just cleaned all the cupboards and closets and there was no doll." Becky looked so forlorn that the woman continued, "But you can come in and look if you would like to."

Becky ran to the pantry and desperately looked on all the shelves, but her doll wasn't there. She thanked the new owner and reluctantly went back toward her new home. She had been so sure it was there. Her mother told her many years later that she had discarded the old doll thinking Becky would like the new one she had gotten at Christmas and would forget about the old one. But Becky never forgot.

Becky had seen that forlorn look on a child's face not so many years ago. She had brought a large doll to a mother-daughter banquet since Lissa couldn't be there. A six-year old child whose family had just broken up sat and held the doll all evening. Becky knew she just had to give this child the doll. She chastised herself for being childishly attached to a doll. She told the little girl that she could take the doll home, but if she decided she didn't want it, she should give it back to Becky. The little girl's face lit up in wide-eyed amazement. "Can I really have her? Really?" Becky nodded.

The girl's mother came to Becky as they were leaving. "I know how hard it was for you to give up that doll. It is a wonderful thing you just did for my daughter. She has been so sad. Thank you, and we'll take wonderful care of it, I promise."

It made Becky feel better that this woman somehow knew how she felt and was kind enough to reassure her.

Becky's house had gotten full of dolls over the years, but there was always room for one more. She called it her orphanage for abused and abandoned dolls. She had only one doll from her childhood, and couldn't remember what had happened to all the rest of them. Even the big doll that came at Christmas to replace her old one. Her mother had a way of quietly moving them on when Becky went to school.

"Now that you've gotten your doll can we please look for scenery and props?" Georgina, hands on her hips, pretended to be long suffering as she waited for Becky to complete the purchase. "This happens every time we go poking around in second hand stores. You'll have to rent an apartment just for your dolls. There won't be room for you pretty soon."

"They are an investment," Becky said feeling an old need to justify herself. "I do have some valuable ones, you know. And then I have some not so valuable ones that are just cute. I can even give them away if the occasion arises. You never know when a little girl will need a doll."

"Right," snorted Georgina. "I know exactly which little girl needs the doll. It's O.K." She didn't know how close she had come to touching the place in Becky that was bruised so long ago.

Little by little they collected old worn checkered table cloths, half used candles and tarnished candle holders, battered goblets, cloudy ale glasses and old velvet draperies. The hardware store was having a sale on paint and brushes and the lumber company by the railroad tracks had some old barn wood that would be good for something. Nick would know what to do with it. They loaded Becky's vehicle and drove down the street to a café for some lunch.

"Georgina, didn't you have a hobby or some favorite things when you were a kid?"

"You mean like dolls? Not really. I gathered music stuff along the way. Old play bills from the musicals, old music scores and stage props like we're doing now. I would fix up a stage and get the neighborhood kids to help me put on a musical. We made costumes out of our parent's old clothes. There was an old back room attached to our house that I could use to create scenery. We thought up stories and silly songs. It was a lot of fun. I guess my family's musical history was a big influence. You could say I've been on the stage ever since I was old enough to build my own."

"What fun! The neighbor girl and I used to act out stories with our dolls, but we never thought of staging a whole play."

Georgina glowed with memories. "I was with my Dad so much. He would conduct orchestras and choruses, and I pretended to play and sing along until I was old enough to really do it. He would perch me on the platform beside him while he rehearsed the musicians. I would turn pages for him and rush to pick up music if the musicians dropped theirs. They all sort of adopted me and even let me try to play their instruments, very carefully or course."

Becky sadly remembered her Dad listening to his opera on weekends and yelling at her if she made a sound in the house. She wasn't included in his music interest. Rather she was shut out and chased away. When she went to college she was relieved to never have to listen to or tiptoe around his opera again.

Her first year in college was a lonely time. The girls in the dorm were nice to her, but they didn't fill that empty place inside that seemed to be growing. Her dorm mates felt sorry for her. "C'mon, Becky, we're going to the pizza place."

It was privately owned. The owner flirted outrageously with all the girls while making the pizzas. He kept music playing on a stereo and Becky began to be aware that she recognized it. It was somehow comforting and made her feel happy. It was La Boheme! How many times had she heard it all through her childhood? The very thing she wanted to get away from she was now missing. Of course it wasn't really the music she wanted to escape from, but the irritable temperament of her father.

They drove to the storage building on the college campus. Georgina called Nick before they started home. He agreed to meet them at the school and help them unload. They culled through the chairs in the back of the building and found a dozen or more suitable café chairs. Nick thought he knew where he could get the tables. He remembered that Grandma Jones stored some in her barn hayloft when she got new ones for her restaurant. The old ones had gotten too wobbly to be trusted with large heavy platters of home fries and eggs and farmers' elbows.

Nick and Becky cleared and swept out a place where they could work. Georgina sat down to make a sketch of the stage, the placement of props, and the details of the background. Then she also sketched the whole finished product complete with characters to get a sense of the overall effect. Becky tacked the drawings up on the wall as Georgina finished them.

Nick opened paint cans and lined up the barn boards and chairs to be used. Becky and Georgina couldn't continue the work all day, but Nick insisted on staying. "I can get the first coats on and paint up the back drop so you can put in the details later on. It won't take me long and you can work on it whenever you have time."

"We owe you a pizza, Nick!" chirped Georgina. "Thanks so much for your help. By the way how is your daughter doing?"

Nick's daughter Laura was crippled from birth. She had several bouts with surgery and ongoing physical therapy. "She's coming along fine. We discovered that she likes to sing in church. She doesn't talk hardly at all, but she will sing. Her mother and I have been very excited about that, and the therapist too."

"Nick, bring her to my studio and let me try to work with her singing." Georgina was excited too.

"Well, we have so many medical bills that we really can't afford to right now, but maybe sometime…"

"Now is the time, Nick. She needs it now while this is developing in her brain and nervous system. Forget the money. I've had lots of training in music therapy and voice therapy, and I would love to help her. Just bring her in if she wants to do it. We'll set up a time. I'll call Doris this weekend."

Nick was speechless for a moment. "I'll tell Doris to expect your call. We hadn't thought of her singing as anything, but maybe it is. You sure, professor? We don't want to impose."

"Nothing could make me happier. It isn't an imposition, it is an invitation. I'll call Doris tonight if you are going to be home."

"We'll be home for sure. I'll tell Doris. We'll be there."

Seven

"Hello, Beck, this is Karla."

"Hi, I just talked to you. What's up?"

"Yup, well I need a huge favor. The guy who had my radio show until the first of the year is incapacitated and I suddenly need a call-in interview."

"Oh, gee, when?"

"Right now. I'm calling from the station. Five minutes to air time!"

Becky was stunned. "Ye gods! Ah…, what will we talk about? What will I say? Gee whiskers! How long is it?"

"We talk about your field, psychology and religion, and it's an hour. Just stay on the line."

Becky spun around to her computer and brought up some recent class notes. She was scanning them when Karla came back on the line saying, "Our guest this evening is Dr. Rebecca Lawrence Richardson Temple of South Bennington College, Johnston Crossing, Connecticut. Welcome to the show, Rebecca."

"Hello Karla, glad to be here." Becky wasn't quite sure of that as she hurriedly put notes in order on her desk in case she needed them.

"I need our listeners to know that George Trent was suddenly incapacitated and will not be able to continue with the show. I was scheduled to take over in January, but it looks like that schedule is moved up starting tonight. Rebecca is a long-time friend of mine and has agreed on five minutes' notice to be on the show. She is professor of psychology and religion and is exploring many new ideas in this area. Rebecca, what is the central theme in your work? Why religion *and* psychology?"

"Karla, religion is as old as the psyche itself. Humankind has always had a sense of something larger or greater and more powerful that is in charge, and religion has sought to form the psychological response to it."

"So, it sounds like religion is a form of power over people. Can we say that?"

"Yes, you can say that. The power has a focus which is to create a society for the purpose of survival. If people are working together, responding similarly to events, there is a protecting cohesiveness that begins to form a society. Since much of the religious fervor is based on fear of the unknown and fear of dying, religion seeks to explain unknown forces and formulate a response that will allow humanity to survive. Since the human psyche has many facets, these facets were envisioned as human-like forms and expressed in religions. Yahweh was one style of god who walked like a human in the garden of Eden and, like a parent or master, chastised Adam and Eve for disobedience. Obedience was their ticket to survival. If they ate of the forbidden tree they would die. If humanity partakes of the tree of destructive behaviors it will die. Elohim was the transcendent god, absent in human form, but residing in the spiritual realms.

"Jesus referred to God as Abba or papa, an endearing term. He introduced the love of God, rather than the Hebrew Testament reward and punishment. God went from being a punishing force to a loving force."

"Could you say that God has evolved over the millennia?"

"Well, Karla, I prefer to say that humanity has evolved in its thinking and understanding. Man tends to recreate God in his own image. Mankind's image evolves and you might say it improves with age. Humanity's psychology grows and matures, and takes in more possibilities, sees a widening horizon of choices. We no longer fear the thunder and lightening as an entity that is out to get us. It is a force of nature that we respect and treat with caution. We even used the lightening to learn about electrical power."

"So, what's the downside of religion and its effect psychologically?"

"The downside is always when a person or a group of persons seize control of the religion and its practices to give themselves power over the people. They distort the teachings and use them as threats of punishment if the population doesn't do what they want. Horrible things have been done in the name of religion, as we know. Fear, guilt, anger, resentment, cunning, violence, all of those are born of this unfortunate use of religion."

"Where does self-help psychology fit in? It is called secularism, humanism, and other nasty names."

"Self-help psychology is indicative of the individual at last freeing him or herself from the tyranny of misused power, and the effects of that misuse upon their very lives. Their thinking, reactions, emotions, and responses to life are all tried up in this morass of error thinking. Support groups such as Alcoholics Anonymous, Adult Children of Alcoholics, Overeaters Anonymous, Emotions Anonymous, and all the offshoots of those, are an attempt to heal ourselves emotionally and physically. Co-dependence is a word coined to explain unhealthy, unbalanced, and abusive relationships."

"We have a caller, Rebecca, who has a question. Go ahead caller."

"Who are you to explain God to the world? Everyone knows about Satan, evil and sin. Those are real. Or are you saying they aren't real?"

"First of all, I'm a seeker of the truth who has devoted her life to study, listening to, and interacting with people of all walks of life everywhere. God gave me a mind and intelligence with which to do that seeking. I honor my God-given gifts by using them for the benefit of anyone who is in pain or confusion.

"Are Satan, evil, and sin real? They are very real in the human mind and they have been given great power to do harm. Since the beginning of time humanity has given them this power by naming them, giving them human characteristics, and then forming destructive responses to them. You said that everyone knows about them. Yes, they do. They give them a lot of attention, which engenders a huge amount of fear, which then creates a negative energy field that is indeed dangerous."

"So, you don't think Satan can come after us?"

"Oh yes. The more you fear Satan, the faster you draw that satanic energy toward you, which makes it appear that Satan is chasing you. But actually you have made a magnet of yourself which draws that energy to you."

"Well, am I doing it all by myself? It is all my own fault?"

"You have lots of help. All of humanity is doing it and we are all part of humanity. Don't heap all the responsibility on yourself. Humanity has to learn better, and I believe we are doing just that."

"Thank you, caller. We appreciate your participation. It is time for a station break and we'll be right back. The number to call is 800-531-0008."

"Phew, I'm glad for a little regroup time," said Becky. "We're off the air I hope?"

"Oh, yeah, we're off. Great job! Wow, I didn't know you were, uh, so smooth with all this."

"Your comments help too, Karla. They really helped me get going. Nice caller. I didn't know where he was going with his questions, but he seemed more sincere than confrontational. I really appreciated that."

"It was a good beginning, Beck. Four more minutes and we go again." Karla reached behind her for the coffee pot.

The whole show went well and they were both pleased. Becky was exhausted from the hyper-alert frame of mind she held through the whole hour. She amazed herself at how much she had put together in her thinking from her research, Chaim's class, and John's test questions. She made some hot chocolate and settled down to watch a movie for a while to calm her jangling mind.

It suddenly dawned on her that she hadn't had a chance to notify the college this was happening. They liked to know in order to use it in publicity or field any phone calls it might generate. She promised herself to let them know first thing in the morning.

Morning arrived with a flurry of call messages at the college office. Becky picked up the phone and called the administrative assistant's office. "Jenny, I'm so sorry I didn't have a chance to let you know about the radio broadcast I was on last night. It all happened suddenly, within five minutes last evening, and I just went on the air for a friend who has the show."

"Slow down, Becky. We're O.K. I'm bringing the messages over to you. You still have time to go through channels. Actually, the messages look really interesting. A few cranks, but there always are."

"Oh, jeez, Jenny, I promised myself I would call you first thing."

"Like I said, not a problem. Take your time. We're fine here."

"Thanks, Jen. See you in a while."

"See ya."

Becky called Georgina who was just getting out of the shower. "Hey, Beck, what's happened? You're not usually awake enough to be all wound up this early."

"Karla called last evening and needed a call-in interview immediately. It was an hour show. I have a bazillion messages here. Jenny brought them to me. I haven't read them yet."

"Hang on, I'll jump into my clothes and come over. We'll read them together. Are you getting a tape of the show?"

"I forgot to ask. I'll give Karla a call later. I'm sure they taped the show."

"Oh yes, radio stations always do. We'll listen to that together too. I can't wait. I know you were great!"

"I don't know if I can stand to hear myself on tape just yet. Glad you're coming over. I'll have the coffee on."

"I'll be there. Bye."

Becky checked in with all the powers-that-be at the college and promised a copy of the tape. Everyone seemed pleased overall and Becky settled down to her day of classes. Having survived a trial by fire gave her a sparkle and animation she hadn't felt in a while.

"How's the celebrity? I heard you were on the radio." Chaim was hauling a load of books toward his office.

"Heavens, is it all over the school? Let me help you with those."

"Thanks. Just grab those few that are sliding off the pile. I can handle the rest. So how did this all come about?"

Becky went over the questions and all she could remember of what she said. It was good to talk to Chaim. He was always so encouraging, and had such good input that would help her out the next time.

"Say, I'll bet Karla would like to interview you sometime. Maybe even soon. Would you like me to give her your number?"

"Yes, would you?" He dropped his books on an existing pile on his work table. "Here, let me get my card for you so you'll have my number. I think it is working. I haven't gotten around to giving it to my friends and relatives yet. That means things will stay quiet a while longer."

"A method in your madness?"

"Yes, that too. Once they all have it, I'll have to unplug the phone to get any peace. They are blissfully unaware of time, especially in the middle of the night."

Becky was sure it wasn't for the same reason her father called in the middle of the night. He was anything but blissful. But she wouldn't allow herself to think about that anymore now.

Monday evening had rolled around again. Mom & Pop's was packed with the students waiting for class time. The group had stabilized in numbers and had divided itself into small discussion groups around the tables.

When Becky arrived in the classroom, John was already there. He was leafing through the books and handouts. Chaim was setting up the slide show. They greeted her bowing and scraping with overweening deference to her celebrityship. They were hilarious. It was amazing to Becky to see those two, who had been strangers a few months ago, be such a fun part of her life now. Well, she wasn't sure about John. This joviality was new for him in her experience.

The class picked up on the energy and was lively as usual. They became engrossed in the metaphysics of describing the invisible and it's meaning in their lives. They went around in circles verbally until Chaim had to rescue them with his clear understanding. He could bring it all out of thin air and make it all so down to earth without losing the mystery. It never ceased to astound Becky and Georgina.

John had to leave a little early, something about calling Jim before it got too late. Becky wondered if he was uncomfortable with the class, or had he used up his sociability for the day. Immediately she berated herself for judging him, for mistrusting him. She made a commitment to find what it was in her that triggered her reaction to him.

Matt had been secretive, private. When he turned away from her, Becky always felt it was her fault. Had she pried? Had she shown up at wrong times? Was she too intrusive? Was he running from her, from her persistence? Their relationship was like a train running off the track car by car until it wasn't there. They took a walk one afternoon and Matt ended it. He said, "I don't have anything more to give to you. I have to end this and say goodbye." Then he simply walked away up the street, into the distance, and was gone. For months she looked for him on every street corner, wanting to see him and afraid she would see him. The pain was overwhelming for a long time. She wrote about her pain in a journal and then burned the pages. It helped each time the pain threatened to engulf her. Eventually it subsided to manageable proportions. It had never completely gone away.

She had to stop thinking she was the cause of everyone else's problems. She had to disconnect herself from trying to figure them all out. She had to deal with her feelings of abandonment now before they caused her to do or say something embarrassing. She would find something in one of her self-help books about it. She would look through them tonight when she got home.

"Coffee, Beck? You look really far away. Anything wrong?" Georgina had been standing beside Becky's chair waiting for her to gather up her coat and purse.

"No, just thinking. Coffee sounds great. Maybe Mom & Pop's won't be crowded tonight."

Chaim begged off on the coffee this evening. He had a conference call with his family coming in. He wasn't expecting good news.

There was a message on Becky's answering machine when she arrived home. It was Juliette Farone, Nathan's fiancé. She had a slight European accent. "Dr. Temple, this is Juliette Farone. We have not met, but I would like to speak with you. I have not heard from Nathan and I am very worried. Perhaps it would be easier to endure his absences if I could talk with you. I hope this would be all right. I hope I am not intruding."

Becky called immediately. "Juliette, I am so glad you called me. Nathan didn't leave me any way to get in touch with you. I guess he is so used to not being able to tell me anything that he forgot to give me your number. What is causing you to worry?"

"He always leaves me a message, a code, when he can to let me know he is all right. I haven't received one and it scares me."

"How long has it been?" Becky's heart was in her throat.

"It has been a week. That is a bit longer than usual. Of course his office will tell me nothing. I called them once and Nathan wasn't very happy about that. They don't even acknowledge they know who he is. It gives me the creeps."

"What can I do? Anything? Where is his base office located, do you know?"

"It is somewhere in Boston. He can't even tell me that. He doesn't know I accidentally overheard him responding to a pager call."

"Juliette, I know he is the best of the best. He can take care of himself. I've had to live with that faith in him since he began this line of work. It isn't easy, but it is all we have."

"Thank you, Dr. Temple. I appreciate your confidence in him."

"Becky, please call me Becky."

"Yes…Becky. Would they notify you if anything was wrong? Are you in the loop as you say?"

"I don't think so. I really don't know. I haven't considered that it would be necessary. I don't let myself think along those lines." Becky's thoughts were beginning to race. Was this real or was it just Juliette's fears? She really didn't know Juliette. But Nathan must trust her so maybe there is something to it.

"Perhaps I must have a little more faith too. It is more difficult than I thought to bear the uncertainty alone. I'm sorry if I have disturbed you unnecessarily."

"Please, Juliette, call me anytime you need to, and do give me your address so we can be in touch."

Juliette repeated her number and address to Becky. Becky thought Juliette was very sweet, but was she strong enough to deal with Nathan and his independent nature?

Becky began looking in the phone book for CIA offices in the Boston area. Under U.S. Government she found one reference. She couldn't be sure exactly what it was. She pulled out a map to get a location. It was near the harbor. Becky sat for a while regarding the map and wondering if she should take some action. She decided to try the phone number in the morning. Considering it made her feel a little foolish, but despite her misgivings, she resolved to make a call or do something.

Leaving a message on Jenny's answering machine at the school to cancel her classes for the day, she was in the car before dawn. The phone call had connected her to a phone tree which required codes for everything and was essentially a dead end.

The map brought her directly to the parking lot of a non-descript brick two-story building. There were no identifying signs anywhere. She sat in her vehicle for several minutes with conflicting feelings. Was she going too far or not far enough? Slowly she opened the door, got out, and started toward the unmarked door.

"Mom? What's happened? Why are you here?" Nathan came striding across the parking lot.

Becky almost tripped in surprise to see Nathan. He caught her arm and she gave him a big hug. Over coffee in a nearby shop she told him about Juliette's call and how she couldn't get through on the CIA listed phone number.

"Mom, I'm so sorry. I didn't call Juliette because I went on a job after I turned in my resignation and before it was filed and accepted. My usual access routes were cut off prematurely. I planned to let you and Juliette know when my exit interview, which was an hour ago, was completed. I just got out. Everything is final and I'm free. I didn't realize she would panic about a few extra days. There was nothing I could do anyway."

"I didn't mean to get Juliette into trouble, and I hope I haven't embarrassed you too much." Becky hadn't thought about the effect her actions might have on their relationship.

"No, not at all. What other guy do I know whose mother is ready to take on the whole Central Intelligence Agency for her son, and probably win?" Nathan was laughing now.

"Darned right," said Becky, "They released you just in time before I was forced to do them some serious damage." They were back to their usual easy communication exchanges.

"I almost forgot to tell you that I have another job. I have to run in a few minutes because they want to complete the negotiations and paperwork today."

Becky needed to finish up their conversation. "Juliette was really feeling alone and scared. I was glad she called me. It helps to have a little support in this cold world."

"I'll call her today as soon as I finish my appointment. I hate to rush off. Are you staying around or going back home?"

"I'm going back, Nathan. Maybe we can make plans for the holidays now that your work is a little more predictable. It will be, won't it?"

"Well, I hope so. I have some negotiating to do around that. I'll call you tomorrow and let you know how it went and what it is about." Nathan got up, pulled Becky to her feet, and gave her a hug. "Thanks for loving me so much, Mom."

Becky closed her eyes and held him tightly. She walked to her vehicle with tears welling up in her eyes, climbed in, checked her map, and drove toward home. Her connection with Nathan was something very special. When he was born, he looked so familiar that Becky thought we was looking at a miniature of herself. It was such a surprise. She thought a newborn was like a stranger that you had to get to know. This was not the case at all. He was completely familiar. He was definitely her baby. This feeling had not changed on all these years.

When Lissa was born, Becky was expecting that familiarity and she wasn't disappointed. But it was a little different. Lissa looked like other members of the family. It was as if she was more the family's baby, even though Becky had the same strong heart connection with her. When Lissa fell out of her little bed onto the floor she cried for a moment, but Becky cried all day. Lissa was only a few weeks old and hadn't moved around at all until the first time Becky turned her back to do something. There was that sickening thud on the floor and Lissa's cry of surprise and rage. Guilt overwhelmed Becky. She kept checking Lissa over to be sure she wasn't injured, her own tears dripping on the crib sheet.

Becky's ride home was filled with memories of her children's childhood events, good and not so good. Mostly Becky's mind was filled with the emotions that went with those events and they were overwhelming her again.

"Why am I torturing myself with this stuff? There's nothing I can do to change anything. The kids don't want to hear about it. They think everything was fine. Why can't I let it be fine? I guess because I wasn't fine. It was me."

She had read that we can't change the past, but we can change our feelings about the past. We can neutralize those painful feelings by remembering that events are events, not torture chambers for the future. We can forgive ourselves, because if we had been able to do better, we would have. It wasn't her fault that she sustained childhood emotional damage from her father's unavailability. And there was no use blaming him either. The point now is to heal those wounds by not picking at them and opening them up constantly. She took a deep breath and resolved to do just that, let the wounds heal. Whenever her mind wandered into those dark alleys she would take the author's advice, and bring her thoughts back into focus with some good idea to work on.

It was late when Becky drove into her garage and she was glad to be home. Her exploration of her feelings had kept her energized all the way home, but now she was ready to drop into bed. It was good to be able to come to a sensible resolution when she had to work through something so painful. She was grateful for the authors that made it possible for her, and many like her, to get on with life in a happier more productive way. She was asleep as soon as she felt the pillow touch her cheek.

Eight

Geez, Beck! You high tailed it all the way to Boston and back yesterday? You must have started before dawn. Jenny said it was some kind of family emergency. What happened? When did you get back?" Georgina was breathless.

"Whoa, slow down." Becky filled her in on the whole story including how foolish she felt, especially when Nathan showed up. She left out the sorting process she went through all the way home.

"Becky, a mother's love and concern are never foolish. We have too few parents in this world who are passionate about their kids. Too many just don't give a damn. I think you are amazing. Oh, yeah, John volunteered to take your classes since there were only two and at different times from his.

"Really! I didn't expect that. What did the classes do?"

"He had the students answer a few provocative questions. You should have some interesting papers to look over. I think he left them in your office with a note."

"What did he ask them, do you know?"

"Something about what they came onto this planet and into this life to do. What did they think their life purpose is?"

"Ye gods! That should be fun stuff. Want to read them with me?"

"I thought you'd never ask," chuckled Georgina. "See you at your office in the morning?"

"Yup, I'll be there."

Nathan called about his new job as he promised. Becky wasn't used to such a quick response from him. It had always been weeks before she heard anything.

"I'm head of the security department for a very old corporation. It is computer security as well as physical security. There are a lot of interesting aspects to it and I'm going to like it a lot. There will be trips to Washington D.C. and the big military bases. I'll be conferring with top security people, giving seminars and doing research."

"Sounds great. At least your travel won't be top secret classified, uh, will it?"

"No, not to the extent it was before. I can't talk about security structures and plans, but where I'm going isn't classified."

"What a relief. Good to have you back in my life. Did you call Juliette? Is she O.K.?"

"Yes, she's fine. A little put out, but when I told her about the new job, that sort of mollified her."

"What do you mean 'sort of'?"

"She's not sure she wants to be engaged to someone so, uh, mobile I guess."

Mobile? Unpredictable? Uncontrollable? Becky was immediately suspicious. Was this girl backing out? Didn't relationships require a little more staying power than that?

Becky always knew when Jeffrey turned to other women. It was usually a one-night stand or one-time liaison, but she always knew when and who. He didn't know she knew. More and more he simply turned away from her affections and became like a housemate instead of a husband. Once again she had married one that was not strong or dedicated. She was better educated, more ambitious, and more aware of human complexities. Those traits always attracted men with fewer qualifications. She and Matt had split up, and Jeffrey was like a hospital for her broken heart. He was a lovable teddy bear at first. She and Jeffrey had been good for each other for a few years. Then he began to be distant and keep to himself. He began to lie about little things first and bigger things as time went on. Becky discovered more about his step-father and the similarities between them, another father-influence destructive to the children.

Becky went back to school after the breakup. Life always called her to move forward. That calling seemed to leave her relationships in the dust, but she could do nothing else but answer that call. It had become obvious that no one was going to look out for her, move her forward, or see that she fulfilled her potential. It was all up to her. She wondered from time to time about husbands who promoted their wives, and where were they in her life? She wondered if that was as wonderful as it sounded. She didn't even know where to start looking or what to look for. She wondered if she lacked what it took to attract that kind of person. What did it all have to do with love anyway? How could she connect it all to make it work?

Her phone rang after she and Jeffrey called it quits. It was Catherine, dean of student life of the university. "Becky, you are the vice president of your class, right?"

"Yes, yes I am."

"The fellow who is president is withdrawing from school, so you are needed to step into his role. You need to preside over the orientation ceremonies this Monday afternoon. I'll brief you on what you need to do Monday morning. Please be in my office at eleven."

If Becky had any doubts about her calling, it was like a sign from God to keep marching to the tune. There was more for her to do and be. It was as if the road kept rolling out in front of her, beckoning her to keep moving forward.

Nathan sounded pretty upbeat, but Becky knew how much he wanted a wife and family. Like her, he seemed to have a calling elsewhere and the women he met didn't fit into it somehow.

Chaim was pushing his tray along the food bar in the cafeteria. Becky and Georgina were right behind him. It had become a given that the three of them would head for the same table together.

"Your friend, Karla, called me and we're set up for next Thursday. She said there was a great response to your interview, and she is eager to do another one. She received letters from everywhere, even outside the country."

Becky's eyebrows went up and she set her fork down. "What's she going to do with them all?"

"She'll call you. Tried to get you yesterday, but you weren't here."

Becky told Chaim about her mission to Boston. Georgina was happy to hear the details again, nodding her head in support.

"I think I would have done the same thing," said Chaim. "I wouldn't have been able to just sit here and do nothing. I'm a warrior. I have to ride into battle. Mostly spiritual battle, but sometimes it manifests into the physical realm of action too. I do have three sons in the Israeli army, so I guess they come by it naturally."

"Really?" piped in Georgina. "I don't think you've mentioned them. They're not here?"

"No, they live in Israel with their mother and her relatives on a kibbutz. All Israeli kids, boys and girls, have to do a stint in the army. They've decided to stay in. They like it. It scares me. Every time I hear about a conflict or bombing, I hold my breath."

Georgina couldn't give up until she had all the information. "Are you separated or divorced?"

"No. Don't be surprised. The culture is a little different there. The boys are grown and gone, and she has her own career. She is a clinical psychologist and her practice has grown enormously since the conflicts intensified. We meet for vacations in Rome, Paris, or wherever she would like to go. When I take a sabbatical, I spend it in Israel. I do research and, of course, fix things around the house, while she is at work. Some things never change."

"Wow," exclaimed Georgina. "That's amazing. I've heard of long distance marriages, coast to coast ones, but you're the first international one I've actually met. Is it hard to keep things going? I mean how do you maintain the closeness, the intimacy?"

"Maybe you could call it the Jewish bond. In Israel we have a diversity of peoples from all around the world and from every country, but we are all Jews. We have history, rituals, celebrations, customs and an ancient language all shared nationally, even if we aren't all religiously observant Jews. You see, our families are close knit with ties back to Abraham and it all serves to support our bonds to each other. Yael and I know what to expect with respect to each other and confident that we are both on track with what we planned to accomplish together."

"Amazing and fascinating. I wish we had a little more of that in this country." Becky was wistful. "We need a little more support and a little less fracturing of the bonds in families." She told them about Nathan and Juliette, and about her doubts. "There is really nothing to support them. They are blowing in the wind and this latest episode demonstrates it so clearly. There is nothing to help them hold together, and they don't seem to be aware that something is needed. If it doesn't work, it doesn't work. That's where it stops."

Chaim had lived in the United States long enough to know exactly what she was talking about. "I couldn't find a partner here that was rooted in our culture. I didn't go to Israel to find a bride necessarily, but that is what happened. My parents were sure that was a mistake since they didn't have much interest in Israel or even visiting there themselves. All they could think of was the women were all in the army and carried Uzis or something equally masculine. Yael is just a little more intense than they are comfortable with, but they agree she is very special."

"So, what are your sons' names?" Georgina was still fascinated.

"The oldest is Yacov after my father Jacob. The second is Uri after Yael's father and the third is Avram after our patriarch Abraham. All have ancient spelling and pronunciations. More of our Jewish bond."

"Isn't this Jewish adherence to tradition how your people survived all the persecution and remained a committed nation?" Becky had read some of the holocaust literature.

"Yes, that was our strength. Many of our young people struggle against those bonds now in the modern world. They want to be free of Jewishness, and later in their lives, will long to return to it. Many countries have tried to destroy us as Jews and our culture. Fortunately, it has remained strong and is always there for them to return to."

Georgina asked quietly, "Do you think the Jews are the chosen race?" She wasn't sure how to approach the subject.

"Well, that's the scuttlebutt. Personally, I think the Jews were the first choosing race. They were the first ones to choose the idea of one god. 'Hear O Israel, the Lord our God is One.' Most cultures were polytheistic. The Greeks and Romans thought that the more gods they worshipped, the more pious and religious they were. They couldn't imagine a culture that worshipped only one god. It was sacrilegious to them."

"Interesting perspective. I hadn't thought of that. I thought God just pointed his finger out of the sky and said, 'You're it.'"

"I think that's the popular notion." Chaim was completely at ease with the conversation. Georgina was relieved and became more relaxed as they talked. It was always easy to be around Chaim, as Becky had said many times. He was always thoughtful about the topic at hand, and not at all defensive about it.

"Do you remember the story of the Apostle Paul and his speech to the Greeks on Mars Hill?" Chaim didn't wait for an answer. "Paul chose the pedestal that was without a statue. The Greeks always left one empty in case there was a god they didn't know about. They didn't want to offend any of them. Paul pointed to the empty pedestal and preached to them about the unknown invisible god that he worshipped. They had been prepared to jeer him, but he got their attention. It was exceedingly clever of him and true to his teaching."

Georgina and Becky were still reading the student papers from yesterday's class when John stopped in. "How's it going? Anything interesting come of yesterday's questions?"

"Yes, John, lots of stuff. Thanks so much for your help. Things came up so quickly that I thought the classes could only be cancelled."

"As I remember, you and Georgi jumped in for me on the spur of the moment."

"Our pleasure. Have a seat if you have some time and look at some of this with us." Becky handed him some of the papers.

"I glanced at them before I left yesterday. Similar reactions from my classes. It took them the whole period to get something down and they were writing like crazy when the time was up. I told them they could continue their answers like a journal as ideas came to them."

"Oh, journals are a great idea. Mind if I use it?"

"Not at all. I'd like to stay and chat but I have an appointment. Glad you like the idea."

"Right," sputtered Georgina. "Was that a brush off? I always get the idea he thinks we are somehow beneath him. Stay and chat? Excuse me, but we don't need to be trivialized as 'chat'."

"C'mon, Georgi, the guy is socially challenged. Give him a break. If we get insulted every time he comes up with something like that, we may be feeling insulted a lot."

"You're right, I don't think there's much hope for him."

"Well, that isn't quite what I meant. Let's not give up on him so soon."

"It's just that every move he makes is a power move. He has to be top dog or he splits. You saw him leave Chaim's class with some lame excuse or other. We don't have the academic jealousy and backstabbing here that bigger universities have, and I don't care to see it start."

"I think you may be right. He comes from that competitive atmosphere and he's good at making a target out of himself." Becky was glad to know it wasn't just her perception that he was always trying to be one-up. "The students have started to call him King John. Not a good sign."

"I think they half admire him and half fear him. He keeps them off balance, like he does us. It's not healthy. You can't trust him." Georgina scowled at the papers in her hand that he had given back.

That was part of Becky's discomfort. She had problems with men who purposely kept her off balance. Becky herself was clever, so it was a fun contest for a while. But it wasn't a real relationship, and it would become tedious. After a while she would avoid them or become aggravated at them. She always ended up feeling she had been made fun of. She was attracted at first and then sorry she had gotten sucked into the game.

"I'm not sure I'm glad he took my classes. I was asked to take his. Was he asked to take mine or did he sort of grab them?"

"He was in Jenny's office when she listened to your message. Let's go ask her."

Jenny confirmed their worst suspicions. He had insisted. He wasn't asked. "I probably would have asked him if he had time to do it, but I didn't get the chance. He sort of jumped on it. Why? Is there a problem?"

"Not really, I guess," said Becky.

"Just an ego problem," said Georgina who wasn't going to just let it go. "He has been lording it over us in his own inimitable style."

"I think I know what you mean. He's kinda that way here in the office with me. I thought it was just me. You know, lowly me without even a masters?"

"Jenny, we know you have an advanced degree in keeping this college together. He'll find it out one of these days. What goes around comes around."

Georgina wanted to continue the conversation, but Becky dragged her out of Jenny's office. "C'mon, Georgi, before someone overhears us and we get accused of starting something. Let's just forget it."

"For now," Georgina said resolutely. "I'm not going to let my guard down."

"Let's go sing it all away. We need to practice and check on the scenery for the recital." Becky was enjoying the preparation for the recital. It reminded her of her early theater days. She wanted to leave the recent events behind and get on with something fun.

They sang for an hour and a half, penciling in notes on the music, coming up with more staging ideas and over-dramatizing until Georgina collapsed on the piano keys laughing. A few of the music students opened the door carefully to see what was happening and decided to join the merriment.

It was almost dinner time when they checked out the scenery in the storage building. It was good to have the paint be dry enough to move things around. Becky pulled out a few of the tables and set the chairs around them. She sang parts of her arias trying out different arrangements. Nick poked his head in the door to see if everyone was O.K. He was on his way home when he heard them. He said goodnight and left immediately. Becky and Georgina covered their mouths to keep from laughing out loud. They weren't sure if he was serious about them being O.K. or if they really sounded to him like alley cats on the back fence.

Lissa's voice sounded very far away on Becky's answering machine. "We're coming home, Mom. I don't know if you've seen the news, but there is a rebel uprising in a neighboring province and we want to get out before it comes here. We are O.K. and the danger doesn't seem immediate, but Mark is close enough to completion and the company wants to ship us home now. Call ya when we get back. Love ya."

Becky was at once shocked and relieved. When Nathan and Lissa first started traveling, it seemed that the world was a safer place. When Becky, herself, traveled to now troubled areas, she had felt relatively safe. But the world was becoming more dangerous. Governments were falling like flies and rebels were jumping up everywhere. Terrorism was on the rise and no one was safe in many of these places. Becky wanted to know that Lissa and her first grandchild were going to be safe. She hadn't realized it was the nagging little fear in the back of her mind since they left.

Mark was handsome, smart, steady, and made a good living. Becky recounted all his good points when he took Lissa into some situation that was a little questionable. She wasn't sure if she thought Mark didn't care enough for Lissa, if she wasn't high enough on his priority list, or if they were just young and choosing their adventures a bit carelessly. Becky wasn't sure she could trust Mark to take care of Lissa, or be aware of what it meant to take care of her. He always seemed make the decision to be off to somewhere and Lissa would be left to follow along or not. She dared not approach the subject. It was Lissa's business and Lissa seemed happy. Becky would keep her worries to herself for now, and just be glad they were coming home.

Nathan called to confirm plans for Christmas with Becky. "I'll come there where your friends are. I really don't know anyone here and it will be fun to see what you and Georgina are up to. How about doing a Christmas concert? I'll be the tenor. We can work up something."

"Uh, Nathan, is Juliette coming?"

"Well, I guess not. We are spending Thanksgiving together and then she is going to her family's home in Minnesota for Christmas. They have been wanting her to come and she has been away from them a long time."

"Of course you can come here and we'll plan a great time. Some of Georgina's Italian family is coming and they are always good for a great party. So, Juliette hasn't invited her fiancée to meet her family? Is that what I am hearing?"

"I doubt if this will last until Thanksgiving. It isn't what I imagined a love relationship should be. She doesn't seem to know what an engagement means. "The two become one" doesn't register with her. She's a lovely person, but I don't think she wants what I want."

Becky thought back to the conversation with Chaim about the Jewish bonds. Nathan was a free spirit and independent. He also knew that marriage was not about being a free spirit, but about being a true and dedicated partner with someone he loved.

Nathan continued, "Juliette's family came to this country a few generations ago and they all scattered and integrated into city life in

Chicago and Minneapolis. I haven't been able to get a line on who they are and what they want in life. Sometimes I think she doesn't know them at all. It is hard to get her to talk about them."

"Does she have a religion? Is she involved in a faith of any kind?"

"No, she thinks religion is stupid. She said something about 'looking into the void and calling it God.' I don't know what that is about, but she obviously has no respect for it."

"So if you became involved in a spiritual path, might she be critical and think you were weak?"

"Yeah, I think so. And I have been doing some interesting reading along those lines, Mom. I really want to know more about what you have been doing. By the way I heard the broadcast of Karla's radio interview with you. Wow, it was great! It was rebroadcast on some fundamentalist station in order to be torn down and roundly criticized. But I think that plan backfired. The callers were quite complimentary, and the host was more than a bit frustrated."

Becky's mouth dropped open. "I had no idea! I wonder if Karla knows. Well, hey, it will be good to have you here. Stay as long as you can. And I'm sorry about Juliette."

"Yeah, me too. I'm fine. The new job is great. Good people to work for. They like me a lot. I should be able to get some time at Christmas. I'll let you know the details soon. And I'll send you an address. Love ya, Mom. Thanks for being there."

"Love you, Nathan. Bye." Becky was a bit choked up as she hung up the phone. She managed to keep a normal tone and not let Nathan know that she was emotional.

It was the weekend. Becky and Georgina went to Grandma Jones' for a long leisurely breakfast. They wanted to plan for the holidays and compare notes on family members who were coming. There would be a songfest in Georgina's studio and they would invite any faculty members and students who happened to remain over Christmas. They discussed music and decorations, and thought about borrowing the café tables and chairs after the recital.

Grandma Jones overheard their conversation, as she always did, and offered to do some cooking and baking for them. She also told them she used to sing. Becky and Georgina were in shock. It was hard to imagine since they only saw her in the kitchen with her oversized apron full of flour, blueberry stains and such. Her hair was always in a babushka and she never wore makeup.

"When did you sing? What did you sing?"

"I used to sing with a theater group before I married Mr. Jones. He saw me on the stage and fell in love." She had a dreamy smile on her face. "I sang in 'Naughty Marietta' and 'The Chocolate Soldier." I was a soprano. I don't suppose I am any more. Too many years in the kitchen tasting the pancakes and sausages. I guess I've put on a little weight."

"So, sing something for us!" Becky was fascinated.

"Well, I don't think I remember anything. Let me see…" She looked around to make sure the customers were all gone.

She started uncertainly to sing the Wedding Song from 'The Chocolate Soldier.' Her voice wavered at first, unused to the demand made upon it. After a few lines, she became more confident, as though the memories were carrying her voice on wings. When she sailed into the finale with gusto, Becky and Georgina leaped from their seats in applause and shouts of 'bravo!'

Mrs. Jones covered her mouth with her hands. "I can still remember it. I don't sound too good, but I remembered it. It was always my favorite song."

"Mrs. Jones, may we call you by your first name?"

"It's Hattie, dear. Hattie Jones."

"Hattie, would you consider coming to my studio for some brush up? I would love to spend a little time with you. Maybe you would like to be part of our Christmas songfest." Georgina reached out for Hattie's hands and gently pulled them from her face. "You just need a little vocalizing, a little practice, and you'll be in fine shape."

"Do you really think so? When can I come? I'll pay you."

"Come Tuesday afternoon, Hattie. And no, you can't pay me. We'll have a wonderful time."

Georgina and Becky got into the car together, drove back toward town, and broke into giggles, cheers, and high fives. What fun this would all be! They felt like talent scouts and the adventure had just begun.

Nine

Becky's mind was on John Sherman and his behaviors that were disturbing to her. She resolved to emotionally distance herself and not pay attention to what he did that caused her discomfort. From now on she would watch for the behavior that hooked a reaction and sent her on a downward spiral that would leave her sifting the ashes of her past for answers. Taking note of that hook would free her from future responses to it, as the book she was using said. This technique had worked for her in the past.

But keeping her distance wouldn't be so easy. Nathan's next call was a real surprise.

"Mom, I met a guy named Jim Sherman on one of my security inspections. He says his dad teaches there."

"Yes, he does, Nathan. I met Jim a few months ago when he stopped in very briefly to bring his father a book from a seminar. The conversation was short, but he seemed like a good person."

"Yeah, he is. We really hit it off."

Becky's heart sank. What would this mean to her resolve to keep her emotional distance. What if Nathan and Jim became close friends? It sounded as if it were already happening.

"Actually, Mom, he was in an engineering class with me several years ago, but we didn't get to know each other then."

Becky tried not to let her voice show her distress. "Good that you had an opportunity to talk at length this time."

"We did. We were in a discussion group together and he really has some great ideas. He's very much in tune with things you and I have been discussing. We're going to be working together on some future projects. They sound pretty exciting. Oh, yeah, and he's coming to our Christmas shindig."

"Well that's great!" Becky was getting the energy back into her voice and her turmoil was subsiding. "I wondered if he might be here. We want to gather everyone who is staying around here, and their families too. Georgi and I have recruited a few local people who are now working with her on their singing. This is going to be really fun. Jim's dad is a bit hard to get to know. I'm not sure he'll be interested."

"No kidding! Jim talked about him quite a bit. His dad is really a smart guy, but Jim never knows how he will react to anything. It's a real roller coaster for him."

Becky felt a little guilty about the relief she was now experiencing. Knowing that she wasn't the only one who felt the roller coaster ride, and knowing she didn't have to explain anything to Nathan made her a bit more secure in talking about it.

"Well, perhaps we can be there for Jim and see that he has a good time anyway." She sat down to reorder her thoughts and plans after Nathan hung up. The same things would still apply. Nathan and Jim would be more of a shield against her discomfort. It would be O.K.

Becky walked into Georgina's studio as Laura was finishing her lesson. She couldn't believe the mature sound that Laura was producing. She didn't sound impaired at all. She was singing quite well, sweet and smooth.

"Come in, Beck. Isn't Laura doing well?"

"Wonderful! Laura, you sound so good! Are you going to sing for us at Christmas?"

Laura smiled shyly and nodded her head. Slowly the word "yes" came from her lips.

"She's making wonderful progress with her singing and her speaking, aren't you Laura?" Laura grinned and this time said quietly but quite clearly, "Yes, I am."

Nick came to collect Laura, beaming with pride.

"Nick, she sounds just great." Becky still wasn't over her astonishment.

"She's beginning to talk to us at home too. If she can't speak it, she sings it to us. She makes up little songs to tell us what she needs. We even sing back to her. It has been fun. Doris sings to her, and I didn't even know she could sing."

"Maybe we can train you all to be an abbreviated version of the Von Trapp family." Georgina had that half kidding, half serious smile on her face.

"No way! You won't get me to sing. Nuthin' doin'! He continued to wag his head as he and Laura left the studio.

Becky turned to Georgina stifling a giggle too. "Have you worked with Hattie yet?"

"Not yet, but she's coming in early next week. I wanted her to come sooner, but she had some traveling and stuff to do. I can't wait to hear what she can do. Those rusty vocal skills have a way of polishing up very quickly."

"Hey, you've got some great people there, Beck!" Karla was elated. "The interview with Chaim went really well. Of course we had a lot of Jewish callers, but some others too. He handles things really well. What a nice person he is."

"I haven't had a chance to talk to him about it yet. I'm glad it went well. Yes, he is a nice person and so easy to be around. He's hugely helpful and never judgmental."

"How old is he?"

"Down Karla, he's lots younger than us and married." Becky started to laugh. "That kind always are, aren't they?"

"I know he is. I was just kidding. It seems that we find the best male friends and I'm not sure I want to spoil that by trying to make something else out of it"

"Well, in my studies I see that Jesus seemed to think that friendship was the highest relationship, not marriage. He said, 'I have called you friends and I have told you all that my Father in heaven has told me.' So those with whom we share our highest spiritual understanding are sharing in the highest relationship."

"Awesome deep, friend. That's really interesting."

"I think we got that screwed up because marriage meant physical survival until the last hundred years. Friendship at this higher level means spiritual survival. When I look back over all the friendships that have lasted, they all have this spiritual component. You and I grew up together. When we got past all the sturm and drang of parents, high school, romances and all that, we finally got around to sharing spiritual stuff. Pretty neat, huh?" Becky was in her element now.

"You had to drag me kicking and screaming into it, Beck. But I couldn't help noticing how much more centered and confident you were than me. Even though I had no religious upbringing, it made an impression."

"I think it has given us another dimension to our friendship that created lasting qualities. How long can we be fascinated by talk about kids, mortgages and growing older?" Becky was so glad to have Karla on board, even if it was just an occasional discussion. Karla had explored Buddhism a bit and some metaphysical teachings, and they could sift through ideas together.

"You bet. So, how about another radio show? I have people asking for you. Actually swamping me with letters!"

"I heard! Chaim told me. I'm amazed. Were they positive? Negative? Right wing?"

"Mostly they were from people who felt they had always been in tune somehow with what you said, but never articulated it. They want to hear you say more about lots of things."

"Hmm, like what?"

"Like God being Principle, reaching God through the mind, the influence of religion on our country and on our thinking. You name it, they're asking it."

"Guess I'd better come prepared! Can I see the correspondence?"

"Yeah, I've sent it to your office overnight mail. You should have it."

"Oh, I haven't been to the office. Guess I'd better check it out. When do we do it again?"

"I thought in two weeks. Give me time to announce it. Sort of advertise. You may get questions about Christmas and all that since were coming up on the season."

The call sent Becky scrambling to gather up some research materials to take to her office. Jenny had been away for a few days, so the envelope should be in one of the two offices. Becky was eager to see what people had written.

"You in on a weekend, Becky?" Chaim was at her office door.

"Yeah, you too?"

"I wanted to clean out a few more boxes. Almost done with them. It's been a long haul. I've even forgotten about some of the stuff in them."

"Oh, I've done that, forgotten what I have. Right now I'm going through the correspondence that Karla sent me from the show. I understand things went super well for you. Karla was raving about you."

"Really? I didn't think anything too spectacular happened. Can I help you with some of that? I'm curious too."

"Sure. Dig in." They began reading, categorizing and listing questions to answer. They discussed ideas for the answers and Becky plugged in notes under the questions. "As hard as we're working, you'd think we were getting paid or something."

"I can never stop myself once I start. Pay ceases to matter. I turn into an idea maniac. That's why I'm not a millionaire yet. I expect the money to pour in automatically." Chaim was buried under letters.

"And does it?"

"Sometimes. I believe in the tithing principle found in Malachi 3:10. Abraham tithed to Melchizedek too. I'm always bringing my work into the storehouse of Spirit and there is often an unexpected return."

"How do you know it comes from that? Maybe it's just coincidence."

"I keep track. The return is supposed to be tenfold. I used to look for the income that was exactly ten times the value of the work that I put out. I believe it's an exact science, but it is hard to understand how to do it. I've experimented with it for a long time."

"You've experimented? Is that allowed in religious practice?" Becky was definitely hooked by this idea. She loved to have her ideas work out exactly. Practice hadn't occurred to her.

"I think it should be. How will we ever learn if we don't try things? God said, 'put me to the test' so I do just that. It is great fun. I've learned a lot. I see God as a partner, not a stern tax collector or slave master. God sets up the game and I search out the rules and play. When I play it right, the rewards come."

"Fascinating! Where do you start? What do you do?"

"Well, let's see. A tithe is something I give back to God. Since I can't give physical stuff to God, I give to those activities, places, or authors that spiritually inspire me. I suppose I've surprised a few writers who didn't expect to receive a tithe from a reader."

"Why did Abraham tithe to Melchizadek?"

"He was the closest to God that Abraham could find. Melchizadek was said to be without genealogy. He was a founder of Jerusalem, God's own city. He was a spiritual mystery and benefactor to all. There are priests after the Order of Melchizadek. In order to be a priest, Jesus had to be made part of the Order of Melchizadek because he was not a Levite. Complicated."

Becky was silent for a while. How had she missed all of this in her studies? How had she not brought her findings into practicality in her experience? She had allowed all of this to stay in her head and not play out in her life. Listening to Chaim, it seemed that he somehow found it all and she had missed so much. While feelings of embarrassment began to rise in her, she put them down with a determination to find how this all worked. If he and others could find it, so could she. She would find a book on practicing metaphysics or spiritual principles. She would begin there, as she always did.

In her library Becky found what she was looking for. "How to Understand and Live Your Life Spiritually Every Day." She began reading.

"This book is about living in a larger world than we now see. It is about being involved in a celestial tapestry of our own choosing and yet of God.

This book is about understanding who, what, and why you are at any given moment. It is about understanding our greater purpose, our higher nature and how it all fits into divine order.

The word metaphysics simply means 'beyond the physical.' The American Heritage Dictionary says: 'Investigating the nature of first principles and the problems of ultimate reality…the study of being…' That 'being' referred to is spirituality, which is non-tangible but of the soul.

We have reserved this area for the mystic and the scholar, considering it beyond our comprehension and probably of no earthly use anyway. However, spiritual teachings are to be aimed, ultimately, at the spiritual interpretation of one's own life, and the practical every-day living of spiritual principle."

Becky read on late into the night. There was so much to understand and assimilate. How would she ever take it all in, much less embody it all? But it had to be done, she vowed to do it, if it took the rest of her life.

Nick and some music students were carrying the scenery for the recital into the recital hall. Everything had been painted and the smaller pieces packed in boxes. It would be easier to assemble everything on the stage. Nick was busy hammering the background onto a frame that would keep it standing, and the sections could be moved around until they had just the right effect.

Tables and chairs were set in place. The boxes were unpacked. Table cloths and candle holders appeared on the tables. It all looked just great. Becky and Georgina sat back in awe. The students were excited to have their first rehearsal on the set. They were busy all evening at the café tables addressing fliers to be mailed and creating posters to be placed in the downtown businesses.

The students had become enthusiastically involved in the whole production. It was more like theater instead of just a recital. They even choreographed their entrances and movements between numbers. Becky was practicing with them and they accepted her as just another music student. It was like being a student back in college again and it was fun. Georgina was glowing as she directed the production and coached the musicians. The singers were more confident and the musicians had electricity in their numbers.

The recital continued to grow right under their noses as the plans for it filtered out into the student body. There were offers from non-musical students to act as waiters on stage and a milling crowd. The musicians were creating preludes, intermezzos, and a huge final number that included all the musicians and the audience. It was taking on the proportions of a gala event.

Performance night arrived and people streamed into the recital hall. It seemed that everyone from the college and town came. Relatives came from out of town and out of state. Nick, Laura, and Doris were in the front row with Laura on the edge of her seat. Georgina was at the piano in the rehearsal room warming up the singers. Becky was helping students get last minute adjustments made to their costumes. The audience walked into a production that had already begun. The waiters were flicking the table cloths, lighting the candles and pretending to sweep the floor. The prelude music was in progress.

It was such a whirlwind of an evening that Becky could hardly remember herself singing. Georgina assured her that she did sing and that it was wonderful. The students did their very best and the audience gave them an enthusiastic standing ovation. They hadn't prepared for an encore, so Georgina stepped over to the piano and sang a popular number from a long ago favorite musical. It brought everyone to their feet again, including the recital members. It was a perfect finale.

As the audience filtered out, expressing their congratulations, parents collected their student daughters and sons. Becky and Georgina started to help in the cleanup, but Nick and the students chased them out of the recital hall. "You two go and have some coffee somewhere. We'll take care of this." They were too tired to argue.

Once again, they drove to Northwick to the Patrician Grille. They were hungry and tired, and the quiet of the place would be most welcome. They dissected and analyzed the whole production all the way to Northwick, and twenty-five miles went by like an instant.

"Beck, I saw the board of trustees and all the other bigwigs there. I'm sure I saw the mayor and a local television anchor. Do you suppose there will be something on the news or in the paper?"

"I never thought of that. I know the television news anchor, and her niece was in it, Donna Jenkins. I saw some camera flashes and I figured those were parents. But, we'll look in the paper. Maybe we should think of inviting the press next time. I'm sure they saw the posters, but it might be nice to actually contact and invite them."

"Yeah. So what if we look like publicity hounds! Those students deserved some publicity tonight."

"Sure did. Well I think we just got our feet wet for future productions. GeorgaBeck Productions, cast of thousands! What can we do next?"

They sipped their wine and the steaks arrived sizzling on a metal platter. The evening was ending in quiet reverie. The owner came out of the kitchen. "Your dinner is on the house. My nephew was in your production tonight. You can't imagine what you did for him. He was just a waiter, and now he wants to be an actor! God, it is time he wanted to be something in life besides a couch potato. His name is Jack. Thanks again!"

Becky flew to Hawaii for Thanksgiving break plus a few extra days. It was a terribly long flight, but her sister Melissa had been begging her to come for years. "God, Melissa, it's half way around the world! I don't think my butt can stand those airplane seats that long." But it was time. Melissa Margrove had been ill and recovered. Becky decided that some things were too important to keep putting off.

Peter Margrove met Becky at the airport. He was tall, tan and solid with a twinkle in his eyes. He had always been a good-looking man, urbane and genteel, yet fun. How fortunate Melissa was. Becky never found a mate that even came close to having his qualities. He placed a lei over her head, hugged her, and picked up her bags. "What's all this? Don't you know we go practically naked here?"

"Care packages from the mainland. Thought you islanders might be deprived of some New England flavors. I have some pictures of the family and other stuff that I thought Melissa might like to have. They all got dumped on me when Mom and Dad moved, because I was closer and I've had them in storage ever since."

"We can never get them to visit us here. You'd think Hawaii was on another planet the way they reacted when we moved here. I think they thought I was spiriting their daughter away."

"Good move, Peter. Spiriting her away was a good thing. She'd been the good daughter, making up for my truancy, long enough."

They stepped onto the tarmac and boarded a small island hopper. Becky wondered how they managed to deal with always having to fly from one place to another. The islands weren't even large enough to wear out a car.

Melissa looked great. She gave Becky an energetic hug and her eyes were dancing with happiness as they entered the house. "Your room is here overlooking the beach. Just leave the windows open. It doesn't get cold here."

"I can't imagine it. Nice all the time?"

"Nice all the time. And the beaches are always clean too. There's no seaweed and junk. We're too far out. Just clear aqua water, white sand, and beautiful sky. We'll take a ride up into the mountains tomorrow. For now, let's grab some food and take it down to the beach. You do have a bathing suit, right?"

"I bought a new one before I left. I used my old one so little in New England that the elastic rotted. Hung like a sack. I didn't know they did that. Rot, I mean."

They were off to the beach with the most delicious food Becky had ever seen. "I thought they only served this kind of food on cruises. It's so beautiful!"

"Well, we sort of went all out. We wanted you to try everything. Thanksgiving will be a luau with the neighbors on the beach down the road."

"What neighbors? I don't see any neighbors."

"Oh, they're here. We just don't live on top of each other. Actually their places are closer going along the beach than the road. We take a dune buggy to visit instead of the car. We modified it so it's quiet and we can carry stuff on it."

"What else do you do here? It's so quiet." Becky was beginning to relax and the fatigue of airline flying was ebbing away.

"Well, we have a movie theater, mall, a couple of eighteen-hole golf courses where Peter and I spend a lot of time, hiking trails, festivals and whatnot. We volunteer in the school system and work in our church. It keeps us pretty busy."

"Do you ever wish you were back on the mainland?" Becky was trying to imagine herself living like this.

"Oh, occasionally. We take the redeye flight to San Francisco and drive into the wine country. We went to Los Angeles once, and the traffic and crowding immediately reminded us why we don't live there anymore!"

"You mentioned that you were starting to write again. I remember the dog stories you used to read to me when you were in high school and I was in grade school. They were always about collies. Lassie was big then."

"Right. Lassie. I'm not writing about collies now." Melissa laughed. "I've written some stories for Christian magazines and some Lenten series articles. It keeps my mind in the creative mode. I get writers' magazines and journals. Even occasionally take a writing class at the local community college."

"Do you still have those dog stories you wrote?"

"No. Someone said they were childish and I threw them away before I left high school."

"Oh, too bad. Why can't people keep their mouths shut. I might have been fun to have you read them to me for old times' sake."

"Never mind, Sis. Forget the dog stories and the old times. They remind me too much of the pain of being home with Mom and Dad. I shut that out of my mind whenever it wants to come up."

"Yeah, well, we had good times together, even if we did fight like cats and dogs."

"Yup. Ever learn to make your bed?"

"Nope. I still leave it the way I climbed out of it until the covers fall off and I have to tuck it all in again. Just kidding. Yes, I make my bed. I live neat so I can find stuff and not have to do heaps of laundry and cleanup. Papers would engulf me if I didn't do something."

Peter quietly strummed his guitar. They sang a few Hawaiian songs together. The tide gently lapped the shore and they fell into silence, each remembering. It was good just to be together again. It was the only thing that came close to feeling like home for Becky.

Ten

Christmas was coming quickly now. Plans for the family gathering were unfolding. Georgina scheduled the President's Fireside Room at the college for the gathering instead of her studio. The room was large with comfortable chairs, divans, a piano, and a fireplace. Louvered doors opened into an additional space for a food buffet and tables.

There would be only one day between the arrival of the families and the Christmas gathering. Since the success and excitement of the recital was still fresh in their minds, Becky and Georgina had to remind each other that this was not a command performance, but a fun, informal family time.

Nathan arrived early and began carrying in boxes of decorations. "Wow, Mom, will there be any room for people when we get all this in there? This looks like a lot of stuff."

"Lots of room. Decorations are fragile, so the boxes aren't stuffed full."

"Right. I know you. I'll believe it when we unpack them." Nathan was in high spirits and ready for a good time.

"Oh, ye of little faith. The boxes you are carrying are full of food. That's why they're heavy. You do want food, right?"

"Definitely!"

Jim arrived not far behind Nathan and began to unpack boxes too. Jim seemed to be an accomplished decorator. He was creating wonderful table arrangements. "One of my minors in college was design. It was engineering design, but it seems to spill over into other areas. Sometimes I think I should have been a florist."

"Have you seen your father yet? Are you staying with him?" It occurred to Becky that she hadn't seen John since before the recital.

Jim was hesitant. "Well, not really. He isn't set up for guests. Never has been. I prefer to get a hotel room somewhere anyway. I think there's one close by."

Becky was a little taken back. She wanted to offer him a place to stay, and lamented that she had no extra room at all.

"Jim! Why don't you and I split a hotel room. There's a quaint historical hotel downtown. Pretty funky, but interesting to explore. It has some unique ideas in its construction." Nathan caught himself and glanced at Becky.

Becky was trying not to look disappointed. She had been looking forward to having Nathan with her this Christmas.

"Don't worry, Mom." He put his arm around her shoulders. "I'll be as close to you as a hip pocket."

"Promise?" Becky was a little embarrassed to show her feelings in front of Jim. She smiled right away and assured him, "Of course, it makes perfect sense. We always have to turn my place upside down to make a space for Nathan. That hotel always decorates for Christmas with lots of old fashioned things. A church group does it every year." Becky knew she had to release her guilt and confusion over the past once and for all, and this was a good opportunity.

Nathan kept his promise. He included Becky in exploring the fascinating history of the hotel. The three of them climbed through the attic, basement and closed-off back rooms. The owner was accommodating since things were usually a little slow. Except for the decorating, this was the most excitement he'd seen for a long time. Nathan became the social organizer throughout his visit and they were having a great time. They had dinner and cocktails, and exchanged gifts in the quaint hotel dining room. There was a small music combo playing Christmas music and a fire in the fire place. It was the best and most wonderful Christmas atmosphere.

Jim was free to be with his father or join them any time. John made only a very brief appearance and Jim went to dinner with him once. Georgina was busy with her extensive family, who demanded much of her time. She said it was the old Italian way. Chaim reluctantly left for Los Angeles to be with his family.

The gathering in the college Fireside Room was warm, full of fun and music. Everyone seemed to be in a joining mood, chatting with each other at every table and in every corner of the room. The music performances, rehearsed and impromptu, turned out well. Laura's eyes were sparkling as she sang. Her speech was coming more naturally, and people were interested in hearing her story. Her mother, Doris, was misty-eyed watching her daughter. Doris and Nick held hands much of the evening.

Becky missed Lissa, who promised to make it there for New Years. There were snags getting out of South Africa. She and Mark had been diverted to Germany for some debriefing about an attack that happened close to their hotel. The Johannesburg airport was in lock down by security forces for a short time and no flights came in or went out.

Mark's family decided at the last minute to have their family event in London right after Christmas. Mark and Lissa flew to London before coming back to the United States. It was difficult for Becky to share Lissa when she herself felt unwelcome. A polite invitation was sent to her, with a note that they would understand if she couldn't be there. Becky was sure she made his family very happy when she declined. She knew they didn't approve of her and she wondered if they really accepted Lissa as good enough for their son. Mark seemed oblivious to it all.

He said he was used to his family's snooty ways, and he ignored them. He always seemed so preoccupied and Becky wondered if he really noticed Lissa or her needs. Becky's heart ached at all the warm fuzzies Lissa had missed at Christmas with her, Nathan, and everyone at the party. She shuddered to think of Christmas in a hotel in frigid London with Mark's equally cold family. But knowing Lissa, she would see the sights, go to an orphanage with gifts, and generally take charge of her own joy. She reminded Becky of Princess Diana, always thinking of others.

How did she have this daughter so unlike herself? Becky was projecting her own feelings of being shut out on Lissa, wanting to draw Lissa in and be sure she felt loved. But Lissa always remained slightly out of reach and made her own way. It made Becky feel admiration and guilt at the same time. Maybe that was why Lissa kept her distance. That would be smart, Becky had to admit. Becky didn't like her own guilty feelings either.

Nathan stayed just long enough to connect with Lissa. They always talked as if they had never been apart. Becky took mental notes on how that looked, sounded, and seemed to feel to them. She wanted to be able to feel the freedom they exhibited. What good did guilt and feelings of inadequacy do her anyway? They didn't make her children feel loved, but instead sad for her. She would learn more about this, practice new ideas, feelings and behaviors. Then perhaps she could talk about it without sounding maudlin or stuck in the past. Her heart felt lighter already.

"Mom, I didn't know you felt that way. I knew there was something going on, but I didn't know what." Lissa was truly concerned.

"It's just my stuff and my family's, too. I want to deal with it before it pushes you away. I don't want you to feel uncomfortable around me and keep your distance."

"No way, Mom, am I keeping my distance!" Lissa was shocked. "You always drilled it into me that I should choose my own path, make my own joy and happiness. It was great advice or whatever. It's just what Mark loves about me. Well, among other things, he couldn't stand a clingy dependent child-woman."

"What does Mark offer in the way of support? I've only seen his back going out the door when I've seen him at all. He's always on his way somewhere. The wedding was the most time I spent around him. He seemed quite attentive for that occasion. I'm sorry. I'm not trying to pry. I want to know if you are really O.K. I would like to understand."

"It's O.K. I want you to understand how we are. We talk now, Mom. We talk constantly. He confides in me about personal and business stuff, and we plan everything together. I know when I finally tell you about things, it is on the fly. I probably sound like I'm in this all by myself, but that isn't true. Believe me, he's there for me. We're true partners."

Becky felt her heart slow down to normal. Lissa was not angry with her, and best of all she was not a victim or unhappy. She could ask for and receive what she wanted with no problem. Once again, Becky took careful mental notes. She learned so much from her children. One thing was certain, they didn't pick up her worst traits or fears. Becky was thankful for that.

Chaim returned from Los Angeles just before classes were due to start. Becky remembered that his holiday was Chanukah, not Christmas. The Jewish new year wasn't the first day of January either. Their calendar went back to Abraham somehow, and not just to Jesus Christ. She tried to imagine this time of year without Christmas and New Years, and could not.

At Mom & Pop's Georgina and Becky told him all about the gathering.

"I wish I could have been here. Things were pretty grim with my family. They've always bickered constantly. Then they stop speaking to each other, threatening to leave and never come back. It's been a way of life with them ever since I can remember. For all my father's illnesses, he still manages to rule the roost, shouting from the bedroom, demanding attention, and shaming us all for not being on the spot every minute. It's a circus. I'm glad our house is on a large lot so the neighbors can't hear."

"Phew. I bet you're glad to get back!" Georgina could sympathize. "My family is high spirited in the old Italian way and it's pretty wearing. Everyone shouts over the opera which is always on high volume. They gossip about each other, pile food on the table like we might starve, and generally stick their noses into your private business so they have something to talk about."

"Sounds familiar. I couldn't possibly live anywhere near that energy. Sometimes Israel isn't far enough away."

"Does that make you feel guilty?" Becky was still processing her conversation with Lissa.

"In my family guilt is our first, middle, and last name. We live it, breathe it, bathe in it, imbibe it, and parade it like a family banner." Chaim was definitely starting to relax and enjoy himself.

"So, what do you do with it? How do you live with the impact of it?"

"I keep busy. But when I'm tired I depress myself. I let it eat at my energy and drag my initiative down to complete inaction. Then when I'm on the bottom, I'm forced to look up and start crawling up out of the dark hole."

"What do you mean 'look up and start crawling out?' Explain that to me." Becky was getting closer to the answers she needed.

"It's not a long process. It used to be. I used to let it get me down for weeks, and I'd thrash around in self-pity until something would snap me out of it. Then I learned that I could choose not to enter the process and let it have its way. I could turn my thoughts to something I really enjoyed, like my research. I could rest and turn my mind toward all the good stuff in my life. It took some time and practice at first, but now I can make it work much more quickly."

"Where do you start? How do you keep from entering the downward spiral?" Becky wanted to take notes on a paper napkin, but thought that would be rude.

"I figured out what the hooks are that grab me. Family is great at knowing just where your vulnerable spots are and then say the very thing that throws in the hook. It is the same hook each time, so once I found it, I was on my way."

"Do mean like 'you never do what your father wanted you to do and now look at you?'" Becky had heard something like this.

"You got it! That's exactly the kind of thing I mean. Shame on me for not being the doctor they wanted. So here is my father with a bunch of illnesses and what good am I to him? I'm not a doctor!"

"Holy Cow, Chaim." Georgina was engrossed. "I, too, am just a music teacher. Why am I not at the Metropolitan Opera? Why not La Scalla? If I had just listened...gone to the right school...had a famous teacher. It goes on and on."

"Do you like being a teacher?"

"I love being a teacher. The Met isn't the glamour job they all imagine. They just want to say their daughter sings at the Met. It's actually a terrible life."

"I love teaching too. I couldn't see me as a doctor. I nearly get sick at gory movies. It's not for me."

Becky was still sorting her thoughts. "I don't know what my parents wanted me to be. I just know it wasn't what I am. They can't attack my profession and my degree, so they attack me as a person. I don't do enough, come home enough, call enough, and I'm just not a good daughter. My sister is the good daughter who lives the American Dream. I fell through the cracks every time I tried."

"How does your sister feel about it? You don't talk about her much. This is the first I've heard that you have a sister." Chaim was genuinely curious.

"My sister and I are good friends. She is very accepting of me and always encouraging. Her experience of our parents isn't any rosier than mine. She just managed to get out earlier, before things got really bad. She stays in Hawaii, far away. We don't see each other too often because of the distance. I went there at Thanksgiving and the flight was grueling. However, when you get to Hawaii with the warm air, palm trees swaying, and gorgeous beaches, you forget about the flight and your aching rear."

"Do you have any other siblings?"

"I have two brothers, Andrew and Carl. They're older than my sister and me, sort of like two separate families. They went off to the military when I was young, so I don't know them very well. They are career military and are always off to some exotic place. I think that's where my kids got the wanderlust." Becky hadn't thought about Andy and Carl for a long time. "They never send Christmas cards or keep in touch. I still send cards, but there's never a response."

Becky felt the old guilt arise. It brought on the thought that she should be doing more to connect with Andy and Carl. How many times had she kept up contact with someone out of duty even though they weren't reciprocating? The harder she tried, the weaker the connection got. It always left her feeling abandoned and somehow at fault. But now she was learning to immediately counteract the guilt with a freeing statement to herself. "Connection occurs at the right and perfect time, and has nothing to do with any short comings on my part or theirs." She was always amazed at how much better she felt after saying that a few times. It was as if a weight were lifted off her mind and body. She could breathe more easily and she almost wanted to skip down the hall.

The books she was studying advised that the guilt feelings would stop coming up because her subconscious mind would neutralize them before she even felt it. Becky couldn't wait for that to happen. She was weary of feeling down and guilty for days at a time. It was wonderful to feel good again. It was even better to choose to feel good and have it happen at will.

Monday evening class was beginning again with a different focus. The second phase would be about what religion left out and the damage it did. It left out compassion and personal responsibility for one's actions. It was new territory for Chaim, Becky, and Georgina. They would be researching and teaching at the same time. Growing with the students would be an exciting adventure as well as hard work. But it would keep things real and alive in the classroom.

Becky wanted to begin with the roots of guilt. Chaim thought it was a good idea too. There would be enough material to last for several weeks of class. Georgina offered to research Catholicism, Chaim would bring in Judaism, and Becky would take Protestantism. A question they needed to answer was whether guilt caused the need for religion or religion caused the guilt in the first place. The chicken or the egg?

John became interested in their project and offered to work on envisioning the world and society as guilt free. Was guilt the only basis of order or could something else be more powerful and safely effective? Becky and Chaim were elated. What a great component this would be. They wouldn't be leaving things mired in the downer stuff, but be lifted up by a look at a hopeful future.

There was some puzzlement in the class. Many hadn't thought about guilt other than as a natural occurrence in every-day life. Doris came to class with Nick. She volunteered that she felt such guilt over Laura's birth accident. There was nothing she could have done, but she thought people might think she was a bad mother or something. Nick owned that he had felt some guilt too. Others began to share their stories and the class time flew by. Chaim had just enough time to introduce what they were planning for the next several classes.

"Do you think we got too personal?" Chaim was a little concerned. "Are we getting in deeper than we should? You're a psychologist, Becky. What do you think?"

"I think these things need to be talked about as openly as possible. People help each other that way. If someone gets in over their head, I have some good referrals I can make. There are counselors they can go to for more personal help. I'll keep careful watch, but I think they are good so far."

"Hi Beck. Ready to go on the air?"

"Lord, is it that time already?" Becky was still munching down a salad and sandwich at her computer.

"Well, we've got about five minutes to air time. What's up with you? Anything new we can talk about?"

"We're starting to talk about the roots of guilt in religion and society. Started it in Chaim's class. Folks were a little surprised, but took to it very well. Lots of interaction."

"Terrific! Let's go with it."

"Go with what exactly?"

"Guilt, of course. Everybody's got it. Just dive in any way you want to."

Becky's mind was whirling when the first caller cued up. "How in hell are we supposed to keep order, morality, and peace without guilt? How do we keep people from getting out of line?"

"Hello caller. Do we have order, morality, and peace now? Guilt is so thick in our culture that it forces the population into guilty behaviors such as stealth, dishonesty, inadequacy, fear and anger. Not a pretty picture. Guilt is misery and if guilt were going to save the world, it would be saved a thousand times over by now. There is another way and we have to find it."

Becky thought she was just a little more vehement that she intended to be. She had to restrain herself from calling him an idiot. It scared her.

"Oh, no! You were great! Passion is good. True, he may have gotten more than he bargained for, but there is a world of listeners besides him out there that need to hear it just the way you said it. Next caller?"

"I've been guilty all my life. Seems like I got blamed for everything whether I did it or not. So, I started doing the stuff I was being blamed for. I thought that would help me feel better, but it didn't. I felt worse. How do I get rid of it?"

"Guilt isn't totally bad if you know you've done something hurtful. A little honest guilt pain will cue you to do better. It's that undeserved guilt that religion and culture heap on us through parents, teachers, priests and whoever else has a little power. We can't do much on a grand scale, but we can do something personally. We can counteract it through our thinking. Fight back. Tell yourself that you are innocent and refuse to feel bad. I don't have time on this show to teach all the details, but there are some great books on dealing with guilt. They have really good stuff in them. "Lose Your Guilt and Start Living" by Martin is a good one. Read a few pages of several different books at the bookstore and see which one feels right for you."

"What about people who have no guilt at all? No conscience?" Karla was leaning into the microphone with intense interest.

"We call them sociopathic. Those people don't know right from wrong. They are seriously underdeveloped in some pretty basic human compassion and they are destructive to human society."

"So, living in a guilt free world, is that a good thing or a dangerous thing?"

"We are talking about evolution here. Evolution of the soul. It is about maturing spiritually to the point of choosing to function in integrity without the coercion of punishment or pain. We're beginning to look at these things through self-help psychology books and futuristic visioning. We all need to evolve out of this lower level of functioning and rise into a higher understanding of our purpose in living. We need to discover that power and riches are only temporary in this world, but they are permanent and unlimited as spiritual power and riches of the soul."

"Next caller?"

"Hello. What is all this guilt stuff? Don't you know that Jesus hung on the cross for your sins? Jesus paid the price for you and now you are whining around feeling sorry for yourself. Why don't you get off the air and go back to your kitchen?"

Karla shut off her microphone. "Don't worry, Becky. That didn't go on the air. We have a five-second delay for call-ins. We don't need that stuff." She flipped the switch again. "Next Caller?"

Becky took a deep breath and glanced at her notes.

"Hi. Thanks for taking my call. I'm Steven Jennings and I've been fascinated with your program."

"Thanks Steven. Do you have a question?"

"Yes. Professor Temple, do you have an organization and how do I get in touch?"

"I don't have an organization, Steven. What do you have in mind?"

"Well, I'm an administrator with a lot of experience and I want to be involved with an organization that is concerned with teaching people to live more successfully, within themselves, you know? How can I do that?"

"I see. Well I can't offer you anything at this time."

"We have to go to break. Stay tuned. We'll be right back." Karla turned her mike off and came on the phone line. "Sorry, Steven, we can't discuss this on the air, but if you'll send a resume to the radio station, to my attention, I'll have a look. No promises, though. My assistant will give you the information."

"Great. I'll do that. Thanks again."

At the end of the show, Karla and Becky talked off the air for a while. "I'm glad you knew what to say. I was flabbergasted."

"Well, Beck, it won't hurt to check this guy out. You are coming on fast with this whole spiritual thing. Maybe there's an organization in your future, and you'll have some contacts ready to go. I can have the station do a background check on him. We have a department that runs down all security concerns. I don't think we have a kook here, but you never know."

"But Karla, I wouldn't know where to start or what I would want to start. I've never thought of doing anything but teaching at the College."

"Hey, I know someone else who might be interested too. Sandy Stratford our high school classmate. I was just talking to her a few weeks ago and she would like to do something else. You know she's been running her husband's family business ever since high school. She'd be great."

"Whoa! What are you going to tell her?"

"Well, just that there might be something interesting coming up and she has all the skills that would be needed. And if this Steven is half the administrator he says he is, he might be just the person to kick it all off. He can look at what you are doing so far and figure out how to put it together."

"Chaim is part of this too. I'm not doing this alone. In fact he's the one that got me started with all this. It isn't just my stuff and ideas. It's his too."

"Yeah, I know. Run it by him. Make him an offer he can't refuse."

"Oh, right."

"I'm serious. Talk to him. He's really a smart guy and might welcome a partner in crime. He might be stagnating, and this is just what he needs."

"O.K. I'll start thinking about this. I'll talk to Chaim and let you know if anything comes of it."

"By the way, I want to be your security officer. I want to run interference when needed. There, see? You already have an organization of five: you, me, Sandy, Steven and Chaim. What shall we name it?"

"The Way Home," Becky quipped. "I'm kidding."

"No, no! That's great. Haven't you told me a zillion times that you were dropped off on the wrong planet? That's a good description of the alienation that many people are feeling these days."

Becky spent the rest of the evening and late into the night on her computer, sketching out ideas. They were just random, but who knows what would work. She hadn't been much for prayer and meditation up until now, but Becky decided that perhaps it was time to try it out. Others said they used it all the time and stuff just came together in meditation. She had several books on meditation. Tomorrow she would begin.

Eleven

"Georgi, I gotta talk to you before I explode. I was on an interview with Karla last night and I'm a little blown away with what happened. Don't worry, it's all good. At least I think so."

"Have lattes and scones, will travel. I'm dressed. I'll be right over."

"A non-profit organization? That loomed up pretty fast. What do we need an organization for? Pardon me for assuming that I am part of it."

"Of course you are!" Becky gave Georgina the whole rundown word for word, five and now six people involved already.

"Well, hey, talk to them all and see what ideas come up. You don't have to do this by yourself, Beck. You don't have to run home to a book to figure it out. Let everyone help you. It's Karla's brain child. Let her run with it."

"I promised I would talk to Chaim. After all, most of this was started by him and his ideas. I'm just trying to catch up."

"Yes, Chaim started this, but don't sell yourself short. That stuff you are coming up with on the radio and in class is yours, regardless of where it started."

Becky sipped her latte thoughtfully. "I guess I'll know how he feels when I talk to him. He might want to be part of this and he might not."

"Knowing what I do about music copyrights, it wouldn't be a bad idea to set something like this up at the beginning. Then everything produced belongs within the framework of the corporation and it is protected."

"Right. Assuming I produce something. This is like building all the boxes before there is anything to go in them." They laughed and started to peruse Becky's meditation books.

"I would like to do this with you. I think a short meditation time together might be beneficial. Lots of people start their days with prayer. Some companies have meditation groups among the employees. They claim it makes things go smoother. They even get creative ideas during that time. I used to write in a journal every morning. I've sort of gotten away from it, but I remember how calming it was, like everything was under control before the day happened."

Becky stopped turning pages and slid the book across the coffee table to Georgina. "Here, on this page, there are six steps. Might be a good one to start with."

They settled into a quiet state, paying attention to their breathing as suggested, and then read the steps together, taking some silent time for each one. Becky asked to know what needed to be done next about the organization. Georgina asked to know her part in it and how her music would fit in.

Chaim was crossing the campus when Becky and Georgina caught up with him. "We have to talk to you when you have a few minutes."

Chaim began to laugh. "Karla called me last night. She couldn't wait. I have a carrel in the library. I'm heading there. We can talk."

The library was empty, and the carrel was quiet. "I'm not sure what kind of participation Karla had in mind, but I would rather not take a large part in this. I could be a consultant and would be happy to do so. I have many commitments here and in Israel, and don't want to add another just now."

"I'm on the same page as you are. This all mushroomed last night in conversation and I don't even know what I need to do first. Georgi suggested I let Karla run with it and see what it turns out to be."

"Sounds good. She has tremendous energy and is looking for some place to aim it. I think she would really like to do this. Anything you want to use, any ideas you want to explore or publish, feel free to use them. I don't have any interest in claiming or copyrighting anything other than what I draw from my research. I'm sure you'll give credit where it is due, and I'm glad to be a silent contributor."

"Are you cutting me loose to go with this, even stuff from your class?"

"Actually, Becky, it has been our class and I've been glad of it. Yes, go with it. It belongs to the world and you express it very well. I'll be front row in your cheering section."

Becky had never met such a selfless, generous person. She was speechless in the presence of his quiet confidence. It was power at its finest. It was a likeness to God as she thought it should be. It felt to her like what she imagined heaven would feel like.

"Chaim, you're amazing." Georgina was not speechless. She was thrilled. "I can't imagine us doing this without you, so we'll keep your number handy, O.K.?" She had that special twinkle in her eyes that spoke volumes about her love for them and her excitement about their new adventure.

"Deal. I'm with you in spirit and will do what I can. Just don't put my name on the work schedule."

Indeed, Karla did have energy for this. "Hi Becky. Just wanted to leave you a message that we are incorporated. I called Sandy. She did the paperwork and it's coming by courier for your signature. Well, we had to write up articles of incorporation and all the legal stuff, but we copied from a similar organization and got enough together plus a small fee, and we're in! You are now "The Way Home!"

Becky burst out laughing. That was the last straw before she just let it all go. Georgina came into her office. "What is so funny? I can hear you all the way down the hall."

Tears were rolling down Becky's cheeks and she couldn't stop laughing long enough to tell her, so she punched the message machine button and let her hear it.

"I'll get us some iced tea from the cafeteria. Don't choke, I'll be back fast." Georgina raced to the cafeteria and back in record time. She was really worried that Becky was hysterical.

"I'm O.K. Really. I just built up so much pressure and tension over this that it all came loose at once. I just couldn't stop it."

"You've been working really hard, Beck, in all areas. I wonder if that meditation this morning had something to do with it."

"I think it did. I was unnaturally calm afterward, and couldn't keep my guard up. It's a good thing, I think. I feel better. Thanks for the tea."

"Well, we're incorporated, and we have five board members, you, me, Karla, Sandy, and Steven. Can you believe it? Steven is in. Karla did a thorough background check on him and he is sterling, solid gold. We're in!"

"We will be when the paper work arrives for us to sign. I wonder…" Becky started at the knock on the office door.

"Courier service!"

"Good God, it's here!" they said in unison.

John Sherman's contribution to the Monday evening class was an eye-opening challenge for all. Futurism wasn't a buzz word in little Johnston Crossing. John began with the work of Teilhard de Chardin and wove a picture of cosmic proportions of the evolution of humankind.

To the amazement of Becky and Georgina he brought in parts of the Bible, astronomy, science, and even music. He created a tapestry that fascinated them all, so fascinating that they overlooked his abrupt answers to their questions and seeming condescending manner.

"What do you think of John's part in this class?" Georgina was concerned and even a little put out, which was unusual for her. Their late evening dinner arrived, which was their Patrician Grille favorite. Becky was pondering her own discomfort. "I was a bit embarrassed at first, but like everyone else I was so caught up in what he was saying that I soon forgot about it. Do you think he really means to come across that way? Do you think he is aware of it?"

"Surely he has gotten some feedback somewhere along the way and doesn't care. Why be that way? What's the payoff?"

"Believe it or not, Georgi, it's fear. It looks like bravado or super confidence, but that's a cover up. Fear is the basis of all human negative emotion. The more I learn about it this stuff, the more convinced I am of that. I'm learning to trade discomfort or embarrassment for fascination. Big jump for me."

"What do you suppose he fears, O great oracle?"

"Very funny," Becky smirked and went on. "Who knows? People fear abandonment, rejection, all sorts of nightmares created by just being alive. Even being born upside down, nearly falling on your head right off the bat."

"Now you're making sense," grinned Georgina.

"I'm kidding."

"I think you've got something. Someone did a study on coming into this world upside down, creating a fear of falling as the first emotion."

"Do you think they'll want to continue to have him in the class?"

"Yeah, I think so. Who cares about his personality if the material holds up. Lots of famous singers have fantastic voices but can be pretty nasty off stage. It's called a prima donna complex."

"We're probably making too much of this where John is concerned. I propose we make a concerted effort, or at least a small effort, to keep him in the loop and be his friend regardless of his quirks. Let's be fascinated!"

"O.K. Doctor Do Good, let's go for it."

"Nut."

"Hello, Doctor Temple. This is Steven Jennings. I guess I started something the other evening. I hope things are working out O.K. and I would like to meet with you. I'd like an idea of what you want and any plans you might have. I want to know how I can best help you."

"You sure did start something, Steven. Actually, it was Karla who ran with it and I'm still a bit dazed. But yes, I think it would be great for us to start sorting some of this out early. Where are you located?"

"San Francisco, with an office in Asbury Park, New Jersey."

"In the Trump buildings?"

"Well, no, but close. On a clear day I can almost see them from my window. Asbury park is a childhood haunt. My grandmother used to bring me here to the board walks. Nostalgia brought me back when I needed an east coast office. I'm in one of the old houses along the boardwalk next to Ocean Grove. It has huge porches where folks used to come to 'take the salt air' as they would say."

"So, you're in Asbury Park right now?"

"Yes. Whenever it is convenient for you I can hop up to…Johnston Crossing is it? I'll have to find that on the map. I had planned to be here for the rest of the month and finish up some things before I go back to San Francisco."

"Is San Francisco your home?"

"Yes. My partner, Loren, is a free-lance writer there. We actually live in Sausalito north of the Golden Gate Bridge, if you are familiar with the area."

"I am familiar with it. One of my favorite restaurants is Horizons on the water."

"It's still there. It's one of our favorite haunts too."

"Small world. Pick a day when you can be here, and I'll work around my classes. All evenings are open except Mondays."

Steven came to Johnston Crossing two days later. Any fears or misgivings Becky might have had about him disappeared in the light of his genuineness. "What a neat little town this is! I love it! It's a perfect place for a small college, like a post card. I've always loved New England."

Becky gave him a tour of the college and introduced him to Georgina and Chaim. They arranged to get together for dinner, which left Becky and Steven a few hours to talk and get to know each other.

"Tell me about 'The Way Home' and what inspired the name."

"It just jumped out of my mouth when Karla asked for a name. But it feels right. Did you ever sense that you were dropped off on the wrong planet? That's how I've usually described my relationship to life here. I never seem to fit, like I'm on the other side of a window looking in. I didn't feel I belonged, even in my parents' home." She told him about looking at pictures in the family album taken before she was born. "It was as if I was too late to be included and missed whatever I needed to be part of things. I'm still a late bloomer. I started singing only a few years ago and I'm already too late for a music career. All auditions say, 'no one over thirty please.' Not that I'm looking to audition, but it always brings up those old feelings."

Steven was smiling ruefully, "Being born gay on this planet definitely has that effect. San Francisco comes closest to being home for us. At least we have a huge community there which gives the illusion of belonging. Gay organizations and activities are plentiful there, but competition is brutal."

Becky's mind spun for a moment. She assumed that Loren was a woman. It had been many years since she was in the company of openly homosexual people.

"I'm sorry. Did Karla not mention that I was gay?"

"No, she didn't. It's not something she would bring up. We were in San Francisco many years ago working with a theater group. Our questions were pretty much resolved during that time. I just haven't been in the company of gay people since, so I just didn't click in. I'm sorry."

"No problem." Steven took a deep breath. "Back to 'The Way Home.' What does it mean? Are you in the process of finding your way home?"

"Well, sort of. I've been turning a corner. You'll hear more about that when you meet Chaim and Georgina. They are a big part of it. I'm beginning to discover that home isn't where I thought it should be. It doesn't have a physical location, but a psychological/spiritual one. We're taught that home is where you are born, a street address. The journey is to find the true home in our spiritual nature, our innate sense of being alive and knowing the source of that life as home.

"What caused you to begin this journey?" Steven was paying rapt attention, jotting a few notes when she paused to think.

"I think it was a combination of guilt and misery overload, and the publishing of books on the various aspects of the subject. The new spirituality and self-help psychology that are just coming on the market are two great sources. The push of misery and unhappiness gets so powerful that it ether breaks you, or pushes you to break through to a journey of discovery and eventually joy."

Becky, Georgina, and Chaim introduced Steven to Mom & Pop's. Their favorite booth in the back had just been cleared. They knew everyone in the place and introduced Steven as their new corporate partner.

Steven wanted to know all about everyone, Chaim's research, Georgina's music, and Becky's religion and psychology classes. He asked about the lifelong relationship with Karla and Sandy. With their input, he began sketching out a framework of how things might evolve. They could plug in components as they were developed.

The word "components" came up several times and stuck in Becky's mind as what she needed to focus upon, one piece at a time. Usually she became overwhelmed with trying to process all facets of an idea all at once. But this was too big.

As Steven was leaving to go back to Asbury Park he said he would call Karla and find a time for a conference call. He had access to a telephone network and they could create a schedule with the network so they could confer as often as needed. He would send them all copies of his notes and progress reports.

Chaim came to Becky and Georgina's table in the cafeteria on the trot. "I have interesting news. A friend of a friend is coming to see me the end of next week. He is Alexei Rusnov from Leningrad, formerly Saint Petersburg, Russia, in the USSR. He is in the country on an educational grant and heard our broadcasts. He wants to meet us and take these ideas back to Leningrad in a month."

"Oh, did you tell him all we have is empty boxes so far?"

"Well, they're worse off than we are. Russia has no spirituality going on at all. It's prohibited. Just the old people, who have no family and nothing to lose, go to the few churches that are still functioning. He's interested because, among other things, he has a family life organization of some sort, and can pass the ideas along to a lot of people without involving the orthodox church or the government. They have mostly social, educational, and medical components. They pass information word of mouth so as not to arouse the suspicion of the authorities, but have no way to get new ideas from the west. He thinks we will be the perfect source. He is really intense and determined."

"Well, where do we start? What do you want us to do?" Georgina was ready to jump in. "How can we help him? I know their window of opportunity rarely opens and can close any moment. It may not open again for another forty years. My aunt has relatives there and from time to time tries to get a letter through. She is rarely successful. The only way she knows that it was received it is when a message comes back to her, usually through a private courier such as this man. Even then they can't tell her much because the courier could be searched and get into trouble. They may even nail this guy on his way back and he knows it. He's taking a huge risk."

Becky was aghast. "I'll start pulling stuff together right away." She was thinking of the fragments she had filed in her computer so far and how they might fit together in some cohesive form.

"Try to use simple explanations. I mean stay away from colloquialisms, idiomatic language, and anything that has a double meaning. It's amazing that we speak in so many idioms that we aren't even aware of. They don't read the Bible and psychology is used only for torture, so the only imaging we have in common is physics. I'm familiar with this because there are a lot of Russian Jews in Israel." Chaim was drumming his fingers on the table trying to think it all through quickly.

Georgina patted his hand. "Stay cool, drummer boy. We can run everything by you and then this Alexei. I suppose his English is good?"

"Yeah, but it's British English. They teach British English in their grade schools. The philosophy of the government is that everyone should learn the language of their enemies. However, the people are eager to learn English because it is the language of the free world."

"O.K., I have a book on physics and metaphysics. I'll scan through it and get some ideas on how to express things." Becky was already visualizing just where that book was on her book shelves.

When Becky and Georgina came into Chaim's office with what they had put together, Chaim was speaking in Russian on the telephone.

"Why am I not surprised?" Becky had been listening to Russian language tapes herself, trying to get a sense of how they said things, sentence order, etc. She knew from dealing with Mexicans in San Francisco that it was better if she could mimic their broken English and voice inflections. They would understand her more easily. She always hoped they wouldn't think she was making fun of them.

"Dosvedonya." Chaim hung up the receiver. "He'll be here tomorrow. I'm still not sure what he is expecting. He tends to skip from one subject to another so fast that I never quite get closure on any one area. He sounds like he is super smart or a super con man. I'm not sure which."

Georgina frowned a bit. "Maybe years of oppression does that to people. They have to get it all into one minute or all is lost. Desperation can make anyone sound like a con."

"Yeah. We'll have to give him the benefit of the doubt. Wait and see what happens when he gets here." Becky was concerned too.

Alexei came running through the door of Chaim's office, coat tails flying, almost out of breath. "Hello. I am here. Tell me please that I am not too late."

"Have a seat Alexei, you are not late. Alexei, this is Dr. Becky Temple and Dr. Georgina West."

"Ochen priatna. Oh, sorry, pleased to meet you." Alexei bowed and shook hands with both of them, smiling broadly.

"Ochen priatna," said Becky graciously. "That's about all the Russian I know besides please and thank you."

Georgina spoke a few more words inquiring after his health and he was pleased. "It is so good to hear my own language, if only a few words."

"I have relatives in Peterhoff. I've tried to learn a little about their language, but of course we haven't been able to see them for many years."

"Give me their names and I will visit them when I return home."

"Can you really do that?"

"Of course, of course. It is possible. I can deliver a letter to them if you wish."

Georgina was not surprised. "I hoped you might be able to, so I've already prepared a letter." She pulled the envelope from her purse and handed it to him. "Bolshoi spaseebo."

Becky spread the work she had pulled together on the table before Alexei. She explained that she used the examples of physics to make things understandable. He was most appreciative of her efforts as he perused the pages.

"This will work very well. We must be sure to tell the people they must do the work and not just sit around dreaming about things. That is what the communists have told the people for forty-two years. 'Just dream about good and you will be happy.' It has crippled them."

Becky showed him the exercises she had created so the Russian people could put the mental work into practical applications. They took some time to practice them with Alexei, so he could explain them more fully.

Georgina suggested they order pizza or Chinese so they could continue working. Alexei was agreeable. He hadn't eaten since early morning and he had a midnight plane to catch. A limo would be coming for him.

It was an intense evening and they were all exhausted when Alexei left. He promised to be in touch, but could not leave an address where he could be reached. He was making several stops before he returned to Russia and his itinerary was in the possession of a KGB official who was traveling with him.

"That's how they are," said Georgina. "The KGB watches everyone like hawks, even when they are out of the country, to be sure they don't give or receive any information not approved by the government. It's scary."

"I wonder how he managed this side trip then." Becky looked around as if spies would be coming out of the woodwork. "Surely this was not approved material that he is collecting. I'm starting to understand the "con man" side of him as a necessary survival mechanism."

Twelve

"Nathan, we've had a visitor from Russia, Saint Petersburg area. He said he was here on an education grant. It seems that the KGB was accompanying him wherever he went, keeping his itinerary secret from him. Somehow he made it to South Bennington because he heard Karla's radio broadcast when I was on it. Should I be suspicious? Are we in trouble? Could the KGB have us on a hit list?"

"Geez Mom. A visitor from the USSR! Highly unusual. This guy must be pretty high up, and/or highly suspect. That's the way their government allows their people to travel, if at all. He could be in trouble if he is off the itinerary, but you aren't. What did he want?"

Becky told Nathan all about the visit and what they gave Alexei to take home with him.

"He'll be lucky if he makes it into the Soviet Union with anything but his underwear and toothbrush. The KGB searches everyone very carefully. I was there once, and they confiscated the few bogus phone numbers I had for fictional people there. Fortunately, I had memorized the real ones before I went. I let them find the bogus list to satisfy them and so my real contacts wouldn't get into trouble."

"You were inside the iron curtain? Well of course you couldn't tell me, I know. Can you tell me what it is like there? In Russia, I mean."

"Well, I can tell you some things." He described the landscape, the buildings, the people on the streets, and the constant presence of the KGB in people's lives.

"So, is this guy in trouble?"

"Most likely yes unless he is unusually clever. He is probably accustomed to slipping through their surveillance nets. It is the only way to get a taste of the western culture and freedom. Saint Petersburg is only a few hours from Helsinki and many of them slip out there. Actually, Peter the Great spent a lot of time in Europe. He wanted a navy, and got his navy officers from Holland because the landlubber Russians wouldn't sail."

"He said he is from Peterhoff. Where is that?"

"A suburb of Saint Petersburg where the summer palace of Peter the Great is located."

"Another thing. Are Russian men usually so flirtatious or was I just not used to their culture?"

"Flirtatious, huh? The unwritten rule is that foreign men are not married if they are outside of their own country."

"You mean he's probably married, but it doesn't matter since he isn't at home?"

"Yup. Did you ask him if he was married?"

"Well, no! I mean, I wasn't even sure if he was coming on to me or what."

"Well he probably was. Just ask him if he is married. He'll tell you he is, but that it doesn't matter or that they are separated. That's a word they've learned from us. To them, however, it usually means temporarily separated by an ocean. Do you wanna give me details?"

"Not really! This is embarrassing enough, having to ask my son this stuff."

"Be cool, Mom. You're a gorgeous woman and European men like older women. Well, you know, older meaning not twenty anymore."

"I get it. You're a good son. I can take it from here." They both broke out laughing. "I love you. Bye." She thoughtfully replaced the receiver.

The next day Becky decided to go to the library and get what books she could on the cities of Russia and their historical sites. A whole new world was opening up for her and she was curious to get whatever information was available.

Thinking about Alexei was making it all ever so much more interesting. Georgina had taken to winking at her during Alexei's visit, whenever she looked up from the paperwork. It must have been obvious to Chaim too. Or maybe not. She didn't want to ask.

John was presenting another phase of his futuristic ideas in Monday evening class. Becky's head was awhirl with all she had been reading about Russia and its backwardness, contrasting it with what John was talking about.

It was enough of a jump from present day democracy to envision this higher level of personal responsibility and freedom to co-create a new and just society. But to imagine how the Russians would get there being forty-two years behind the free world in industry alone was really difficult. Their society was mired in the idea of the aggregate and not the individual as most important. How could they quickly adjust their values to see the individual consciousness as all important.

It was as if there were many evolutionary stages present in different countries and different segments of the population. East and west Germany. Palestine and Israel. Central America and the United States. How would it all fit together, or would the gap become greater and greater.

Becky raised her hand and posed the question to John.

"Indeed, there are many levels. Evolution is like a spiral, every round going higher. When we were separated by oceans we could not readily cross, and airplanes had not yet made the world smaller, each level could exist in its own enclosed location and progress at its own pace. So isolated were these civilizations that the tales of Marco Polo were not believed in his time. Eventually populations expanded and wars broke out. The Tartars invaded Russia destroying everything in their path.

"Eventually, civilizations learned about each other through wars because they were exposed to different ways of living even if it was destructive. Without wars, we could have gone on for centuries without ever learning about others on our planet. It is the only good aspect of war I can think of. Fortunately, we have learned to cross the borders in peace for purposes of commerce instead of conquest. Of course, commerce is its own brand of conquest as we practice it in this country.

"Now we are face to face, neighborhood next to neighborhood, with disparate beliefs, values and customs. One civilization at once rejecting and assimilating another. Cultures are living side by side scaring the wits out of each other. Some of the people within each culture become open and accepting, some closed and territorial.

"Our proverbial melting pot has caused people to try desperately to preserve their own culture instead of letting it be dissolved into the whole. Which is better? We nearly lost the American Indian cultures, stamped them out, stuck the people we largely destroyed on reservations. We obliterated the Hawaiian culture too. Some melting pot. More like a cooking pot. Now at least we are trying to recover those cultures from the remnants that are left.

"Dr. Temple, we have so many questions to answer and it seems the more answers we find, the more questions arise. Until now we have only asked small questions, so we got limited answers. We need to learn to ask much larger questions. Ask questions of universal proportions. That is the only way we will get beyond the minutia of our struggles and see the greater picture.

"And let us not think that the Russians are lower on the spiral than we are. They may be behind materially, but they are deeply spiritual. They have fortunately been deprived of their Orthodoxy that is as repressive as the rulers of their country. This has driven them inward to their own spiritual nature. They have healers because they have been without wide spread medical assistance. Their arts are pure because they have no distractions. Their Olympians are top flight."

For the first time Becky found comfort and upliftment in John's words. She sensed a safety in his presence that had nothing to do with personality. He was not looking down his nose at others, but opening a door that had a high sill to step over. And he was helping them step over it into a higher way of thinking. She saw for the first time his compassion that extended to the whole human race.

Georgina and Becky invited John to go to the Patrician Grille after class. He declined but thought perhaps another time.

"Well it's a start, Beck. Maybe it just takes a little time with John. There might be a person in there after all and we just need to stay with it."

"It is hard to know if you might be stepping on toes or touching old wounds with someone like him. I know how it is when someone pushes a little too much with me. I close up until they back off."

"What did you think about the evolution idea?"

"Well, I was really blown away by Teilhard's idea that "Omega" draws us from the beginnings of complexity consciousness in an upward curve toward the Omega or highest point. Sounds like either image will work."

"I like the idea that we are drawn, invited, beckoned instead of pushed by biology. I like the idea that there is a higher power that draws us to itself. It's heady stuff." Georgina stuck the menu back into its holder.

"Did you ever feel that drawing upward happening to you? Have you ever had a sense of it?" Becky placed her usual order.

"I guess musically I have. Just about the time I thought my voice had come to a plateau, it would take a jump to another level. I was always sure I couldn't go further and yet there was the urge to continue working. Suddenly I was there, like going through a gate into a new level. It never seemed that it was a simply a result of the exercises I did. It was something more that I couldn't explain."

Becky frowned. "I've always believed in God, and have studied religion and all. But the actual experience of God like that I'm not sure I've had. Maybe when I was a kid at church camp."

Becky was twelve when she attended Christian Camp. They each held a candle and sang Jacob's Ladder. "Every round goes higher, higher." Becky described it to Georgina complete with singing a little of Jacob's Ladder. "That's the only spiritual experience I can remember. I remember the awe it inspired in me. Adult church never did much for me. In an adult church service I would sit and draw caricatures of the people around me on the back of the bulletin. My mother would hide them so no one would recognize themselves and be insulted. She let me do it because it kept me quiet."

Georgina laughed. "You're an artist?"

"Haven't done it for years. I took a few art classes in high school and college."

"In the Catholic church we spent most of the time on our knees. Our kneeling benches were not padded. We were told that the pain was good for our piety. Lord, we hated that. I couldn't imagine the Orthodox church where they kneel on cold stone floors for hours. My elderly relatives in Russia do that. It's no wonder they can hardly walk for the arthritis."

"Did you ever have the spiritual experience other than your singing?"

"I don't think so. My cousins and I were too busy getting into mischief for which we were soundly punished after church. My father, who never went to church, insisted we go and behave. Go figure!"

The next morning Becky and Georgina met for their joint meditation and prayer time. They went through the six steps in the book, and asked to be open to the spiritual experience in their lives. "This is a little scary," said Georgina, "sort of like asking for the roof to fall on you or something."

"If it was only the roof we'd know what to expect. This feels more like calling the whole universe down on our heads!"

"I think we're still too superstitious. I've got Catholic traditions, punishment, and God's will all mixed up into a nasty brew of something I won't like. Now I'm starting to remember the fear and anxiety I used to have about religion." Georgina took a sip of her coffee.

"It's a bit difficult to unload the stuff we were filled with in childhood. It is down there so deep in the non-verbal reaches of consciousness. We don't know it's there until it shows up in the form of irrational fears." Becky joined her and they were quiet together for a moment.

"So, what do we do, O Great White Mother?" Georgina had that impish look again.

"Well, little one, we keep talking to ourselves and each other about the positive stuff we find. Sort the chaff from the wheat, the goats from the sheep. Biblical ya know."

"Right. Sort the goat thoughts from the sheep thoughts!"

"Georgi, that's brilliant. We'll work on it. No more goat thoughts!"

Georgi raised her coffee cup. "Here, here! No more goat thoughts!"

Karla's radio program was causing a stir and gathering a wider listening audience. She had several new age speakers on, but Becky was the most requested guest.

Karla began after the opening trailer, "Becky, can you share your thoughts on what spiritual evolution is? What powers it? What your experience is with it?"

"I can only share some word pictures and images of what is unfolding for me. We begin mentally asleep to our true nature. We are involved in the physical world always looking outward for our future and fulfillment. Something jogs us and we open one mental eye to see what it was and go back to sleep again. What we saw drops into our subconscious mind and stays there until summoned.

Enough of these images start to create a body of thought or belief. They push our consciousness to awaken."

"Sounds like gas on the stomach, Becky." They laughed.

"I guess you could say that. It gets uncomfortable. Nothing fits the way it did before."

"So, something moves us to awaken? It doesn't sound like we can force the awakening or cause it to happen on cue."

"I think we can fill the conscious mind with ideas that go in that direction, but they stay in the intellect. Often they don't really become our experience. Many people stay at the level of intellectual exercise. Others seem to ingest it and it becomes part of them in a deeper way."

"Go ahead, caller."

"Yeah, thanks. This is Jack. I was taught that God has to touch you. That you can't do anything yourself. And if God doesn't touch you, it means you aren't worthy."

"How do you get worthy, Jack? Did they tell you?"

"Uh, I don't really know. You try to be good and help other people. Don't cheat anybody. But no guarantees. God may still not choose to touch you."

"And you don't think we can have any part in our own spiritual progress, Jack?"

"I don't see how we can. It's God who decides."

"Well, I believe that God's decision is already made for all of us. God's answer is yes, and our part is to spend our lives preparing our minds and hearts to live as closely to God's likeness as we can until we arrive at what some call enlightenment and other's call being touched by God."

"Sounds like a lotta work to me. I think I'd rather wait for God to decide and if He doesn't touch me, I guess that's the way it goes."

"Jack, don't you think we need to do our part?"

"Oh, Yeah. But it doesn't change anything. Only God can do that."

"It sounds like you might think any effort is hopeless. Do you think that was Jesus' message?"

"Well, there's something about considering the Lilies of the field that doesn't work and God takes care of them."

Becky wasn't sure where to go with this one. Karla joined in. "We have to go to break, Jack, but we want to take time to thank you for your call. We bless you in holding to what feels right for you."

"O.K. Bye."

"Some of those old beliefs die hard, Karla. I'm afraid that a large segment of the population doesn't see their position as anything more than a pawn in God's chess game."

"Next caller. Jane is on the line. Hello Jane."

"Hello. I have to say that I hate the idea of being a victim. I couldn't love a God that treated me that way. I believe God gave me a brain to use and intelligence to figure things out for myself. The idea that someone died for my sins without asking me is ludicrous too. More victim stuff."

"What kind of God do you want, Jane?"

"Well, certainly not one who threatens or punishes, or ignores me altogether. I want the kind of God that gives me the power to live well and who is my cheering section all the way."

"What might you think of God as an all-pervading creative principle. A god that is the first cause of all creation and is a sustaining power in every atom and molecule as life and intelligence? A god that has given us the power to choose?"

"Wow, that's a mouth full. I'm jotting some of that down, because it is something I would like to know more about. It's kind of intellectual, but I think it has the best chance of leading to something more than being a victim or a pawn. Can you give me some references to look up?"

Karla jumped in. "Yes we can, Jane. Stay on the line while we go to break, and our producer will give you what we have. Thanks for your call."

"Next caller?"

"No, I'm not going to give my name to a bunch of witches. You'll all burn in hell…"

Karla let Becky know that one didn't go on the air. Becky took a deep breath and a sip of water.

"Hi, I just came to this country two months ago. My name is Helga and I have never heard of what you are talking about. In East Germany we have no such words, no such hope. How can you say we are not victims when that is all we have ever been? We are victims of whatever governments we have. How can we be anything else?"

"Good questions, Helga. Thanks for calling. God created us with free will to think what we want to think. You may not be able to give voice to your thoughts in some countries, but you can still think them. God intended you to be free to use your thoughts in your life. Victimizing is a human thing, not a God thing. Thoughts are more powerful than we have ever believed. "God meant us to be the hero of our lives. To use our thoughts to create our lives. Even the oppression you have experienced is the result of a way of thinking, a destructive way. Because you have always felt victimized doesn't mean that is the way God intended it to be. When you direct your thoughts toward the creative and positive, you can change your life in that direction."

"I still don't understand. How do I do that?"

"Helga, how did you get out of East Germany and into this country?"

"Well, we escaped at great risk to our lives. We planned for a very long time and had to pay bribes."

"Didn't the thought of escaping to freedom start your actions? And here you are."

"I thought we were just fortunate that all went well."

"Didn't you intend for all to go well? Didn't you plan to succeed?"

"Yes, yes, of course. But I didn't think it was connected. I didn't think about that. Is this for everything? Can I do this with other things?"

"It works for everything, Helga. Direct your thoughts in the way you want your life to go. Welcome and I hope you have a happy life."

"Thank you. Yes, thank you."

After the broadcast Karla and Becky reviewed the calls. "I just want you to know, Beck, that we run down some of the crank calls. We find out who they are and whether they are a danger of any sort. We haven't published the name of the college and we don't mention it on the air now because we don't want a crank to show up there. I should have thought of it the first time you were on the show, but I wasn't looking far enough ahead. We haven't done it since the first time however."

"Should I be worried?"

"Well, not worried. We just want to be careful from now on. I'm going to keep a security system in place. It's a service of the station while we are on the air. However, if someone should contact you directly, I want to know about it immediately. And if someone shows up or is the least bit antagonistic on the phone, call the police and me in that order."

"Don't worry, huh?"

"No, just be aware. The world is full of cuckoos and as soon as you go public it's a concern. That's why we have a security office here at the station."

"Hi Mom. Just wanted you to know everything is going well. I'm glad to be out of South Africa and that mess. I'm in good health and the doctor said the baby is doing fine. We have a few months to go which seems like an eternity now. I think I'm starting to waddle."

"Oh, I hated that part. I always felt like a walking blimp. I learned not to glance into store windows as I walked by. Didn't want to see myself in full bloom."

"Mark is making up for being gone so much by bringing home baby clothes and flowers. He's trying to arrange his schedule so he can be here more. He wants to be in the delivery room, if you can imagine. I expect him to faint. He didn't even want to visit me in the hospital and thought maybe I could come home the next day. The doctor cleared that up."

"He's a good doctor."

"She."

"Right. Where is Mark this time?"

"He's back in London, but only for a few days. Business, not family stuff."

Becky was ashamed of her feeling of relief that Mark's family wasn't dragging him back there.

"I spoke to Nathan. He told me about your Russian friend."

"I don't have a Russian friend and tell Nathan to put a sock in it."

"Well, we share everything, you know."

"I guess that's good. Far as I know the guy is back in Russia and they may have drawn and quartered him by now."

"Likely. Gotta go, Mom. Literally. Love ya. I'll call again soon."

"Love you, too."

Thirteen

The invitation arrived seemingly out of the blue. It came from an organization of citizen diplomats.

"Georgi, this group wants me to go with them on a citizen's diplomatic mission to the USSR next year. I didn't know just anyone could get into the USSR these days."

"That's strange. Especially since Alexei was just here. How did they select you? Get your name and location? Surely not through him."

"No. The radio. The first time I was on we mentioned the college name. Karla checked them out and said they are legit. They're O.K. It's a new organization of peace makers who want to diffuse the cold war atmosphere. They are in touch with a peace committee in the soviet government. The meeting is to be in Moscow. I think Alexei is just a coincidence. Maybe the USSR is opening up and we're just seeing bits and pieces of the evidence of it."

"Scary. Totally scary. I'm amazed that the KGB would even allow it. They'll follow everyone right on their heels and listen in on every conversation. I vowed I would never go there knowing how my relatives live in fear under that system."

"Yeah, I've never experienced that kind of oppression. Not sure how I would react. I wouldn't know what to do and not do. Be in Siberia in a heartbeat."

"What are you going to do? Ignore it?"

"No. I'll call them. Accept the invitation if it sounds right, if I like what I hear. Find out what it will cost for the two of us." Becky grinned at Georgina. "Don't think I'm going by myself, do you?"

"How 'bout taking Nathan? He knows the ropes."

"His security clearance rating is too high. They'll grab him the minute he sets foot there. He told me that a while back. No, good buddy. It's you."

"Uh, I need to check on my own status because I have relatives there. Maybe Nathan can find out for me if that would be a problem. Like I said, it's scary."

"Just think about the Bolshoi opera singers, Georgi. What fun it would be to hear them! Focus on the positive."

Jim Sherman called the college switchboard Thursday noon from a dealership service department. His car had stopped outside of town and he rode the rest of the way in the tow truck. His father wasn't in, so he asked for Becky.

"Hi. This is Jim. I've taken a few days off and wanted to attend the Monday evening class. I thought maybe psychologically freeing architecture might have a place in your topic."

"Hi. Well, great. Would you like to present something to this class? I think Chaim would have no problem making room for you. When will you be here?"

"Well, I'm here now at the service department of the dealership on Main. My car quit. It will be tomorrow before they get the part and fix it. I don't know where my father is, but could I ask you to come and get me? I can wait for him at his office."

"Oh, sure. I'll be there in a few minutes. Have you had lunch?"

"No. Shall we do lunch, as the corporates say?"

Becky and Jim found a table in Mom & Pop's just before the place filled up. "What are you talking about with the psychologically beneficial architecture?"

"The Japanese have something called feng shui. It is a way of arranging working and living space so that the energy can move properly. They claim it has a good effect upon the people there. I've been studying some things about it and it makes sense to me. I've even arranged my apartment according to their ideas and I can feel a difference. At first it seemed to be just visually pleasant, but I began to feel slightly exhilarated when I walked in after work."

"I really want to hear about this. My place is probably as un-feng shui as it can get."

"That can actually drain your energy, so you have to work against that depleting force the whole time."

"Are there any books about it?"

"Only in Japanese, but I have a translation that a friend in Japan sent me from Tokyo."

"Jim, have you heard about the organization that is growing up around me despite my best efforts to resist?"

Becky told him about The Way Home and all that had transpired. "Your architecture ideas might make a great addition to whatever else we can put together. It is in the idea stages right now and I'm thinking I'll be doing seminars and stuff. Right now, I'm just a regular on a friend's radio program talking about religion, self-help psychology, talking to callers and all that."

"I'll keep that in mind. I don't know enough yet, but I may by the time things come together for you. By the way I think this is wonderful of you to help me out. I appreciate your friendship and Nathan's so much."

Becky's heart went out to Jim. She wasn't sure what all precipitated his declaration, but she was sure he had some feelings of loneliness and abandonment. She was sure that John's aloofness had something to do with it, but hesitated to ask.

Instead, "Jim do you have a girlfriend?"

He laughed. "No, not really. I have lots of friends who happen to be girls, but no one special. I guess I really like my freedom and I move about a lot. That's not too attractive to someone who wants to settle down."

"Actually, I have similar feelings. Even though I don't move around, I really like to go home to a quiet place and shut the door on the world. I love my friends and my students, and I love to go home alone."

"I have friends who lament being alone and not having someone in their lives. I figure it may happen down the road at the right time and with the right person, but I'm not going to spoil things now by obsessing about it." Jim was ready to let go of the subject.

"Your father gave quite a presentation in the last Monday evening class. Sort of blew everyone away. Gave us a lot to think about. He even answered questions."

"Yeah, he's way out there, isn't he?"

"He certainly is!" Becky still couldn't read Jim very well. "Does he share any of this with you?"

"Yes, sometimes. He stays holed up with his thoughts and papers, and just doesn't touch terra firma very much. So I don't have a lot of contact with him unless he needs something done. It's just as well. He doesn't like company and becomes irritated if anyone is around too much. Even me."

"Do you have any idea why? What makes him that way?"

"I think maybe it happened because he is an orphan and being extremely bright, he just made up his own world in his mind. He is still doing that, only it has taken on this futuristic direction. He works for the good of all mankind because he can't deal with individuals. My mother was a Dane who didn't want much attention anyway. She was preoccupied with her business and traveled between the United States and Denmark every month. Their marriage didn't last long. I was born after they split."

"Did they get a divorce?"

"No, they just left each other and have no contact. They didn't own anything in common, except me I guess, so there was nothing to divide up or dissolve."

"Did she raise you?"

"Actually, her mother did for a while and then I went off to boarding school. She was a nice lady, and warm hearted. I guess she made a human being out of me as best she could. I was pretty rebellious."

"Do you ever see your mother?" Becky hoped she wasn't pushing too far.

"No, not for years. We drifted apart when I went off to school and I just sort of found my own way. My father did send me to college and saw to it that I had enough money and all. He tries. She doesn't."

"And your grandmother?"

"She died when I started graduate school. Her illness was sudden, but I did get to say goodbye. I grabbed a flight to Copenhagen just in time. Got to thank her for taking care of me and apologize one more time for being such a brat."

John was in his office when Becky and Jim returned to the college campus. He seemed pleased to see Jim and generally interested as they spoke about plans to include Jim's work in a segment of "The Way Home" organization. Becky was a little more relaxed while talking to John since Jim had given her a little background on their lives and circumstances.

Becky had worked in a manufacturing company in her early twenties. "That sales and marketing department has done it again." Her boss stormed through to his office. "They promise deadlines we can't possibly meet and tell the customer it is our fault. Each sales person thinks their order should have priority."

Becky completely agreed as she finished her typing and brought the paperwork to his desk. Sales and marketing was the elite and seemed to get all the credit for the good stuff while manufacturing got the bum rap. A few months later Becky's boss was promoted to the executive offices and Becky was transferred to sales and marketing.

"How does manufacturing expect this company to survive, let alone progress when they can't meet the easiest deadline?" Her new boss was mirroring the reverse of what she had believed about the situation. "They have many excuses and our customers will be going some place else if they don't get on the ball. We already lost one big order this month."

Becky remembered feeling guilty for all the things she thought about it, knowing only the manufacturing side. How freeing it was to see both sides now as she listened to Jim and John.

Nick and Jim dragged furniture and other props into the theater for the Monday evening class. Jim had drawn plans to demonstrate the power of surroundings according to his Japanese books. He and Georgina planned music to go with the scenes to represent the energy flow in each one. During class his explanations about the arrangements that created peace and the ones that created anxiety kept everyone on the edge of their seats. Becky was already envisioning what she could do at her place and in her office.

Becky, Georgina, and Jim went to the Patrician Grille for a late dinner.

"I wish you could come to my house and give me some pointers." Georgina was thinking of the piles of music and books everywhere, old Italian decorations and crooked drapes she had neglected for years.

"Actually the place needs an overhaul, but maybe there are a few things I can do to improve it."

Becky exploded into laughter. "I'm sorry. Tell you what. If Jim is willing, we'll all go together to your place and pitch in."

"Oh God, my place is a major mess!"

"We don't mind, do we Becky? We'll just dive in with our eyes closed."

"Very funny. Guess I shouldn't refuse help. Lord knows I've needed it for a long time. My mother goes cluck-clucking around like a bossy hen about it every time she visits me. 'See what a failure I am as a mother? You can't even keep your place nice. What is all this stuff? Can't you put it away or throw it out?' It goes on and on."

Jim confirmed with Becky and Georgina there were no classes the next day, turned a place mat over and began to sketch Georgina's house as she described it, windows, doors, furniture, piano, and orientation to the sun.

Becky arrived an hour ahead of time to help Georgina gather up music and books. Georgina cleared the kitchen table and counters. Jim arrived, plan of action in hand and ready to go. He also brought a hand truck, measuring tapes and gloves. Fortunately, the service department where his car was being repaired was open early so he could retrieve them from the overcrowded back seat and trunk. The mechanic dropped him off at Georgina's on his way to get the parts.

"First let's go over the plans and do some measuring to be sure everything will fit." Jim spread the sketches on the kitchen table. The excitement rose in Georgina's voice as they went from room to room discussing the changes.

"I'll bring the small stuff into the kitchen out of the way." Becky had a feather duster in the back pocket of her jeans and a cleaning rag over her shoulder. Her hair was tucked into a baseball cap.

The transformation began with amazing speed once the preparations were made. By noon everything was in place and they stood back to admire their work.

"Oh, it's amazing, Jim! I never thought my place could look, uh, larger, freer or lighter somehow." Georgina was all smiles as she walked around and around taking in the view from every angle.

Jim called John to see if the service department had left a message. The vehicle wouldn't be done for a few hours yet. The three of them stopped at Mom & Pop's for carry out and headed for Becky's.

Jim looked around Becky's place and began to sketch a plan while they ate. The work began with a flurry of items being moved in every direction. Becky's place was more compact. They bumped into each other and laughed a lot. Becky was sure they would never make order out of the chaos or that she would ever find anything again. But little by little, following Jim's expert directions, it began to come together. What a mover and shaker he was.

John called and came to pick Jim up before they were completely finished, but enough had been accomplished. Jim hugged Becky and Georgina thanking them for a great time. "I really enjoyed this time with you. Thanks for letting me practice on your places. Hope I wasn't too intrusive. I'll be in touch."

Becky and Georgina met Chaim at the Breakfast Nook. He listened patiently as they described the previous day with Jim Sherman.

"Maybe you can do my place next. Probably better to wait. I still have a jumble of boxes and unsorted stuff. Even a slight breeze would render my life inoperable."

Georgina laughed, "What do you think our places looked like? We weren't in any better shape. But it was no problem for Jim. He's a genius."

"We learned a lot," Becky added as Grandma Hattie came bustling in with a steaming platter of pancakes and blueberries. She was singing something from the musical "Roberta." Hattie hadn't stopped singing since the Christmas party. Becky and Georgina often joined in. The farmers would ignore them and just talked louder about their farming concerns.

"I'm going to Israel for summer break. I was assuming we would have ended the Monday class by now. What do you think we should do?"

"Let's suspend it for the summer. Let the energy build up again for the fall, if it's going to. I would like to focus more on "The Way Home" and put something solid together. It seems to be still floating in the unformed state and I don't want to lose the little momentum I have."

"I was hoping you'd say that," said Georgina. "Steven has been updating me too, and I'm eager to get to work on my part of it."

"Is everything O.K. in Israel? Your family, I mean?"

"Sort of, Becky. There was a border skirmish and Avram caught some shrapnel in his leg. He had surgery and is walking with a severe limp right now. He's on desk duty until this heals. Something in the shrapnel caused a reaction or infection. They're not sure what it is. He's the hot headed one. He was going ahead of his team when he was told to wait. He always had to prove himself by being first. I guess that's the result of being born last."

"I know exactly how he feels," said Becky ruefully. They set the date for the class to close in the next few weeks.

Summer break came quickly and with it Becky's first grandchild, Sarah Rebecca Melissa Davies, six pounds and eighteen inches long, born in Middletown, Connecticut.

Becky looked in amazement at the tiny face and fingers. How familiar this child looked to her, a bit like Nathan. It was as if she'd always known her. Was there something to that? Somewhere in the cosmos, did they know each other at another time and place?

"Are you sure she has enough names?" Becky was amazed that her name was among them. She hadn't even thought of that possibility.

"Quite sure, Mom. We worked it out over several months. Sarah is Mark's grandmother, and then there is you, aunt Melissa and me. His father's mother was his inspiration and helped him live past the folderol and pomp of his parents' lives."

"How about Mark's mother?"

"She was appalled that we might name the child after her and forbade us, so we didn't. If her feelings are hurt, it was her choice. I can't worry about it."

Becky knew that Moira Davies always said the opposite of what she really wanted. She always gave herself airs and feigned distain of what she thought was unworthy of her. She wondered if Lissa knew that and chose to ignore it.

"Yes, Mom, I know it. I can't play those games, so I just repeat back to her what she says and act accordingly. Mark does the same. She gets pretty impossible if you play into her games. I guess George understands her because he seems to live with it without complaint."

"I wonder what the attraction was between them." Becky didn't want to appear catty, but she couldn't imagine that woman was capable of intimacy.

"Position and old money. When they were married, 'putting on airs' was classy and people didn't 'reeeely relate' like the current generation. They had a sheet with a hole in it in order to get Mark."

"Lissa!"

"Right from the horse's mouth, Mom. Well, if you consider his grandmother the horse's mouth. She's the one who told Mark."

Becky couldn't help but laugh. "She didn't pass the sheet on to you?"

"No, but I'll bet she thought about it. She was always complaining that we were much too romantic with each other and should take a cooler look at life. She meant he should take a cooler look at me."

Classes were over. Georgina would be traveling in Europe visiting opera houses and music schools. Chaim had already left for Israel and Becky decided to take a sabbatical to Cairo to study the beginnings of the Coptic church there. That was one segment of her studies that was not as fully developed as she would like. She would start with Israel, visiting Safed, Capernaum, and Jerusalem. There would be some rest and relaxation time on the shore of the Mediterranean near Tel Aviv. She knew Chaim would be busy with family and there were no plans to connect with him there.

Through her college connections, Ruben and Aviva Ne'er would be her guides in Israel. They were overseeing a few of the archeological digs and worked with several university programs. Becky was excited as she boarded the plane and began her journey. She had packed very lightly, glad to shed the trappings of home and school for a while.

She was armed with a list of things she wanted to see and know more about. Ruben and Aviva smiled looking at the list. "This will take at least a year, Dr. Temple!"

"Becky, please. I thought it was probably a bit much, but I wanted all the options listed. We can cover a lot of it."

"We will see that you get something about each item one way or the other. All will not be lost."

The trip to Safed took them up a long winding mountain highway with many switchbacks and glorious scenery. Safed was very high up in the mountains, which seemed a strange place for earthquakes. As

Chaim had told her, old Safed was in ruins from the violent quakes over the centuries and the government gave up rebuilding the old places. The artist colony that mushroomed among the broken walls and twisting walkways was rich with paintings and sculptures.

The ancient synagogue with its blue sanctuary and papyrus scrolls was intact. Ruben led them inside where they chatted for a long time about the history, the writing of the Kabbalah, and stories about interesting events that took place there.

While Aviva and Ruben attended to some business, Becky took some time to wander through the shops and art displays, and enjoy the rarified air and sunshine. It felt like the proverbial heaven and Johnston Crossing was just a distant memory.

Becky was not prepared for her feelings about Capernaum. Many of the Gospel stories about Jesus' activities took place here in this area. It felt like he was still here. She sat on the wall of the first century synagogue and wrote poetry for the first time in several years. She wrote about the woman touching the hem of his robe and strangely tears came to her eyes.

As she looked across the northern tip of the sea of Galilee, she could see a pass in the mountains where Jesus must have walked to go to Cana and Nazareth. Or perhaps He walked along the shore. It would have been a seventy-mile walk and she tried to imagine walking that far, day after day, along the dusty roads which were probably little more than goat paths then.

The mount of the beatitudes was so jammed with tourist busses that it was difficult to park very close, so they walked a distance. Aviva said it was always this way. The place was small and everyone wanted to see where Jesus delivered the sermon, and to look out over the sea. From there Becky could see a small town that is now called Magdala to the west and Capernaum to the east. It was a small area indeed.

She had a rude awakening when she entered old Jerusalem. The hodgepodge of buildings and the congestion of people and traffic was daunting. In the old city the pickpockets were thick as mosquitoes, and there was red and black hate graffiti everywhere in East Jerusalem.

Ruben and Aviva led her into the Via Dolorosa where the crush of people was wall to wall. There was a religious celebration ahead of them and they got separated as people pushed and crowded through. Becky was suddenly alone in the crowd and kept a tight grip on her pack. She wondered if this is what it was like for Jesus' followers as they tried to follow Him to the cross, straining to get through, keep up with friends, and see what was going on. They emerged into a market place and things loosened up a bit. Aviva and Ruben were immediately at her side fending off the aggressive vendors.

It was good to return to Tel Aviv and some relaxation. They stopped in a beachside café for a late snack and chatted with other patrons around them. Many were from Russia as Chaim had said. It was a truly international scene and yet they were all Jews. Becky could feel the solidarity even in all the diversity. Soldiers came through with Uzi's on their shoulders ready for action. They also sat down to talk, and danced with some of the girls.

The lights along the beach walkway came on and the waves grew dark. They walked toward the hotel in silence enjoying the night air, the sounds of music, and the mystical healing presence of the vast Mediterranean Sea.

Fourteen

Becky spent part of the day at the Dead Sea and Masada, enjoying the emerald green of the water contrasted with the golden desert mountain cliffs and bright blue sky. She opted to climb down the ancient foot path from the top of Masada that had been used by the water carriers during the siege. It was steep and a little scary in places, but a great adventure.

Ruben and Aviva would be staying behind as she crossed the Egyptian border into the Sinai. They gave her careful instructions on how to negotiate the check points and the possible searches. What lay ahead was exhilarating and frightening at the same time. Her Egyptian guide would not meet her until she crossed the Suez Canal.

Their bus soon arrived at the check point to enter Sinai. The travelers were herded into a low cement block building guarded by armed military. Becky held a handkerchief to her nose and coughed as the air, stale and blue with smoke, closed around her. There were no windows or discernible air conditioning. There were only two doors, the one they came in and the one through which they would exit, if all was in order. She said nothing as they took her papers and looked her over as if she might be a criminal. She kept her eyes directed toward the floor like the others around her, trying to act "normal" whatever that might be.

Two hours later they were loaded into transport vehicles with an armed jeep in front and another in the rear. Machine guns were sticking out of the jeeps in every direction. As she looked at them, the dark woman next to her said in a thick accent, "Robbers. They live in the desert caves. We would be killed without protection."

Becky thought how different it must have been for Moses and the Israelites, wandering around Sinai for forty years, and what he might think of his desert now. Armies, wars, machine guns, marauders, check points and papers. She had pictured Moses' desert differently and it didn't really hit her until now that this wasn't the old world of thousands of years ago. A great sadness swept over her and she thought she would cry. She took a deep breath reminding herself that travel was exhausting, and her emotions were probably just a little closer to the surface than normal.

The Canal was amazing and there was an American ship coming through. She wanted to wave and cheer at the sight of the American flag, but she saw the scowls on the Arab faces around her and decided it would be wise to remain still. She was in unfriendly territory now. The glow of being in the Holy Land was fading from her mind and she wondered if she was going to be happy at all that she came here.

"Dr. Temple, Dr. Temple, I am Akhmed, your guide. Welcome to Egypt."

Becky smiled in relief at the clean look of the handsome young man reaching for her bags. She hadn't seen a friendly face since she left Ruben and Aviva at the bus station near the Gaza Strip.

"Do not worry, Dr. Temple. You will like Egypt. We are friendly here and you are an honored guest."

She managed to smile again and followed him to a small tour van. "Egypt is friendly to Americans?"

"Oh yes. You will see. We will take good care of you."

He was so confident and completely without guile. Becky began to relax. He drove her into Cairo and to her hotel. On the way he told her all the things she needed to know about getting herself settled. Since the hotel had a casino, she could get clean money there. Becky didn't understand what he meant about clean money until later when she did some shopping and was handed filthy, foul smelling paper money. She didn't want to get that smell into her wallet and bag, so she wrapped the money in a travel brochure and stored it in an outside picket as separately as possible.

Akhmed was right about the friendliness of the people. The shop keepers were aggressive, but they didn't crowd her. When she was caught in a crush of people on a narrow street, a shop keeper came to her rescue and made a way for her back to the larger avenue. She had expected that he would take her to his shop and try to sell her something, but he didn't. He spoke perfect English and assured her that she was perfectly safe, even in the crowds that thronged the bazaar after dark.

She was amazed that there were no pick pockets here, as in the old city of Jerusalem. The next day she asked Akhmed about it as they headed for the Coptic church and community.

"We have no pick pockets because our prison system is very cruel. We are not so changed from when a man's hand would be cut off for stealing. No one here steals. Look over there in the middle of the road. You see that man with no legs?"

"Yes, what is he doing. Won't he be run over in all this traffic?"

"No, Doctor. Everyone knows he is there and he is safe. He sells paper towels to the drivers rather than steal and risk losing his hand as well as his legs."

Becky couldn't believe her eyes. The traffic was over ten lanes wide and no one drove within the lanes. There were donkey carts, oxen, trucks, American cars, all jumbled together. No one was blowing their horn in exasperation. Some drivers quickly leaned out of the car window and bought the paper towels from the man with no legs. Meanwhile Akhmed was handily negotiating the impossible looking traffic mess and somehow they managed to get through.

Becky walked through the ancient Coptic neighborhood to the church. She was shown Mary's Tree where they said Jesus' mother sat. She saw marvelous paintings worthy of Rembrandt in the lower levels of the ancient church. Akhmed told her the story of the Holy Family from the Egyptian perspective. Becky thought at first their story couldn't be right. But then she realized that she knew those stories only from her Bible and the Coptic stories were from their writings, not from the Christian Bible. It was difficult at first for her to feel they were talking about the same Jesus, Mary, and Joseph because it all sounded so different from what she was used to. But of course their stories were no more or less historically founded and, therefore, just as legitimate as those known in the western world.

Becky couldn't resist a camel ride around the pyramids. She explored the inner chambers of the pyramids, climbing down the narrow passageways that became more airless the deeper she went.

The low ceilings caused everyone to bend low awkwardly to make the descent. Her lungs were glad to return to the fresh air as she climbed back up the ramp.

That evening she and Akhmed boarded a train that would take them south along the Nile River to Memphis, Karnak, and to the Valley of the Kings. Becky wanted very much to see the temple of Hatshepsut, the woman who was Pharaoh. The enormity of the stones, the pillars of the temples, the steles and statues left her awestruck. Size alone was enough to make Becky believe the stories of extraterrestrial beings as the builders of all of this.

"You see, Dr. Becky, you are welcomed by the children. They know you are good." They sat on the floor in the magnificent mosque as the trip came to a close. Young girls came past them and giggled at Akhmed who was very handsome. He blushed to his hairline trying not to let Becky see.

"You are welcomed by the young girls who think you are very handsome. They smile at you, not me." Becky was teasing now.

"No, Dr. Becky, they are curious about you. Only you." He flushed crimson.

The Egyptian museum was Becky's last stop before she went to the airport and boarded the plane for home. Bus-loads of Egyptian children came through the parking lot. The children leaned out of the windows and shouted "Welcome to Egypt. We are glad you are here!"

Becky was astonished and waved back enthusiastically. She had not expected to fall in love with Cairo and its people. She had not expected the dust covered buildings on every street to turn into a blaze of glory with lighted and colorful bazaars at dusk. She had not expected to feel safe and secure in such strange surroundings. Arriving with one picture of Egypt in her mind, she left with a very different one.

Becky flew to Amsterdam to spend a few weeks alone thinking and writing. She had rented a house boat on one of the canals and rode a bicycle everywhere. Her legs soon became accustomed to the pedaling and she rode for several hours a day. She sat in cafes and on garden walls to sketch and write. Small shops and parks were some of her favorite spots. The square downtown was filled with actors and mimes posing on corners or walking among the crowds. Life here was much more relaxed and seemingly carefree.

Becky wrote about the people she met, her impressions of their lives and beliefs. She would casually interview the ones who spoke English. Sometimes a person in a café would offer to translate for her and her table became alive with people interested in talking to her. They were as curious about her life as she was theirs. The men wanted to take her home, but she declined and quietly moved away into the crowd, hoping she wasn't followed as she made her way home.

Each evening she would buy sweets and thick coffees from a small stand, return to the tiny deck of her house boat to watch the night and the stars. Everything and everyone she knew seemed very far away. She had a sense of there being only herself, God, and the universe. It was intoxicating, quiet, and somehow filled with promise.

Becky's phone began to ring as soon as she set her suitcases down. Everyone knew she was away, so the answering machine wasn't overloaded, but they seemed to know the minute she crossed the doorstep. Georgina and Chaim weren't back yet, so she let the answering machine pick up to give herself time to unpack, sort all her notebooks, brochures, unwrap her purchases, and sleep off the jet lag. Part of her wanted to still be in Amsterdam and the smell of the Egyptian money lingered in her bag. Emotional re-entry would take a little more time.

"I'm so glad you are back! Did you have a great time, great insights? Would you come on the show and talk about it?" Karla was her usual gungho self.

"Half of me is back, Karla. I'm not sure where the other half is. Somewhere between Cairo and Amsterdam I think. When is the broadcast?"

"Tomorrow. Is that time enough to gather yourself together?"

"Yeah, I think so. I have notebooks full including poetry and sketches. I'm glad I didn't go with a group this time because I wanted to put it all down as I was experiencing it. Such a contrast between the ancient world and the modern world crushed together like a crazy quilt."

"Great. Looking forward to hearing about it. Gotta run. Talk to you tomorrow. Can you call half an hour early and we'll chat before we go on? Steven and I have been busy. We've mailed plans and stuff to you when you get a chance to check in."

"I will do that. Thanks. Love ya."

"Love you, too."

Becky sifted through her notebooks, putting the ideas on her computer that she could use on the radio program. There was so much it was difficult to choose, so she selected more than she would probably need. Jenny would be happy to type the notebooks verbatim onto a floppy for her. She was always interested in Becky's ideas.

She opened her mail from Steven and Karla. She was amazed at how well everything was fitting into the segments, and immediately began to put it all together. It was well after midnight when she fell into bed, her back aching and exhaustion taking over. She dreamed of Amsterdam and thought she could hear church bells somewhere in the distance.

It was Steven's voice as Becky came out of the fog of a dead sleep. "Sorry. I didn't want to wake you."

"What time is it?"

"Well, it is eight in the morning here in California. Probably noon at your place."

Becky jumped up. "Noon! Oh right. Sorry. I worked until two or three this morning on your plans, plugging in my stuff. Guess I got carried away. How are you?"

"Doing great. Do you like the work we did?"

"It looks super. Everything I have been working on just slips right in with yours."

"I will be back on the east coast in two weeks. Can we get together? We can be on the speaker phone with Karla if need be. You have access to a speaker phone?"

"Sure. Call me when you get to this side of the continent and we'll set it up. I'm kind of in a fog right now. Don't even know where my Daytimer is."

"No problem. I won't know my schedule until I get there anyway. Have a great time?"

"Amazing. I haven't traveled on my own very much, so it was an adventure. I usually went with an academic group to save money for the college. But I just really needed to be alone to think and write this time."

"I'll be eager to hear about it. See you soon."

Becky looked at her list of to do's and dialed the phone. "Hi Karla. I've got my notes mapped out for this evening."

"Super. You work fast! By the way did you talk to Steven?"

"Yes. I'm afraid I was still really out of it. I worked until two or three this morning on the plans and I was still in never-never land at noon when he called. It's a strange combination to get all enthusiastic in the middle of jet lag. I think it's called burning the candle at both ends."

"True, true. What were you working on? Surely the notes for tonight didn't take that long."

"Oh, no. I was plugging my notes and stuff in to the plans for The Way Home. It was going so smoothly that I just kept at it until I nearly dropped off the chair."

"You must have still been on Amsterdam time. Traveling through time zones makes you crazy. Give me a quick rundown on what we have for tonight."

Becky obliged and Karla was sure it was way more than enough.

"Good evening and welcome to our show. Our guest tonight is Dr. Becky Temple who has just returned from travels in the middle east. What took you to the middle east, Becky? Were you looking for something in particular?"

"Yes, I wanted to focus on the ancient Coptics and visit their community in Egypt. Their experience of the holy family is different from ours. The holy family lived in Egypt for twelve years, so they have their own holy sites, stories and legends. I wanted to know what those were and how they came about. I became acutely aware of how possessive we are about our own Gospel stories, and perhaps how difficult it is to give the same credence to another perspective as we give to our own."

"Dr. Temple, thanks for taking my call. I wonder how you could possibly think any perspective other than our four Gospels would be authoritative. If their stories were true, wouldn't they have been included in the Gospels? Wouldn't the Christian church know about them?"

"Great question. In those ancient times, news didn't travel as it does today. There were no wire services, publishing houses, and the like. Geographic distances played a big part in their ability to communicate. News would come by word of mouth and who knows if it would land on the ears of someone who would write it down or not. And if it were written down, the only copy might have been destroyed in a battle or war. For example, Constantine burned the Alexandrian libraries where all the knowledge of the then-known world was stored. It set civilization back thousands of years and humanity again endured the dark ages of ignorance. We are always longing to know more about Jesus Christ and if we turn away from writings other than the four Gospels, we cut ourselves off from expanding our knowledge and understanding."

"But wouldn't God have seen to it that the Gospels included them if they were true?"

"God works through humanity to bring Truth to the world. There is no other way. Humanity is frail and human circumstances determine much what we can understand and pass on to others. The Bible was written by divinely inspired human beings who did their very best to understand and faithfully record what they understood. God is not a person directing things like a parent or school teacher. God is the Divine Principle within each one of us and it is up to us to interpret how that Principle works in our lives. This is what the early teachers had to do."

"You don't think God wrote the Bible?"

"The word 'man' means hand. We are the hands of God. God inspires us and we do the mental and physical work. Mankind does the actual writing. Thanks for your call. I appreciate your interest and your comments."

"Hello. Aren't you flying in the face of the church and all we believe? Your answer to the last caller was pretty far out there."

"Nothing I say is intended to fly in the face of anyone else's beliefs. Many of our beliefs are theory or theology, but are not founded on scholarly research. They are largely symbolic to give us a sense of the mystery of God. The research of scholars in the languages, archeologists in the physical artifacts, and the discovery of other early writings has given us a much richer basis upon which to base our understanding. Personally, I find it thrilling to read of the discoveries that clarify passages in the Bible and give us new ways of thinking about them. After all, the early Jewish culture is very different from ours. Their symbols have different meanings than we have given them from our culture. The Bible was written according to their understanding of God and their local traditions. Things actually make more sense if we know more about the context in which they were written."

"Aren't we supposed to have blind faith and do what the church tells us?"

"We can make a choice between blind faith and understanding faith. I prefer understanding faith. God gave me a brain and intelligence, and I assume I am supposed to do something with them. We are not intended to be slaves to some else's ideas. We have the power of discernment and we make choices according to that discernment. There was a time when humanity was illiterate and using all their energy to scratch out an existence. They needed the church to give them something to have faith in, something to hope for. But the church failed, giving them nothing to hope for except more guilt and misery.

"I believe the church misused that purpose when it turned to threats of punishments, purgatory, and hell to control the people. It misused its power in demanding money and taxes from a people who were already starving to death, giving them only penances in return. It became morally corrupt in usurping the power of the governments and taking license with every opportunity to rape and pillage. Had the population possessed the literacy and resources we have today, things that were done in the name of God, Jesus, and the church could not have taken place."

"Like what?"

"Like the crusades, like witch burning, holy wars, the destruction of the civilizations of others. You don't have to read very far into Christian history before you find the worst atrocities, the worst examples of man's inhumanity to man."

Karla finished the show. "Our time is up. Thanks to our callers who always add so much to our discussions with their questions and comments. We hope you'll tune in next week for more fascinating interviews and guests. Good night."

"I had all these notes, but the discussion continues to devolve into who is right and who is wrong. I guess I'll save the deeper stuff for seminars and conferences." Becky was a little exasperated.

"Well, that's kind of how public discussions go. But don't give up. It has people thinking. Those who want to know more will dig for it, let us know, or come to the seminars. We are here to whet their appetites. We'll advertise our events when we start having them. Tell me about your trip!"

Georgina and Chaim returned a few weeks before the semester was to begin. The three of them met at Mom & Pop's for dinner. Becky brought The Way Home plans with her should they ask about them, but she was more interested in hearing about their travels.

Chaim seemed quite down. "It's getting harder and harder to fit back into the lives of my family. Quite understandably, they go on about their lives without me and I do the same. I feel guilty. I was looking for a comparably paying position there, but couldn't find one. Things are much more expensive now and we've gotten into a lifestyle that takes a lot of financing."

"How is Avram's leg healing?" Georgina was very concerned about Chaim and his family now.

"Well he's back on the job, crutch and all. The limp turned into something more because he wouldn't stay off it. He may need more surgery and rehabilitation. This time the military will insist that he behave or release him early. His pride couldn't stand to be released. I guess the military is his father now."

Becky knew that feeling in regard to Nathan and the CIA. "And Yael? Is she doing well?"

"Yes, she's really busy. Whenever there is an uprising of any kind, people flood into her therapy groups. She is working in Jerusalem and Tel Aviv both. I would drive back and forth with her so I could job hunt while she was working. It was pretty convenient for both of us, gave us a little more time together. Georgina, you were in Europe?" Chaim switched the subject so abruptly that she was startled.

"Uh, yes, and I'm glad to be back. Their pizza isn't exactly what I'm used to."

Georgina described the opera houses, the way they teach and perform. "It is quite different from how we do things. It is no wonder our young singers have a difficult time, especially in the German opera houses. You have to change your whole personality to get along. And La Scala is like a free-for-all. Sometimes their clackers are so loud you can't even hear the singers. I guess, of course, that is their purpose.

Singers pay their supporters to shout down the booers. In this country you wouldn't dare even sneeze in the opera houses."

They asked Becky about The Way Home and its progress. She took out the plans that she had brought, and they spent the rest of the time reading and discussing them.

"Becky, I think you could start right now writing your seminars, books, and any other literature. When you get on the road, if you do, it will be more difficult to concentrate. Then you can add to them by filling in with experiences, reactions of the people in the seminars and all that. I wish I could be of more help, but I may have to go back to Los Angeles before long. My family is hysterical. The usual. But it gets louder and more vehement as time goes by. If my father dies and I haven't been there, I'll never hear the end of it."

Over dessert Becky took notes on the ideas Georgina and Chaim were offering. They worked almost until the restaurant closed. Once again Becky was so absorbed she didn't realize how late it was getting. They ordered a glass of wine and toasted each other before they parted. They were glad to be together again and sad that Chaim was still a little down. But he was always appreciative of the support they offered.

There was a small package by Becky's door when she returned home. It was from Lissa, and Becky knew what it was. It was a stack of pictures and an album with a note, "For your grandma's brag book." Becky glanced at the clock, but it was far too late to call her. She contented herself placing the photographs into the album and looking through them over and over. It seemed as if Sarah Rebecca had almost grown up while Becky was away. Lissa and Mark looked wonderfully happy holding their daughter and somehow Becky felt more at ease about them than ever before.

In her mailbox was a large brown envelope from World Family of Peace. She tore it open and a handful of brochures fell out. It was the same organization that invited her to go to the USSR with them. They would be going the first of May and all the instructions to prepare for the trip were included.

At first Becky was reluctant to consider it, having just gotten home from a long arduous trip. But then she thought about having her materials written and published by then, and wondered if she could find someone to translate them into Russian. She would need to contact these people and determine if she could even take them into the USSR at all. It might be worth the extra effort if she could share some of this with the Russian people. Would they be receptive? She had no way of knowing. She would call Nathan in the morning. He could probably tell her more so she wouldn't sound like such a novice when she contacted the organization.

"Here I go again," thought Becky, "reading up, hedging my bets, covering my fanny so I don't look stupid." Well, she wanted to talk to Nathan anyway. It seemed like forever since she had spoken to him and she missed him very much. Becky knew when she started feeling like this, a little emotional, she needed to go to bed and get some rest. She wrote a list of what she wanted to do tomorrow. It always gave her peace of mind to know it was all written down and nothing would fall between the cracks.

Fifteen

"O.K., I'll go to the USSR with you. It seems that I won't have a problem even though I have relatives in the Ukraine and elsewhere there. They aren't in any trouble. And I really do want to visit the opera houses. In fact I've applied for an invitation to visit them as a professional." Georgina's eyes were sparkling as she talked about the trip.

"Yea! I'm really excited to share this experience with you." Becky was ecstatic. "It seems that this World Family of Peace has some pull. They've taken about eight hundred Americans into the USSR in the last five years. Trust has built up between them and the Peace Committee in Moscow, which is interesting and perhaps helpful. Maybe I can get my literature in after all. It's a matter of getting through the border and the officials there. That's where things get sticky according to the information they've sent me."

Nathan was on the phone when Becky got to her office. "It's still iffy, Mom. Here's what you do. Take three sets of notes with you. Buy a body belt for your money and passport, and put a copy in your belt next to your skin. Place a copy in the lining of the suitcase, and one set right on top of your clothes in plain sight. Chances are if they find and confiscate the set in plain sight, they won't look much further."

"Oh Nathan, that sounds so undercover-ish! Won't I get in trouble if they find the other ones hidden in the lining?"

"Nah, you just do what they do. You shrug your shoulders and smile wide-eyed. Say nothing. Look like you don't understand, which is actually true. And this is really important, don't try to explain anything. It won't be a problem."

"Will you come and get me if I go to Siberia?"

"They don't want a troublemaker like you in Siberia, Mom. You'd teach them all to be free thinkers. Relax. It will be O.K. Things are changing a little. The cold war is more cool than cold these days."

Becky and Georgina spent every spare minute making arrangements and planning for the trip. They purchased language tapes to learn a little Russian and practiced together. Mom & Pop's became their practice place. People were so accustomed to leaving them alone there, providing privacy as well as food at the same time.

Karla secured a booking for Becky to conduct a seminar at a retreat center in the Midwest. It would be advertised on the radio program. The Way Home would be launched at last. They hoped it would be successful in creating a bridge between self-help psychology, self-awareness, and spirituality.

Karla would be there as Becky's support person, making travel and hotel arrangements, setting up a temporary office, taking reservations, and running the registration table. Steven had made the financial arrangements and secured a guaranteed fee plus a percentage of the door above expenses.

Becky hadn't realized there was so much to do. She was incredibly busy herself just planning the lectures, discussions, and exercises. There would be an opening session on Friday evening, and the seminar would run all day Saturday and through Sunday morning.

Steven secured a booking for Georgina at a nearby college. It housed a musical theater program he knew about. It had a cancellation by a teacher that Georgina could fill. It would work out perfectly. She could provide music for the opening and closing of Becky's seminar, and teach in the theater on Saturday.

Becky and Georgina spent hours at the copy machines collating pages and assembling booklets filled with exercises and take-home handouts. Music that Georgina had ordered for the theater class was secured in folders.

"Time for dinner and wine to celebrate a job well done...and my feet are killing me." Georgina kicked off her shoes while they stacked everything into file boxes.

"I'll get the hand truck and we can load this stuff into my vehicle. Where shall we go?"

Georgina squinted her eyes and thought a moment. "How about the hotel dining room? The South Bennington Arms is it?"

"Yes, it is. Nathan, Jim and I were there several times during the holidays. It is quaint, quiet, and the food is fabulous. Let me call from here and see if they are open, and if we need reservations."

"Reservations? In Johnston Crossing?"

"Who knows? It might be just a tradition. Or they may want to know if someone is coming so they can heat up the stove."

They went over the menu with relish. Surprisingly, there were several other guests and more came in as the dinner hour progressed. There were thick table cloths and linen napkins. The silverware was old fashioned and heavy to hold. The wine glasses were crystal with an embedded design. Someone began to play the piano in the alcove.

"Well I'll be darned. Look what we've been missing." Georgina was completely charmed. The first glass of wine had already begun to give Becky a rush and she giggled. It caught Georgina by surprise and she began to laugh as well.

The mail was waiting at Becky's townhouse. There was an envelope that was badly battered and scotch taped shut. There was no return address and the post mark was New York. Fearing it was some crank from the radio program, she opened it cautiously.

Dear Dr. Becky,

I hope you are well. You will be coming to Moscow soon I am told. It will be very good to see you again. I hope we can have an appointment together when you are here. I can be contacted through your friends.

Sincerely yours with affection, Alexei

Becky sat stunned looking at the letter and envelope, turning them over and over. Could he have mailed it from New York, or perhaps someone mailed it for him? But why would it have been opened? Maybe it came from Moscow through New York.

Besides the condition of the letter, the word "affection" kept jumping out at her. She felt a tingle go all through her that was thrilling and embarrassing at the same time. After all she didn't know the man. And after her conversation with Nathan about foreign men being married but considering themselves available outside of their country, it was an unwelcome feeling. Or was it? She felt a smile on her face and wasn't sure how long it had been there.

"Listen, Beck, girls our age deserve to get 'the make' put on them, too. Sounds interesting!"

"Well, I'm not sure it's 'the make' or anything like that."

"So, what else could it be? Check it out. It could be, like I said, interesting."

"Georgi, I don't care to indulge my curiosity on this one. And what about his wife, if he has one? He may have a family. What would they think?"

"Get a grip girl. That's his problem. Getting a proposition doesn't make you a marriage wrecker. A little flirtation will do you good! Have a little fun. You'll be on the other side of the world."

Becky burst out laughing. "You think I ought to be bad one more time before I get too old, but do it on the other side of the world?"

Dan was the new owner of the company where Becky started to work after her first marriage. Lissa and Nathan were cared for during the day by a high school classmate. "We're going to Indianapolis tonight and you're welcome to come along." Dan was powerful, persuasive and cocky.

Becky was disillusioned with the way things were going in her life except for the kids, and was ripe for something more interesting. She felt inexperienced and ignorant about the racy side of life. She had thought of sex as boring and tedious in her marriage, and was curious about what more there might be. The nightlife, dinners, and drinks that Dan offered soon led to Becky's bedroom.

"So, you want to learn about sex?" Dan had read her mind. He placed a bottle of Scotch on her dining room table and proceeded to shed all his clothes right there in the middle of the room.

Becky snapped light switch to off and took a deep breath. "That will do for openers." She sounded brave, she thought, and began to remove her blouse. Dan brought out responses in her that she never knew she had. He knew everything, what to do, how and when. It was indeed the education she was lacking and during the day she could hardly concentrate on her work. Dan would pass her desk frequently, smiling and chatting with her. He was always interested in conversations with her, but something was wrong with the picture besides the fact that he and his wife weren't estranged or separated, as he had given her to believe.

As the months went by, Dan became more entangled with alcohol and Becky knew she had to find a way to end the affair. It was dangerous for her and now for the children. His call from jail at two in the morning, voice slurry, was a real turn off. It was the final straw. Somehow, she found the courage to extract herself from the situation, quit her job in his company, and move on.

Karl was from Croatia, cultured, quiet, successful, married, and was in love with Becky from the start. She was his receptionist in a research company. He gave her small gifts of music, suggested books, and asked what she thought on many subjects. It was so comfortable to slip into an affair with him. Their connection had a mystical quality that fascinated her. He reminded Becky of her favorite uncle with whom she had been infatuated, even besotted, since she was twelve. Karl gave her expensive gifts of which she felt totally unworthy. He seemed to engulf her with caring and consideration. She had never been treated like that before. Her feelings of not being worthy became stronger as his attention intensified. He paid for her books at the university and whatever else she needed for classes. It was positively overwhelming.

It ended when she met Matt and she felt terribly guilty about betraying Karl. But Matt was immediately and unexplainably the love of her life, and everyone else faded from her thoughts. Lust, fascination, and the fast lane had run its course, and love had begun. Things that had been so important at one time slipped into history. There was a newer, deeper resonance with Matt. Her life had switched onto a new track and there was no going back.

"You're only as old as you think you are, Love. I plan on being twenty-nine in my mind for the rest of my life. What do we care what anyone else thinks? There's more to you than teacher and mother. There's a woman!" Georgina had that impish grin again.

"Oh goodie, and you are going to be there with me cheering me on? You realize you can't know my secrets and live, don't you?"

"You're starting to sound like your CIA son. I plan to have a few secrets of my own. We can be secret sisters!"

"Georgi! What do you plan to do?"

"Everything I can. If one of those Bolshoi baritones has a hankering, I just might be agreeable."

"I don't believe I'm speaking to my friend Georgina Lucia West! I've not heard you talk like this, well at least not seriously."

"I have a past too, you know. I've always been serious, Beck, just not ready to let the world know. Especially my students. Can you imagine?"

"Actually, no. Uh, I'll have to think about all this.

"Well, let's take it into meditation tomorrow when we get together. I'm sure that's legal."

"I'll see what the meditation books says about it. See you then." Becky smiled. Something was stirring in her again that had been dormant for a long time.

She was lost in thought with Alexei's note in her hand when the phone rang again.

"Hi Mom. How are you?"

Her mother rarely started with a greeting. She just launched into a recital of her troubles. "Well I'd be better if I could get some help with your father. But I guess my daughters are busy."

"Mom, we've been over this. I'm not responsible for him and I can't change your situation. Only you can. I couldn't do anything even if I were there. You know how he is."

"I thought you could come here and just help me for a while. I know you're busy but I don't know what else to do."

"I can't come there, Mom. It's the middle of a semester and I can't just up and leave. You forget that I'm not retired like Melissa. I don't have an income other than my work. And where are my brothers in all of this? They're never around." As always Becky felt like she was whining and giving lame excuses.

"Well, I called Melissa and she is coming in a few weeks and I just thought it would be nice to have the two of you here together."

"I know, Mom. But I'm just not free to come and go right now. You could always leave him and go to Melissa's. She offered to help you do that."

"Oh, it's too late. I'm too tired to make a change. It isn't that I don't love your father. But he just does so many self-destructive things, and I can't always help him. He's going blind you know."

"Yes, I know. I told him to contact the Society for the Blind and he blew up all over me for suggesting it. His breathing isn't good either. I can hear it on the phone." Becky hadn't told her mother that he was calling in the middle of the night. Hoping she didn't notice the implication, Becky rushed on. "He needs to be willing to do something for himself. Maybe your home health care people can work on him."

"Well, they are. I just hope he'll decide to stop drinking and cooperate. It's good to hear your voice. That at least helps. I love you."

"I love you too, Mom. Maybe I can make some plans for later on."

Becky always hated the way she felt when she got off the phone from one of those conversations. She had great compassion for her mother and was always fighting off the guilt feelings that came up. Her feelings were so mixed. She never told her mother how angry she was with her for marrying him, and putting up with his running around and drinking. But it was really not her business to say so. It wouldn't help in any way. She was out of their home now and dealing with those feelings as best she could on her own.

Melissa rarely called and Becky was surprised. "Becky, Dad took ill several nights ago. He's been in the hospital. Mom didn't want to worry us, so she didn't call. He just couldn't breathe and was out of his head. He died an hour ago."

Becky glanced quickly at the clock. It was five in the morning. "My gosh. Oh, my gosh! How's Mom? Where are you? What do we do?"

"She's doing O.K. Really sounded calm. I don't know if she was expecting it, is in shock, or just relieved. You can't tell with her. She always says she's fine. You know Mother. If she doesn't want to tell you, she won't."

"I guess that tells us she's herself at least for now." Melissa's big sister manner always calmed Becky. She was always grateful to have someone like Melissa to reassure her. They lived a continent apart, but they were never far apart in spirit. They always talked as if continuing a conversation that had never stopped.

"Yes, I think she probably is. I'm at home. I'm starting there tonight on the redeye. Will get to Anderson about three in the afternoon.

Layovers are interminable, but affordable last-minute flights at decent hours are hard to find. I got the last seat out of Honolulu and that's a miracle."

"O.K. I'll meet you there as soon as I can. I'll call my administrator, Steven. He is great at finding flight cancellations and all."

Becky was on a special flight into Indianapolis by two that afternoon. Steven was truly a genius. It was a company charter flight and she was listed as a consultant. She shared some of her materials as a precursor for spirituality in the work place with them during the flight.

Her mother and Melissa had begun the cremation arrangements. Becky settled down to the paper work, getting copies of the death certificate for his retirement and insurance companies. It appeared that her mother would be financially secure, which she found amazing. Becky wasn't sure how her father handled finances and alcohol at the same time.

There was to be no funeral. Her mother told Lissa and Nathan not to come now, but to visit her when things were settled. She would like that.

"Melissa, you've asked Mom before if she wanted to come and stay with you. Is that still an option? Would she do it?"

"I've been talking to her about it. Peter said he would find a suitable residential place for seniors on the island. She could have a life of her own and still be near us. It seems to appeal to her."

Becky returned home feeling like she had done her part. Melissa was well organized and everything was covered. Peter was so supportive and they all felt the security of his efforts on their behalf. When those tremulous feelings of guilt tried to surface, Becky quickly reminded herself that her life had taken a different direction and there was nothing to feel guilty about.

In fact, the family members were always interested in what she was doing next. She was seen as the adventurous one. That secretly pleased her. She turned her attention to the Midwest seminar and reached for the phone to call Georgina. It was good to always be able to return to her own work.

Eighty-seven participants filed into the auditorium. The seminar began with a greeting and meditation. Becky's soft voice floated over Georgina's quiet music. Karla was busy with the registration work and preparations for the next day. She stopped to join in the quiet time with everyone, and resumed the organizing when Becky began the opening introductions and material. She started with a quotation from Jesus:

"Life more abundant! he said. What could that be? Are we not as alive as we will ever be? Yes and no. We are not as aware of aspects of it as we must be to experience and utilize the full force of being alive. We refer to it as potential, capacity, growth, development, latent or undiscovered power. Colleges and universities are geared toward exploring potential, but mostly at the intellectual levels. 'Life more abundant' is not usually how the nature of the subject is described.

"We are looking for spiritual pathways in life where we can walk confidently. We are seeking a conscious expansion of our ability to live in greater dimensions. We deserve to be in a safe place where joy reigns supreme. We need to be able to see clearly to the heart of everything we experience, and invoke divine wisdom to accompany us each step of the way.

"Well, if God knows what we need before we ask, why bother to pray? We pray to get ourselves clear in our own thinking and feeling. It is like cleaning a window to let the light shine through. You make of yourself the clearest channel possible to let more life and energy to flow through you. If you want the highest and best, your life according to your divine nature, then you need to be as clear as possible in your understanding of what that is. Hopefully, we can provide some of the mental framework with ideas you can use to bring that clarity to your thinking.

"Spiritually we are one with each other, made of the same God stuff, moving together on an eternal journey of unfolding divinity. We are learning to transform the world by beginning with ourselves, and this is a marvelous learning experience.

"As a new way of being we learn to live in our higher nature. We find ourselves shifted in some wonderful way, and we function differently inside and out. For instance, our thinking begins to change in terms of becoming more positive and hopeful, compassionate, and a sense of seeing life from a greater perspective as we regard any situation. A peacefulness begins to unfold within us that eclipses worry, surpassing human understanding.

"From the book of Second Corinthians, 'From now on, therefore, we regard no one from a human point of view…if anyone is in Christ, he is a new creation, the old has passed away; behold the new has come.'

"The writer of the book of Revelation calls it 'going into the courts of the Lord and going no more out.' We find we have moved slowly and gently over a threshold. The Apostle Paul wrote in Ephesians, 'we are to grow up in every way…into Christ.'

"We do not become exempt from earthly events, but we can choose our responses to them. We no longer need to become panicked in an emergency. We know a higher way of dealing with it now, one that brings peace.

"It is written in the Book of Revelation, 'To the overcomers I will grant you to sit with me on my throne beside me, as I myself conquered and sat down with my Father on His throne.'

"We become aware of our part in life as a co-creative, a seemingly peer relationship with God through our Christ nature, just as Jesus had. We become spiritually empowered to do the greater things. We begin living as a god-like being. In this way we become true heirs to the Kingdom of God, living life more abundantly."

Becky continued throughout Saturday with good responses from the participants. They did their written work with enthusiasm. Their questions stretched her thinking and brought her some ideas to explore in the future.

"We are multi-dimensional, multi-level beings. Part of us is visible, part invisible. Our power comes from the invisible part. We are taught to believe that power comes from money, position, friends, family, good looks, muscle, etc. But you can think of cases where people have all these things and are still fragile, frightened, and confused.

"When we understand the scope of our being, physical and nonphysical, we discover that we can work in the world, enjoy physical and material life, and still live in the greater dimension of spirit. God isn't confused, and when we are in our godlikeness, neither are we.

"From high in consciousness, Earth looks rather like a school where many things go on all at once. Many different classes are taking place simultaneously. If everyone is at varying degrees of learning, we can understand why the world looks so disordered from below. If we take our clues solely from the chaotic physical/material level as to what our behavior should be, and measuring our well-being from that, we lose track of the bigger picture.

"The most popular three-dimensional notion is that power and control equal survival, success, happiness, and the good life. Power and control at the physical level are subject to so many variables and unknowns. It is rather like riding an unpredictable bronco and trying to hang on to it. Sooner or later you will be thrown off.

"All of life's energies are spent trying to stay on top for as long as possible. This is the stuff of our daytime soap operas. At the lower levels no one and nothing is trustworthy for very long. Love does not really exist there, and relationships are for convenience and profit.

"Jesus showed us the higher aspect of power and control. Change those two words to empowerment and command, and you begin to understand at a higher vibrational level. Jesus had command of the empowerment that spiritual law offered him. The story of the temptations is a clear illustration. Jesus simply knew where the true power lay, and the proper use of it. He was not fooled by the appearance of temporal power that was offered to him at the material level.

"It takes practice. It takes a powerful sense of who you are as an offspring of the Most High. When Jesus was distracted, and felt his vibration lowering, he went apart to be alone and pray to raise it. He immediately took steps to return to his interface with God Mind. The moment you have evidence that you have slipped into fear, be prepared to do whatever it takes to keep your vibration high."

Sunday was a mystical day for them all. The effect of the first seminar on Becky, Karla, and Georgina was enormous. They were elated, exhausted, filled with new ideas to further the work, and entirely too tired to think about it.

Becky began to glimpse a sense of belonging, a solid place in the world that was hers, but it still wasn't the illusive home. She thought about Jesus' words "my kingdom is not of this world" and "being in the world but not of it." The title, The Way Home, had been just a catchy one intended to gather public interest. Now it was taking on a deeper meaning in her life.

Georgina was quiet, thinking about a new freedom she was feeling in her music. She was filled with new ideas for musical theater stories and compositions, not even sure where it was all coming from.

Karla planned to take up some research on her own. There were things in her life that lay dormant and she had been content to leave them there until now. Now it seemed safer to explore and apply new perceptions, freeing herself from the drag the old ones had been on her life and happiness.

Steven had flown in Sunday morning to help Karla close everything up and be sure that all was in order as they headed for home. He took notes on all their ramblings as they packed, and assured them he had enough to preserve the essence of the experience. It was a beginning and he could see much more to come.

Sixteen

Who am I? What am I? Where did I come from? What is my purpose? The books Becky was reading pointed to the home she was seeking mostly with questions, seemingly unanswerable questions.

Chaim was in the cafeteria when Becky and Georgina came in after the weekend. "How'd it go? You both look a little beat."

"We are!" Georgina sank down into a chair opposite him. "I still have bags under my eyes, I know. We got back really late. I guess it's a sure sign that we aren't sweet sixteen anymore."

Becky shifted things on her tray. "It went really well. I'm still processing it. I'm learning to be adept at exploring with questions rather than giving pat answers. It works wonders. Answers came from the people who asked the questions. And more questions arose. That's what the authors of group-work books say should happen, and it works. It was a little scary to trust it, but exciting."

"Why scary?"

"I've been a lecturer too long. I'm still learning to trust it. It was actually exciting more than scary. I am learning that I have a choice to turn scary energy into excitement. I thought it was my responsibility to bail them out if they got stuck and I wasn't sure how deep the mud would be. What if I just drew a blank?"

Georgina laughed. "You've never drawn a blank that I've ever seen. Students think you can get them out of any hole they fall into. Got lots of faith in you, Beck."

"I guess I need to make how I feel on the inside match what I look like on the outside."

"It's more than that, luv. You're capable. That's why they trust you so much."

Becky glanced up at Georgina a little shocked, half a French fry in her hand. She had struggled to be competent and responsible wherever she was, but hadn't used the word capable to describe herself. She hadn't thought about students trusting her.

"What questions were asked?" Chaim pushed his tray aside and took out a small notebook. "And what discussions resulted? Do you mind? This sounds like something I've been exploring but haven't had the same opportunity to experiment."

"Uh, yes. Sure. Things really jumped when I asked them to write answers to the questions "Who am I? What am I? What is my purpose?" Of course there was material I introduced before I landed that on them."

"Right..."

Becky described the material briefly and went on, "After the usual demographic answers like wife, husband, mother, engineer and all the stuff we think of as identification, the discussion got deeper. I introduced the concept of the observer self and asked what part of them could observe their thoughts. There was a period of dead silence, so I asked them to just brainstorm names for it. They suggested higher self, higher nature, and spiritual nature."

"So, they were sort of forced to talk about the invisible. Was there resistance to that?" Chaim was taking notes as he talked.

"I couldn't tell if there was overt resistance. There was a lack of words to describe it. We started sharing experiences that might relate to it. It was a risk to share those things amid strangers, but no one made any judgmental remarks, thank heaven. Resistance may have come in the form of simply not sharing."

"Can you summarize what the overall sense was?"

"I took some notes on the way home to pull stuff together. They wanted to know how to take action. They wanted to do more than thinking and meditating on it. How do we actually incorporate the awareness of the invisible into our daily lives? They weren't ready to trust the process that a change in awareness would bring a change in attitude, reaction, and eventually action. They wanted it right now. I need to take it a step further and anchor it in behavior. I guess I need to anchor it in my behavior, be aware of how I change, and what exactly changes."

Chaim riffled through the pages of his notebook. "It has been the challenge of the mystic to help students realize that the changes make us appear to others as if we are off on some cloud, not paying attention to earthly matters. While Kabbalah teaches that we are to find God in a new way, it does not mean that we seclude ourselves and only breathe in the ethers. It means that we seek God in a new way in the congregation of the world. It means that we see and respond to the presence of God in others, and treat them with greater respect as spiritual beings like ourselves. Of course that begs the question of how to treat ourselves as spiritual beings first and physical beings second. That alone is a great challenge since we are used to putting ourselves down and being called humble."

"O.K. No more humble pie for us. Anyone for dessert?" Georgina stood up and collected the trays. "I'm ready to go home and be a couch potato this afternoon. My student cancelled, so I'm off for today."

"I'd be interested in anything else you think of if you wouldn't mind my kibitzing a bit more." Chaim declined the dessert and got up to leave.

"No problem. Be glad to. I'll have the fruit cup, Georgi. Thanks."

Becky spent the evening with her feet propped up writing in her journal. She wrote at the top of the page, "How Have I Changed and How Does It Show Up."

Next she made a list:

Changing my thoughts about feeling guilty.
I feel lighter and talk about guilt less often.
Becoming aware of my reactions in situations.
Choose my response verbally and emotionally.
Stop thoughts that put me down.
Take risks without fear.
Becoming aware of how others perceive me.
Practicing seeing myself that way too.
Learning to trust others to do the work their own way.
Delegating to others and walking away in confidence.
Looking for home within me instead of outside of me.

Comfortable anywhere, not expecting fulfillment from outside.

Becky looked over the list and read it out loud several times. She could see it was about living confidently. The chapters she had been reading on how to love yourself began to take on new meaning. Loving yourself wasn't about generating a warm, huggy feeling. It was taking action on your own behalf in ways that supported confidence and emotional health. It was believing in your own capability, your legitimate place in life, and commanding your experiences to go in the direction of your goals and dreams. For the first time she really felt she had a right to that. There it was. People didn't feel they had a right to their own success, so they defeated themselves in various ways through their thoughts.

Ideas began to form in her mind about exercises that would help people practice these things. Dramas! Create dramas where people could act out how they usually are and then recreate the drama to let them act out how they want to be. Form a support group where they could return for more feedback from people they trust who are doing the same thing. People couldn't do it alone. Becky had tried to do it alone for a long time. How much faster might she have learned with that kind of help?

"The Way Home" was going to be acted out with the assistance of like-minded people in a safe atmosphere. She could see taking this into middle and high schools where her pain had been the greatest. People who accomplished their desired changes could become trainers for others. Kids could learn to deal with their lack of self-esteem early and not spend years going through broken relationships, guilt, and loneliness.

She was still typing all of this into her computer at top speed when the phone rang at midnight. "Hi Becky. It's your mom. I hope this isn't too early. I'm not used to being in Hawaii and the time difference confuses me."

"It's O.K., Mom, I am still up. It's midnight here. What's happening?"

"Oh goodness, I didn't realize, I mean I didn't know which way the time went. You're later, not earlier than us. I just wanted to tell you that I'm settled here and give you my address and phone number."

"That's great, Mom. Are you enjoying it? What's not to enjoy, huh?"

"It's lovely but it's different. I suppose I'll get used to it. Everyone is so kind and helpful. I'm going to church. Haven't been in church for years. Couldn't leave your father alone with a bottle and a cigarette. He nearly started a fire, you know."

"I know, Mom. That's all over now. I guess it will take a while to realize that. You lived with it a long time."

"Well, I miss him, even though I don't miss the drinking. There was a time, you know, when things were good. When we first met. We were young. He was nice and even dashing. I always kept those times in mind."

"I'm glad you still have the good memories. Always hang on to the good stuff, and expect more. You deserve a lot of good times."

"Well, I suppose so."

"I know so, Mom. We all do."

How good it felt to affirm that for herself and her mother. Yes, it was all going to work out well. For the first time, Becky felt a powerful confidence welling up inside her. Home was coming into view. She saved her work, shut down the computer, and went to bed tired and happy.

"My new passport just arrived." Georgina danced into Becky's office waving an envelope. "Russia here we come!"

"I just got a call. They moved the date up for that trip. We've got six weeks to get ready. I've heard that happens a lot."

"Yes, I got the message too. Oh well, we're nearly ready, aren't we? I mean with the stuff we, uh you, are taking to Alexei?"

"Are you being funny? Alexei isn't the focus of this trip, you know. It's something bigger like world peace and all that."

"Then how come you're blushing, Beck?" Georgina's impish grin was unsuppressed.

"I'm not blushing. I'm healthy. Now, here's the literature from the group we're going with. We need to designate ourselves as roommates and fill out the medical release forms. The temperature might be turning cold even in September. I would have preferred next May, at least knowing the warm weather was coming."

"Aw, come on. You can't wait to get there and you know it. Adventure is calling!"

"Are we talking about the Bolshoi baritones you are dreaming about? How crowded do you think our room is going to get?"

"Stacks of 'em! Really Beck, you seem different today. What's up? I thought you might still be dragging a bit after the seminar and getting home so late."

Becky handed Georgina her list and the drama exercises she had been working on. "Let's go to dinner at Mom & Pop's. I want to go over this with you. Need your feedback and some ideas."

"O.K., great. Let's go. I'll drive. But there's something more isn't there?"

"Yup, there is. I'll tell you as much as I can. I had an epiphany of sorts last night and it is having quite an effect."

The combo pizza was steaming in front of them as Becky went over the list with Georgina and recounted her conversation with her mother. "It was as if everything that has been weighing me down just let go. Remember I said my insides didn't feel like what people thought of me? Well, I went over and over this list really looking at myself and it just seemed to take hold."

"In the 'twinkling of an eye' sort of way?"

"Yes, sort of like that. I decided it was time to get busy and clear out the stuff that's been hanging around in my mind and jump into the new ideas with both feet. Affirming to my mother that we both deserved good just set the foundations firmly in place. I guess I let go of my reluctance to pull her forward with me and went for it. I don't know what I thought might happen. I guess I thought it would be cheeky for me, the daughter, to go that far, but it felt right. I got off the phone flying. I thought I wouldn't sleep, but I conked out as soon as I hit the pillow."

"I love this drama idea. Why don't we start working with it right here? Let's get the permission of the college to turn the Monday evening class into the seminar with the support groups. The response to that class has been good. I think they will trust us to do it. You're the resident shrink, so that's covered. Let's plan a presentation to the class and to the powers that be, and see what comes of it. We can even try this out in Russia if we can get a group together there, and see how it translates in another culture. That would be really interesting. I'm betting that people suffer from the same guilty feelings the world over. The challenge will be to find out if they are willing to be rid of them. Like Chaim said, guilt is a national treasure in some cultures."

Monday evening class was the first testing ground for the drama idea. People courageously stepped forward to be the cast members for the one who agreed to work on changing a behavior. Becky and Georgina kept careful watch on the action, coaching them through and helping orchestrate the change. Chaim sat in the back of the room carefully taking notes. John was absent which was a relief to Becky. She was sure his condescending manner would hamper things. Trust and security were so important. The first drama went fairly well. The second one benefited from the first one and went much smoother. It even elicited applause. The college agreed that Becky and Georgina should continue with their experiment, but they needed to get parental permission for any students not yet eighteen who wished to participate.

"How is this different from psychodrama, Beck?" Karla was preparing for the next radio program. "If we talk about it, I want to be sure we're on solid ground."

"Psychodrama is much more intense. It involves alter egos, or someone speaking behind the participant as a second voice. We're just practicing alternative behaviors and responses in specific situations. The participant coaches their cast members on how to enact the scene, and then the participant reacts the way he or she normally does. Then the drama is run again and the participant tries out different reactions until he or she finds the best one. There is no pressure or confrontation from an alternative voice and the participant is in complete control of the situation."

"O.K. Sounds good for the seminar. I don't know what will happen with the callers. We probably need to pick a topic and let them respond."

"We've done it in the Monday class a couple of times with good results. I'm working on it for the seminars and will even take it to Russia."

"Siberia here we come! Think of an opening and I'll call ya back ten minutes before the show."

"I'll be here."

"Good evening, Dr. Temple. What do you have for us tonight?"

"Well, Karla, I thought we might talk about the Bible as a handbook for human development. Many of our behaviors and misbehaviors come from an interpretation of something in the Bible. For instance, the wrath of God is taken to mean God exhibits human wrath or anger. The wrath of God is impersonal, however, closer to the result of our ignoring spiritual law. Our own hatreds and prejudices draw to us negative circumstances and painful results. It had been assumed that God was angry and rained thunder down upon the sinners. But God is Principle or immutable law, not personality. You can relate to it this way. If you jump off a ten-story building, gravity is the law that will bring you crashing to the ground. The law of gravity isn't angry at you. It is simply a law and if you do not honor it as such, injury will result.

"If we believe the interpretation that God is angry with us, then we act like victims full of fear trying to appease that angry god. Not knowing what will anger this god, we create a set of violations that we must not commit. All of this puts us in a state of mind that is unhealthy and not in tune with our true nature. Spiritual law will work for us when we work with it. As I mentioned, it is impersonal. If we work against it, we reap the result and cause ourselves pain.

"Hello Dr. Temple. This makes God sound pretty cold and unfeeling toward his people. What about God's love for us? Is that impersonal, too?"

"God's love is impersonal in that it 'rains on the just and the unjust' as someone said. God's love is played out in the immutability of the law that is unchangeable, and always at our service. It is not whimsical. We can always depend upon it. When we learn how to cooperate with it, the results are good."

"Are you saying that a sinner or a criminal can cooperate with God's law and get good, no matter what they have done?"

"Are not some criminals rich? Don't some criminals have families who love them? Don't they experience excellent health? Yes, they can experience good from right thinking as well as negative results of their error thinking. Each of us has that opportunity according to our understanding of the law. Good people have painful things happen to them, too. But everyone has an equal opportunity to observe spiritual law and change their life experience."

"I thought criminals would burn in hell for eternity. You mean they can go to heaven?"

"Friend, we are in heaven or hell at this very moment according to our own choice of thoughts, attitudes, beliefs, and actions. Jesus said, 'the kingdom of heaven is at hand.' Heaven is available now to anyone who aligns their life with a heavenly state of mind."

"Well, if anybody can go to heaven, how to we sort out who is good and who is bad?"

"We don't make that judgment. We restrain people who are doing harm, but everyone is God's child and has the power within them to change. We are like the Prodigal Son who rises up out of the pigpen of wrong thinking, sets his feet on the road of right thinking, and returns home to God. There was rejoicing and celebrating that he finally came home or returned to sane thinking."

"That's a lot to think about. Thanks. I guess I have some work to do. I'll have to spend some time with that story. I enjoy your show. Bye."

Becky and Georgina pulled their bags through JKF Airport looking for the international flights and Czechoslovakian Airways. They arrived huffing and puffing, hoping for a sign of their group. A man walked up to Becky and said "I'm Ben. I thought you might need this." And he handed her a fudge sickle. "I'm with World Family of Peace. Sorry I didn't mean to startle you."

"Oh! Thanks. My favorite." Becky gratefully took the fudge sickle and divided it with Georgina. "Is this where we begin? What do we need to do next?"

"We have your tickets and visas. Let's go over to gate and we'll get it all confirmed." His manner was so easy and relaxed. "No rush. We have a little time yet before we board." He picked up their bags and started for the flight counter.

It was the most interesting flight Becky had experienced. The international rules were different for passenger compartments. The overhead bins had no doors, so all the carry-ons were exposed and shifted from time to time. The seat backs folded down flat, and many people sat cross-legged on the folded seat backs and conversed with those all around them. The meals were delicious gourmet dinners that tasted freshly cooked. There was a storm over the Atlantic. Their dinner trays bounced and leaped with the turbulence. Becky and Georgina laughed as they caught the sliding plates, somehow managing to keep the food in place and eat. They were relieved to land in the morning in Prague.

Without any real sleep, they stowed their bags on their tour bus and began a walking tour across the Charles Bridge, through the squares of Prague. It was more like a running tour because the guide was determined that they should see some government buildings. Not being interested in government buildings many of the group stopped to visit the local stores and markets. The guide suddenly found himself alone and returned to see where his group was. He was very angry that they did not obey him and follow where he decided they should go. Ben patiently explained to him that American's were accustomed to making their own choices and that he should consult the group to see if his plans for them were agreeable.

"The guide is really upset. Who does he think he is?" Becky was a little shocked at his rage.

"We are in an oppressed country where people do only what they are told and don't make choices for themselves. The guide is in charge and making other choices will get people into trouble." Georgina knew from her relatives what oppression did to the people.

Ben explained, "The guide really doesn't understand because he has never experienced freedom as we know it. He only understands that he is the authority and if he can't control a group, he himself could be in trouble. However, it is more of an ego thing with this guy because Czechoslovakia isn't as bad as Russia. The satellite countries are a little looser. They follow the communist doctrine, but they have their own people running their country."

The bus trip to Pardubice, Czechoslovakia, was endless. They were told it would take one hour to get there from Prague. They soon found out that "one hour" was a standard answer, not an exact traveling time. It actually took four hours. The roads were so narrow through the small towns that the bus nearly scraped the buildings. As another bus passed them going the opposite direction, their rear-view mirrors collided and broke off. The bus driver drove very fast through the countryside oblivious to the complaining passengers being swayed and jostled over the uneven pavements. The trip culminated in complete exhaustion for all of them and they were grateful to finally reach the hotel and bed.

The next day Ben reviewed the plans with them and conducted a seminar on what to expect in Russia. They practiced their Russian phrases and shared about themselves to get to know each other. After a full day of review, they strolled into Pardubice in the evening. A young woman approached them in the town square and offered to show them the ancient theater and the church. She spoke broken English but she was easily understood.

The flight to Moscow was uneventful. They had to put their cameras away, being sternly admonished not to take pictures out of the airplane windows. Becky couldn't imagine why anyone would want to take pictures from the windows. What would they see but flat empty landscape? She noticed that the highways far below were completely empty. There was no traffic, not even one car or truck, for as many miles as she could see. The reality of the bleak existence in the Soviet Union was already becoming apparent.

An excited group of adult students from a Russian World Family of Peace school met them, immediately introducing themselves with American names they had chosen for themselves. There was a whirlwind of tours through so many places, that Becky never felt she could orient herself. There were no street signs. First they were in the middle of Moscow and then in the suburbs. Everything looked the same. Georgina told her they did that on purpose so travelers couldn't find their way around. But the taxi drivers didn't seem to know where some places were located either. They had to ask other drivers until they found someone who knew where the address was.

They were visiting a partially finished school in a suburb looking at the educational equipment. The Russian people were so proud to show them everything. Becky became aware that what they were seeing was a prototype and not standard in all their schools. The hospital they had toured was state-of-the-art, but only a few doctors in the whole country knew how to operate the equipment. As she sorted this in her mind, she turned to see a man seemingly flying through the window. He had come up the fire escape, coattails flying, and brief case in hand. Becky caught her breath. It was Alexei.

Seventeen

The large meeting was held in an auditorium somewhere deep in the heart of Moscow. Becky and Georgina marveled at the Metro system, as they hopped on and off trains with Ben. They were fascinated by the four to ten story deep escalators that acted like wind tunnels as they plummeted downward. The stations were full of artwork and lit with beautiful chandeliers. How could the Russians have dug the Metro system so deep in 1942 without modern equipment? It was unfathomable to a westerner.

Becky had managed to keep her notes concealed and intact crossing the borders and through customs inspections. They didn't even seem to be concerned about the notes she left on top in her suitcase as a decoy. That was a big relief. Being in a trusted group might have been the reason. Maybe things had changed from when Nathan was here.

Becky and Alexei found a small room off the conference hall where they could go over her presentation. He made a few suggestions, but was generally pleased with what she had put together. "Yes, yes. They will understand this very well."

He had many, many questions about everything in the United States. "Now Becky," he would begin, "what is this place called Mississippi? Is it like New York?" His intensity was attractive and disconcerting.

"No, it is in the south which is perhaps a little more provincial. Why do you want to know about Mississippi?"

"I was invited to come there, but I must be able to meet people who will help me." He looked a little disappointed.

"Now Becky, do you know anyone who could invite me? I must have invitation so I can do my work for my people. I want to bring books and

American education to them. In twenty years we will be just like United States. This is my job. The voice inside me tells me I must do this."

"Do you ever take time for a life of your own? What about your family?"

"I must work night and day. I am like soldier and obey. I follow orders."

Becky was puzzled. "Who gives you orders?"

"Voice comes from in here," he said, pointing to his heart.

He had a huge plan to help his people. In spite of herself she wanted to help him as much as possible. How could she present his request to the college or to Steven and Karla? Obviously they would have to pay his way. It seemed as though all questions led the conversation back to his work and, in particular, what he wanted to talk about. She couldn't keep his focus on himself.

There were many gaps in his plans that she wasn't able to clear up, but he was confident that his work was absolutely necessary. He gave the distinct impression he knew what he was doing. He repeated often that he was a soldier of his country and all his energies must go to that great purpose. Yet there was another energy that pulled her in, another agenda. Becky was pretty sure she knew what that was, and she wasn't about to be hijacked into a Russian bed on a trip she had paid for. She subtly let him know that he could buy his own ticket to see her.

Georgina and some of the adult students went to the apartment of an art dealer for lunch where they were treated to a mini-concert by Mikhail, a Bolshoi baritone. The studio was not large where the piano was located, and his voice was huge. Georgina was thrilled, but she observed that some of the others with her seemed to be in shock. She guessed they had never heard an opera singer at such close range. He was extremely powerful and impressive. After some conversation Georgina and Mikhail sang a few impromptu duets for the group. They knew the same music, so it didn't matter if he sang in Russian and she sang in English.

They toured the rooms of the apartment where paintings, hangings, and sculptures were everywhere. The dealer explained this was not legal artwork a short time ago because it was not sanctioned by the state. She wanted the World Family of Peace to take some of it back to the

United States for display. She had secured the necessary permits and the paintings would be at the airport when they were ready to leave. There would be someone from a gallery in the United States ready to receive them and take them through customs.

Mikhail offered to give Georgina a tour of the Satirical Theater and the Bolshoi Theater, which she happily accepted. She left with him not knowing how she would get back to the hotel or when. He had said not to worry, so she didn't.

It was late when Georgina and Becky returned to their hotel room. Before anything was said, Becky put her finger to her lips and placed a pillow over the telephone, as Nathan had suggested, before they began to share their experiences. All the guest rooms were bugged, usually through the telephones, so the pillow would muffle their voices. They turned on the water in the bathroom for a sound screen and talked while they were getting ready for bed.

"You went where?" Becky was hanging up her clothes.

"To some park with fountains and for a walk down Gorky Street. It is sort of like Greenwich Village. Lots of students, musicians and interesting things going on."

"Were you doing interesting things?"

"Well sort of. He is very romantic but rather egotistical. He was very busy telling me how great he is. I guess in this country you have to toot your own horn. It's not like there are billboards, tabloids, and talk shows. I just played along, left my 'independent American woman likes non-egotistical men' stuff behind and enjoyed his company. After all this is Russia and things are different."

"They sure are. My class went pretty well. I kept two interpreters busy and I hope they were saying what I wanted them to. It is easy to misinterpret from one language to another, especially with my kind of material. Sometimes they would stop and say, 'May we start over. I believe I have made an error,' and we would do it over. That made me feel like they were trying to get it right."

"Did they ask you questions?"

"Yes. One young person asked what I thought of the Russian icons. I dug keep for that one. I told him they were powerful images of the soul, not necessarily needing words or interpretation. He seemed to like that answer."

"How many were there? Don't mind me if a feel a little guilty for running off to play while you worked."

"That's O.K. Alexei was interesting. I gently turned him down for a liaison in the bedroom."

"Really? Why?"

"I paid for the ticket to get here. Let him buy his own ticket to see me. Make an investment!"

"So, the turn-down isn't forever?"

"Oh, probably. I doubt he will show up on his own. He wanted me to get someone to invite him to the United States. My ticket again."

"You know these people can't travel without an invitation and they can't take money out of this country. They are pretty much stuck. Another government plot to keep everyone under control."

"Yup. Well if he thinks Russia will be just like the United States in twenty years, let's get started on the right foot."

"Right. Good idea, I think. Back to the group. So, how many?"

"About twenty-five. They ranged in age from seventeen to seventy. I was surprised. Then I had an extra hour with them because the scheduled professor didn't show up. He was from Holland. Do you know their teachers come from all over the world? Famous ones! I was honored and a little blown away to be numbered in that elite company! Phew!"

"They're bringing in academic stuff. None of them are bringing to these people what you are, a way to live in the new world. You are unique in that bunch."

"Well, are you going to see Bolshoi Mikhail again? Got any plans?"

"I don't think these people plan. They can't, so stuff just sort of happens. I guess he'll find a way to show up if he's interested."

"And then what?" Becky turned back the beds covers.

"Like I said, no plan. G'night." They took the pillows off the telephone, said a blessing into the phone for whoever might be listening and turned out the light.

The trip to Tblisi, Georgia, was a little disjointed. They flew into Moldavia and took a bus from there. While they waited for the bus they wandered through the bare waiting rooms. A little boy was fussing at having to sit and wait. Becky indicated to the mother that she wanted to give something to the boy. The mother seemed to understand and nodded. Becky had a sheet of children's stickers in her bag. She peeled a couple of them off the sheet and stuck them on his arm. He stopped crying immediately and smiled. Becky gave him the sheet and showed him how to take them off and stick them back on. The mother was so grateful that she gave Becky a fob from her key chain. Becky knew better than to refuse, even though it was probably the only thing the woman had. She also knew that the people in the satellite countries didn't like to speak Russian, so she took it and thanked her in English.

The bus stopped at a school on the way to Tblisi so everyone could have a bathroom break. Becky and Georgina went into the school's restroom and saw that it was only holes in the floor with excrement all around them. The place smelled horrible.

"Let's wait. I'm going back to the bus. I'll hold it, drown if I must, but I'm not using this." Georgina was adamant and Becky agreed. They returned to the bus in shock.

It was on a city bus that Becky and Georgina were approached by a Georgian teenager. She asked them to come to her school with her. They exited the bus and followed her down several streets and into a building that looked like it was closed. They went up a flight of dark stairs and into a room where a class of fifteen students were meeting with the Minister of Culture of Georgia.

"Please tell us about your life in the United States. We are preparing to go to Aspen, Colorado, in six weeks." The minister was very happy to see them.

They answered all the student's questions, sang and danced with them. Then the students gathered at the front of the room and sang all the verses of America The Beautiful to Becky and Georgina. Becky dissolved into tears. It was such a touching and beautiful thing to see these kids so open and loving, even in such a repressed culture.

In the evening, the Georgian National Dancers, fifty of them, came to perform for the group. "Ben, how is it that they would do this for just twenty of us rag-tag tourists? They are famous."

"Becky, it is a great honor to them to dance for the Americans. It is a rare opportunity for them since they are controlled by the Russian government. We are from the free world. We are their dream that may never come true for them. Tblisi used to be an international city, open to all visitors, and a popular destination for travelers before the Soviet Union annexed it and closed it. The people have been brokenhearted, but now things will change. They won't believe it until they see it, and even then they will think they are in a dream."

The streets of Tblisi were tree shaded and the lamps were ornate wrought iron masterpieces. Among the beautiful buildings and parks were ugly Russian white concrete buildings and communist worker statues, as ugly as the Russian name for Tblisi, which was Tiflis. The Russians had covered over the glorious frescoes on the walls of the churches with white paint and used the buildings for government offices.

The Russian students who traveled with the World Family of Peace were beginning to loosen up and enjoy themselves. They were so fearful that they would be punished if they didn't obey some authority figure. But with Ben they were encouraged to make choices on their own, something they had never done in their lives. They worshipped freedom, but had no idea how to live it. They soon began to imitate the behavior of the Americans, learning by example. Becky and Georgina saw how important it was to walk with these people and help them practice step by step what it was to really be free.

Before beginning their work in St. Petersburg they visited the Kirov Theater. It was difficult to remember to say St. Petersburg after knowing it as Leningrad for many years. Sensitivities were high with all the changes coming about in their government and the Russians would remind them that the name was changed back to its founder, Peter the Great. A magnificent statue of him looking out onto the Baltic Sea, seated on a rearing horse, still stood in a park behind Saint Isaac's Cathedral.

Becky was thrilled to find Russian-made dolls for her collection. She and Georgina also bought jewelry and art work from the street vendors and hurried on into the Hermitage. They wanted to see the paintings of Rembrandt and the impressionists that had been unavailable to the world for over forty-two years. Becky spent ten minutes transfixed in front of Rembrandt's painting of Jesus being taken down from the cross. The way he used the light gave it a certain magic.

Elena was Becky's translator for the classes. Formerly she had been a translator for the United Nations. A heart condition forced her to retire and work only occasionally. She and Becky were instant friends.

"Becky, there are many healers here from Siberia and the Ukraine. They were told this was a healing seminar, and spent all their money to come here. But it is lecture and not what they expected. I don't know what to do. It is hard for them to get here. They will be so disappointed."

Becky's heart went out to them. She was now well aware of how hard life was for them and the effort it took for the people to show up. Her mind raced over the energy healing classes she had taught several years ago. Could she recall enough to share with them on the spot?

"Tell them, uh…, tell them I will meet with them if they can find a room where we can hold a class together."

Elena was delighted. "I will find the room and tell them to be there in one hour. Thank you!"

Becky wasn't sure if that was really going to be one hour, so she sat down right away to sketch out an outline to follow. She slipped into meditation to gather her thoughts. After a while she began to see a large red apple. She tried to refocus on the healing energy notes but the apple came back again. She hadn't seen fresh fruit since they left Pardubice two weeks ago and thought that must be the reason. Then she felt something cool in her hand. She opened her eyes and Elena was smiling at her. "I thought you would like this. We are almost ready. I will come back for you in a few minutes. Elena had placed a large red apple in her upturned hand."

That almost brought tears to Becky's eyes. She couldn't remember a time in her life when her heart was touched many times a day. These people had so little and were so generous. Did she have some sort of sixth sense experience about the apple? It seemed that mystical experiences were woven into the very atmosphere. She was having many glimpses that were out of the ordinary, like the apple and Rembrandt's painting.

There were about thirty people in the room when she and Elena arrived. In the first row was a group of the grandmothers, babushka ladies, as they are called. They had bags of herbs and jars of other things Becky couldn't identify. In the middle, several rows back, was a tall handsome man who was whispering to the young women on either side of him. Becky had just said that healing couldn't be forced upon anyone. They could be surrounded with healing energy and prayer, but no one was forced to receive the healing.

The man stood up majestically and announced, "I am very powerful and no one can resist my healing powers! What do you answer to me?"

Becky rose to the challenge with her sweetest smile, "Your personality has a lot of energy that hits and changes another person momentarily, but it does not last. You may strike them with the force of your ego, but that is not healing. It is only shock."

The smile stayed on her face through the translation as Becky held her breath waiting for the reaction. The babushka ladies grinned and applauded vigorously, turning to look at him in triumph. The man turned, motioned to the young women in his group, and flounced out the door with them trotting along behind. Then everyone stood and applauded.

Becky quietly let out the breath she had been holding and continued with questions and discussions. The babushka ladies offered her an herbal drink of some kind from their bags. She didn't know what was in it, but graciously drank it acknowledging their kindness.

As they walked back into the main auditorium, Georgina was leading the singing in the ending segment. It was good to have it all come to a close. It had been an exhausting, but a good day.

Becky ran into the hotel room, tossed pillows onto the telephone and whispered to Georgina, "Grab your toothbrush and turn on the water. I've got some interesting stuff to tell you about what happened in my class."

The last afternoon of their meetings Ben got the news that their dinner plans had fallen through. There was a misunderstanding and the place where they were to eat was not going to be open. "What will we do? We have thirty-five people to feed, interpreters and staff included."

Becky and Georgina walked out onto the front steps of the building to wait for Ben when Georgina spotted a little blue car driving by slowly. On the side and trunk, clearly lettered in English, were the words "Pizza Express" and a phone number. They wrote the number down and dashed inside to tell Ben.

The pizza company was partly owned by Finns and understood

the American way of business. They arrived right on time with twenty pizzas, ten cokes, ten Sprites and mineral water. Becky paid the bill and would collect from the Americans later. She carefully tucked the bill away in her bag, intending to frame it as a memento when she returned home. It was probably the first pizza party in St. Petersburg given by guests. Customarily guests were never allowed to treat the Russian hosts. This was another lesson on freedom for them.

The flight home stopped overnight in Helsinki to change airlines. When they walked out onto the streets of Helsinki they were struck by the contrast against the grayness of the oppressed world they had been in for three weeks. Neon lights were everywhere and everything was clean and bright. They all said in unison, "Thank God for the free world!"

Becky and Georgina went on to Colorado for a retreat with the World Family of Peace people. High in the Rocky Mountains at Grand Lake they spent a few days in debriefing and planning sessions. Their ideas for group work using world peace strategies were fascinating to Becky and she bought copies of their manuals and literature. As she read through them, there was a definite similarity to John Sherman's work. Her way home was becoming clearer and clearer to Becky. She was no longer looking for it, but creating it step by step.

They hiked a bit on nearby trails, dangled their feet in an icy cold brook, sang in the evenings, and laid on their backs on the rocks in the middle of the night to watch the milky way in the clear mountain air. It would be a new and different Becky and Georgina who would return to Johnston Crossing.

Steven was leafing through the manual Becky had purchased while he was talking. "I have several bookings, Becky, and many more inquiries. We are going to need more people to take The Way Home into more communities. You can't possibly do this alone anymore. We also need to publish a more comprehensive manual and workbook like the ones you brought from World Family of Peace. By the way, do you have the option to take a sabbatical from the college to go on the road?"

"Whoa, Steven, one thing at a time. I agree, I agree, I agree! Yes, I have some sabbatical time coming up. I thought about using it to train others to do this, like having them come here or to some camp where we can train them in a group. We can have seminars for trainers only."

Georgina glanced up as she was sorting through her notes and books. "We can start with a meeting for our relatives and friends. I have cousins who would jump at the chance to get involved."

"I totally agree," responded Becky. "I think the world urgently needs what we are teaching and what World Family of Peace is trying to do. Nathan and Lissa have always been interested. I'm sure Jim Sherman, along with Loren, Karla, and Sandy are too."

Steven was on the phone with everyone constantly. "Let's plan for Thanksgiving weekend. Christmas might be a little too much to give up for some. But who can't give up overstuffing themselves with Thanksgiving dinner and all those calories? I'll book a place where they serve healthy Thanksgiving food and have small free-standing cottage-like meeting rooms in the mountains. I know just the place."

With all the plans swirling around her, and her experiences from the USSR still fresh and unsettled within her, Becky unplugged her phone and curled up on the couch under her mother's favorite afghan. She had placed hot chocolate on the coffee table and an open journal. It was good to be in the sanctuary of her own home.

"Who am I and who do I want to be? Who did I think I was as a child growing up and what direction did that take me for so long? Where do I want to go? I am creating my path to home, but where?"

Becky came running home from junior high all aglow. The teachers had a scheduling dilemma and she had solved it. They acknowledged her solution and she was so proud of herself.

"Just you be careful, young lady. You're not as smart as you think you are." Her father shook his finger at her and began to walk away. "You just let the teachers take care of things and you keep quiet, you hear? You hear?"

Becky managed a very small "yes" and then was forced to say it louder. She felt frightened and humiliated, and tiptoed up to her room. She wanted to cry but the mixture of anger and disappointment seemed to keep her tears dammed up deep inside. It wasn't the first time he made her feel small, stupid, and wrong, all wrong.

Becky reached for the hot chocolate and her journal. She wrote,

"Here I am in the midst of success and I feel wrong, as if I don't deserve to be here. I'm like an imposter, a fake. But no one else had ever said that to me. No one else has said that I am anything other than smart, capable, and authentic. Why do I still react so deeply to my father's words?"

She set the chocolate and journal down again and closed her eyes. "God, show me what to do." In a few moments her mind went back to that scene again. She saw the family kitchen, her father at the kitchen table with his usual tall glass of scotch and soda, mostly scotch. She heard herself telling her mother all about school. Then she saw him get up from the table and heard him scold her with those same words. Suddenly she saw her "present self" enter the picture, take young Becky's hand and lead her away into her present living room. "You are smart, courageous, and good, and from now on you will live here with me, not in the past. We will have a wonderful time and you will never be criticized like that again."

Becky opened her eyes in surprise. She felt the stone in her midsection dissolve and her spirits lift. She was almost giddy with the freedom. She repeated over and over, "I will never be criticized by that inner voice again." The unnamed anxieties ebbed away and the experiences of the last several weeks settled gently into place.

She picked up a hand mirror from the dresser top and looked into it. "Becky, you are smart, courageous, and authentic. That is the truth of about you." She looked deeply into the reflection of her own eyes and quietly whispered, "I'm sorry for all the doubt and mistrust I've had about you."

When she was preparing for bed, Becky gingerly tapped back into that scene to see if the feelings were really gone. She boldly tried to relive the feelings through the scene, but they didn't appear. She was really free. She could trust that she was safe from this inner assault on her happiness, and slipped into sleep with a smile.

Eighteen

The Patrician Grille was fast becoming a favorite getaway for Becky, Georgina, and Chaim. More and more they needed the remoteness and quiet of the place. No one knew them there, so there were no interruptions except for their orders being taken and served.

"Chaim, how do you pray?" Becky was curious to get deeper into the practice. "I've been asking God for answers and guidance, and the other night I received a great idea that worked. It had to do with freeing myself from the influences of past experiences, childhood experiences.

"Really!"

"It was wonderful and came out of nowhere! I guess I've always agreed with the principle, that we should pray, but I haven't really sought it. It was a sideline that I would get to someday, or use in desperation. It jolted me when the answer came so clearly and in such detail."

Chaim ran his hands over his placemat as if to smooth out imaginary wrinkles. "Well, when I get over my begging and beseeching that I heard others do when I was a child, and move into a more mature state of mind, I start by giving thanks for what I have and all I have learned. That leads me into Isaiah's words, 'The Lord will restore to you all that the locust has eaten.' That brings me up to date. Gets my mind off the past so I can move forward. It assures me that the ancient promises are still with us, and I feel more in tune with God. Like adjusting the radio frequency."

Georgina was taking notes on a small pad of paper she fished out of her purse. "Where to from there?"

"I like the prayer of Jabez in the first Book of Chronicles. It's a strange interlude in the midst of long genealogies, like someone injected it as a footnote. He asks God to enlarge his borders, keep him from harm or harming others. Something like that. I ask to have my understanding enlarged, and to be aware of my actions toward myself and others. It brings on some interesting results. Something always changes for me. I see some aspect of my studies I've never noticed before even though it has been right there all along."

Becky was engrossed. "Why do you think the part about harming others is there, besides the obvious. I mean, did it suddenly just state that without preamble?"

"Yes, it did. The prayer is just a few terse sentences. For example, the inventor of the atomic bomb suddenly had larger understanding and realized the great good or great harm his discovery could do. With greater knowledge comes greater responsibility to do good, and we don't always know what will be good. We ask God to guide that too." He paused to sample the food placed before him.

"Do you stop there? What happens next?"

"Oh, I just carry on with my day doing the usual things, but I notice that my perspective is different. I try to keep that perspective as long as I can and when it starts to hit the skids, I have a prayer time again."

"And are we supposed get to a place where we level out on this higher perspective and stay there? Or do we just cycle up and down? Becky and I have a joint prayer time and it seems we ask for the same things over and over."

"I have to look at the long run. I seem to function much better than I did, say twenty years ago. My downs aren't so far down and I don't stay down for as long. It used to be weeks and months. Now it is hours, or a day or two. I look at my father who never changes. Maybe he does when forced to by his incapacity, but he really doesn't believe people can or should change. He thinks I'm weak and vacillating because I change. To him strong is being as stubborn as possible even when he is proven wrong. Even when the Rabbi intercedes for the family. Then he narrows his eyes and asks the Rabbi if he is going soft. It's a circus."

"What's changed, Becky? You seem to have made a shift. I can't really put words to it, but you've crossed over some line. I can even hear it when you sing. It's a different, younger vibration in your voice."

Becky smiled at Georgina and touched her hand on the table.

"Thanks for confirming that for me. I've felt it coming on and didn't know if it was wishful thinking or if it was real. When I was growing up, it seemed that everyone was at home but me. I was missing, thinking home was here and I wasn't. I could never reach it. Weird huh? Well, now I am here and home isn't and it is O.K. I guess that's where the name for the organization came from. I'm on my way and seem to be creating home as I go."

Chaim sat back as the table was cleared and coffee was served. "I think we're all on the way home, the way back to God. Ever since Adam and Eve were expelled from the garden, humanity has been on a long journey home. You see, we've had to learn about physical life and creation this way. There is no other way to learn about it but be in it. If we're truly offspring of God, then we have to grow up in God's creation and learn to create too. We must be constantly discarding the old lessons and learning new ones. When I go down into a low place, I'm being weighed down by stuff that needs to be discarded and when I ask for enlargement, the new ideas for creating my life come flooding in and I just lift up emotionally."

"I learned from the operas. Many of the famous arias are prayers. Mostly they are prayers of desperation, begging and beseeching, as you mentioned, Chaim. I've looked for another way to pray because those prayers were never answered. They were a last ditch stand before someone killed the hero or heroine. I never thought that was a good way to operate, so I try to pray ahead of events, at least keeping up to date and not playing catch up." Georgina grinned at Becky, "Of course, the aria wouldn't be exciting without the drama and desperation, now would it?" They laughed. "The lesson is don't keep doing what doesn't work!"

"So, Chaim," Becky pursued, "do you practice any of the Kabbalah rituals that you study? It seems that their stuff is rigorous and demanding."

"Yes, they are very controlled to keep out the vagaries of the world and reach an ecstatic state. I personally believe there are more practical and livable ways to do that. I try to take on the spirit of their ideas in my own practice."

"Like what?"

"Like their teaching of loving kindness toward each other to create an eternal community of God. There's watchfulness, or to be aware of their own thoughts and actions, and there's holiness which means wholeness. They take themselves into the hubbub of the world to practice. It is a heightened self-knowledge, they believe, that enables them to make choices every day to better themselves. Also endurance, which we need in this world, and appreciation of beauty, wisdom and awe-inspiring majesty."

"Wow, I didn't realize that." Georgina was still jotting notes. "I thought they all kept themselves secluded, denying the physical and social world."

"Well, some do. There are different teachers using different levels of discipline and all levels of practice. Their literature was secret in ancient times to protect them, but now it is becoming available to the public. Some of their ideas are getting into the mainstream of society and churches, allowing people to participate at their own level of preference."

Becky wondered if the college would permit her to do some research with volunteers. She wanted to know more about the effect of prayer and alignment on the mental and emotional well- being of people. She needed to know more about God, the Creative Principle, and set up criteria for alignment with it. This would not be easy, but if there was a way the world at large could participate, wouldn't that bring a better world? What would a better world look like? There were many questions to answer and parameters to be determined and set, before a study could begin. First, she needed to look through her research materials to begin putting it together. And maybe she needed John Sherman's expertise in research to help her. She would ask him.

It seemed to Becky that John Sherman had been absent from the college a lot lately. He taught some classes and engaged a student assistant to conduct others for him. Becky stopped by his office several times, but he was never there.

"Jenny, do you know where John Sherman keeps himself these days? I need to talk to him and can never find him."

"Uh, well, I'm not supposed to say. He doesn't want anyone to know. You'll understand when you see him."

Becky was mystified. "So…is he sick or in league with aliens? What? Never mind, I'll talk to him myself. It's O.K."

That afternoon Becky went down the hall to John's office and then up to his classroom. John was working at a large table filled with papers and books. When he looked up she was shocked. His face was pale and strained.

"I'm sorry to disturb you, John. Are you doing O.K.? I mean, I haven't seen you around much." She desperately hoped he hadn't seen her shock.

"No problem. C'mon in and sit down, Becky. Nice to see you. No, I haven't been around, and I'm not well but getting along."

"Maybe I shouldn't bother you with this. I just came to ask for some research advice. Better I should ask if you need some help."

"Oh, thanks. My student assistants keep things in order for me. I'm going through chemotherapy right now. I don't think it is doing much good. In fact I feel worse most of the time. They doctor says to give it a chance. A chance to do what I'm not sure."

"John, I am so sorry. Does Jim know?"

"Not yet. There isn't much he can do, and he doesn't need to run up here and hover over me."

"Would he do that? Hover I mean? He does care about you, you know." Becky couldn't resist making the point.

John shifted in his chair and winced. Becky didn't know if he was in physical pain or it was what she said. "What research are you contemplating? What can I help you with?"

Becky hesitated, trying to gather her thoughts. She hadn't expected this quick shift back to business. She explained her recent experience in prayer, the answer that came, and the research she wanted to do regarding it. Together they sketched out a complete plan of action including some possibilities for funding. Becky hadn't even thought about the expenses it would incur. They spent a couple of hours going over every aspect.

"You're really pale, John. You probably need to rest a bit. Is there something I can do for you?"

"Well, I guess I need some of my work here carried to my car. Let me grab a box here. I hope you don't mind. I get a little wobbly lately."

"Not a problem. Glad to. Show me what to put in the box."

As she carried the box of his work to his car, Becky wondered if John was overdoing it by working even at home. She could see how weak he was, though he did his best to hide it. But how did he get this way so quickly?

"Are you O.K. to drive, John?"

"Yes. Just give me a minute," as he slipped into the front seat and gave a sigh of relief.

"Suppose I follow you to your place and help you unload this?"

"If you wouldn't mind. I hate to ask, but yesterday it was several hours before I could get myself together to make it into the house. I guess I don't want to do that tonight."

Becky was becoming more and more alarmed. John seemed to be worse off than she first thought. John leaned heavily on Becky as she helped him into his house and onto the living room couch. She took note of the medication bottles lined up on the coffee table as she went back out to get the box.

"John, my schedule is clear this evening. Let me stay a while and be sure you have everything you need."

"Oh, I just need a little rest. Could you fill my water pitcher and a glass with ice before you go? I have to take all this stuff. I set a timer to keep track of when to take it, so I don't sleep through it."

John was perspiring when Becky returned with the water and ice. She went back to the kitchen, found a towel, dipped it in cool water and brought it to the living room to place on his forehead.

"Can I call you a little later to be sure you're doing O.K.?"

"I'll be fine. Just did a little too much today. Really. I'll call you if I need to."

Doubtfully, Becky left her phone number beside his medication. "Be sure to call, O.K.?"

"O.K." He whispered and was asleep before she got to the door.

The digital clock read 3:45 a.m. when Becky's phone rang. John's voice was hardly recognizable. "I need…" and Becky heard the receiver drop to the floor. She jumped out of bed, into her clothes, and ran out of the house after she called emergency 911.

John was on the floor, the receiver beside him and pills scattered on the carpet. She checked for his pulse and breathing. They were faint, but there. Emergency medics arrived as she was dialing the phone number of his doctor.

"This is Dr. Becky Temple, colleague of John Sherman. I am at his home. He is unconscious and the ambulance is just arriving."

"Tell them to take him to Northwick Cancer Research Hospital. They'll call me when he gets there."

"Doctor, anything we should do? I mean…"

"Not really. The medics can handle it. I've been trying to get him to go into hospice, but he won't. We are doing chemo, but there isn't much hope."

Hospice! Becky was stunned. As the ambulance left for Northwick, she found Jim's number on John's kitchen counter and called.

"Jesus! I had no idea. Damn him! No one there knew?"

"No one, Jim. Jenny and his students were instructed by him to say nothing. He managed to hide out from us all. We didn't think anything about it since he usually does that sort of thing regularly."

"I know. Sorry. I didn't mean to sound accusing. I'll be there as fast as I can. And thanks for being there." Jim hung up and Becky looked at the clock again. It was 4:30 a.m. She went home, packed some extra clothes and cosmetics in a small bag, picked up her Daytimer, and headed for Northwick.

Becky, Georgina, Jim, and Chaim were in the waiting room. Jim went back to his father's room every fifteen minutes. "He's stable, but not good and not conscious yet."

Georgina brought sandwiches, snacks, and drinks from the cafeteria. "We've been talking about prayer. Let's go downstairs to the chapel and hold a prayer vigil for John."

They finished their sandwiches. Jim was finishing a bag of chips. "You all go ahead. I'll hang out in his room."

They took the elevator to the first floor and found the chapel. One man was there obviously very distraught. Georgina sat down beside him and gently asked if he could care to join their prayer circle. "We're praying for a friend and would be glad to pray with you, too."

"It's my wife. She was in an automobile accident. They don't know if she'll make it," the man whispered.

They gathered around him taking his hands in theirs. Chaim

began with a prayer chant in Hebrew. Becky picked up with a healing meditation, and Georgina ended it singing the Lord's Prayer. As they were leaving the chapel thirty minutes later, a doctor came in and told the man his wife was out of danger. They all looked at each other in astonishment and broke into applause. The man hugged them all and ran to the elevator.

Becky wondered if it would be too much to hope for that John would have a miraculous recovery too.

"They've balanced his medication intravenously. He shouldn't have been trusted to do that himself when he's so weak. He couldn't possibly be accurate in his condition. He's still unconscious but his vital signs are holding steady." Jim was a little lighter hearted and almost smiling. "Think the prayers are helping. With him it's always a delayed reaction to everything, even prayer. I guess that applies whether he's conscious or unconscious."

Becky, Georgina, and Chaim went home later in the afternoon, leaving Jim to wait for John's awakening and make the hospice arrangements. Jim preferred it that way. They promised to return tomorrow and earlier if he needed them.

"Hey, Nathan."

"Hey, Mom. Thanks for the message about Jim's dad. I'm at the hospital with him now and his dad is starting to wake up. He's weak and groggy, but doing a lot better. They'll be moving him to the hospice facility in a day or two."

"Oh, good. I mean I was hoping they wouldn't just send him home alone again."

"You're a hero, Mom. He'd be dead without you."

"Well, at this juncture, I'm not sure that wouldn't have been a better outcome, except that Jim really needed to be there before he just died on his own alone."

"Jim wants you to do the memorial service whenever it happens."

"What? What do I know about doing that? What about a minister or a priest?"

"Well, Jim doesn't want any of those. He wants you. He knows his dad would agree."

"Oh my. Tell him I'll do it. I'll call Chaim. He'll have something

I can use. I don't even know where to start. Yes, tell him we'll figure it out."

"I knew you would, Mom. Haven't seen anything stymie you get. If the CIA didn't scare you, what's a little memorial service, huh?"

"It's God! That's what it is! And yes, the CIA did scare me when they had control over your life, smart guy."

The hospice facility was quiet, elegant, and efficient. Becky was pleased that it wasn't like the hospital at all. John was awake and cheerful when she arrived.

"Hey Becky, thanks for the rescue. I don't remember even dialing the phone."

"Well, some part of you has more sense than the part we usually see. Glad you managed to call. How are you doing?"

"Oh, fair I guess. The drugs are good here. The stuff they pump into me takes the pain, but not the mind. Pretty nice considering..."

"Considering that?"

"Considering I've been a damned fool most of my life and probably deserve Dante's inferno instead."

"You've got a great son. Don't shut him out anymore. He needs to go through this with you."

John heaved a sigh. "I shut him out so he could live his life without my baggage. He's been through enough."

"The baggage could be worse when a father he loves withholds himself and hides out. We don't get to escape, John, or save others, even our kids. We have an effect regardless."

"Yes. Smart late as they say. That's me. So, are you started on your research?"

"Sort of. We held a prayer vigil for you and someone else got healed. Our aim must have been a little off."

"Well, I've always been the great deflector."

"Jim said it was probably delayed reaction. Same thing. I guess I shouldn't divulge his conversations even if they weren't actually confidences."

"I'll keep it to myself. But we're getting to know each other a little better. It's late for regrets, but I should have gotten to know you better too."

"What do you mean?" Becky wasn't ready for the conversation to turn personal.

"I always say the wrong things, make awkward situations for others, communicate badly, and then go hide. I didn't want to do that to you, but I think I did. I'm sorry."

"I was uncomfortable around you, John. But I was busy battling my own demons. I was using that uncomfortableness to learn about myself, searching out the roots of my own stuff."

"Well, Georgina was ready to deck me a few times, I'm certain."

"I can't deny that, but I'll let her speak for herself."

He reached for her hand and whispered, "Again, I'm sorry."

Becky took his hand in both of hers. Hot tears welled up in her eyes. He pulled her close and smoothed her hair away from her face with his other hand.

"I don't know what to say, John, except thank you. No apology needed. You helped me learn something I needed to know about myself." Becky kissed his forehead and got up to leave. "I'll be back tomorrow."

"Promise?"

"Yes, promise." She hesitated a moment, smiled at him, and walked out of his room.

Becky was still in a bit of a turmoil when she met Georgina for dinner at Mom & Pop's. For once the place was quiet. They were early and the dinner rush hadn't begun.

"Why the turmoil, Becky? Do you have feelings for him?"

"It's hard to say. I've been holding the fort against his manner for a long time, and suddenly the walls fell. I feel really sorry for him, and for me I guess. But there is nothing else I could have done."

"True. He is the way he is, and it was up to him to change, to let people in. He was right. I could have decked him a few times. When I get that angry I have to remember that I need my hands to play the piano. That has always tempered my urge to attack."

"Your urge to attack? Georgi!"

"It's the Italian in me. My family always yelled at each other, pounded the table and all that. They never actually attacked each other, but to a kid or an outsider it would sure looked like it was about to happen."

"I would be so angry at my father I wanted to kill him, and then on an occasional day when he didn't have a drink, he would be sweet and nice. The same thing would happen. The dam would burst and I would be remorseful for all the anger I had toward him, and overwhelmed with sentimental emotion. I don't know if I would call it love. More like a mixture of guilt, remorse, and starvation for his love."

Georgina nodded. "Isn't it interesting that the people who give us the most hassle teach us the most vital lessons? I think the people who don't give us problems are there as a safety net and resting place before the battle resumes."

Becky shifted in her seat. "You know what? I need to sing. Let's go to your studio and give Carmen and Delilah a whirl."

"Yes, I would like to beat on those piano keys for a while. Let's go."

Nineteen

The next day Becky brought flowers to John's room. Jim and Nathan were already there. The conversation was animated when she walked in and she almost wished she had come at a different time. Her feelings about the day before were still running high. She had dreamed about John all night, but couldn't remember what went on in the dream. She still felt a little disoriented and flustered.

Of course Nathan picked up on it right away. "You O.K. Mom?" They hugged each other.

"Yes, why?" She busied herself arranging the flowers in a vase.

"You look a little out of it?"

"Could be. I didn't sleep well last night." It was a fib, but she couldn't let the subject go any further right then.

John looked a little brighter and he was smiling at her. Suddenly her discomfort disappeared, and she went to his bedside and hugged him. "You're looking much better. How do you feel?"

"Well, actually, I'm sort of floating. Good drugs and some rest, I guess."

Nathan and Jim gave Becky hugs. "We're going to get a snack. We'll be back in a while."

"It's not necessary for you guys to leave." Becky didn't want Nathan to run off right away when they'd just gotten together.

"We know. We have some talking to do, too." Jim was grinning.

Becky raised one eyebrow and turned back to John. "What are they up to?"

"They mentioned talking to your partners, Steven and Karla. They want to take 'The Way Home' into their field of business. They have some promotion ideas. So, you didn't sleep well?"

"Uh, I guess I dreamed and woke up several times." Closer to the truth, but not quite the truth.

"What do you know about dying, Becky?"

"Well, I'm not sure I actually know anything. I've read a lot of books about it. I guess I'm a little short on the actual experience. What I get out of the books and near-death testimonies is that there is nothing to be afraid of except the pain caused by disease or trauma. It is an easy and rather thrilling transition across that line. I've seen the look of peace that comes over the face of a dying person when they finally go. The doctors, of course, assured me that it is only a reaction to body chemistry. But there's no mistaking an ethereal look. I don't think chemistry alone can produce that."

"Oh, I don't know. If it's anything like the chemistry I'm getting through this I.V., I could smile for a long time dead or alive."

"O.K. nut case. What is it you really want to know?"

"I want to know if I am going to miss all the things I've done and regret the things I didn't do. I guess it's hard to let go of what we're familiar with. Right now, I can't imagine how it will be."

"All of this, John, is planet earth software. What we go to is much greater, lighter, and joy filled. I can't imagine we'll miss this, but I certainly wouldn't want to leave my kids and grandkids. I understand your concern. I don't like to think about that either. Tell me, did you miss anything when you were unconscious? Did you fight to come back that you were aware of?"

"Actually, I was so comfortable that I wanted to fight against coming back. Even if I wasn't in pain, it still felt like pain somehow."

"That's the closest I can come to how the death experience will feel. I've also not wanted to awaken from under an anesthetic. It is the general heaviness of physical life that seems to press, sort of like being pushed to the wall by something too heavy. I tried to push it away, but couldn't. I woke up anyway and I wasn't happy about it. Then there was the nurse that kept shouting at me to wake up, calling my name. I was so mad at her! Of course, I apologized later."

John laughed out loud.

"Things weren't so heavy in the cosmic realm, and I have always kept my studies in that area. I could ignore all that was immediately around me, including my family and friends." His smile faded.

"Maybe that's why the human mind has limits, we will focus on our immediate experience and not be concerned about or distracted by what is beyond."

"By the way, another thing Jim and Nathan are doing is arranging to have my work formed into a library. They are investigating a grant and maybe a website. That seems to be the coming thing... websites. I don't know much about them."

Their conversation trailed off as the voices of Nathan and Jim were heard coming down the hall.

"You youngsters can tell me about your big plans for 'The Way Home' over dinner," Becky laughed.

"Oh, oh. Cat's out of the bag. Dad, did you rat on us?

"...'fraid so. Must have been talking in my sleep and couldn't help it." John was drifting off to sleep.

Nathan was aglow. "Here's what we've worked out with Karla and Steven. Jim and I are going to work together, the feng shui energy flow stuff and your exercises. We thought we would go to companies and offer the ideas for the well-being of their employees, showing them the benefits for their company. We wanted to get a plan put together for you to look at and tell us what you think."

"Lissa mentioned that she is also working on an idea for mothers and children. She wants to take it to other countries when she and Mark travel again. I don't know when that will be now that she is pregnant again."

"Is she, already? Wow, that seems close." Nathan was genuinely surprised.

"Yes, it's easy for it to happen again right away after a birth. She'll be busy, but I understand her college friend, Ginger Lydell, is helping her with the plans. Ginger has been giving childcare seminars and wants to join forces with us."

"I'm so sorry to hear about John. How's he doing?" Karla was calling for the evening program with Becky.

"He's comfortable at the hospice facility. I don't know how long it will be. We're all pretty upset. We didn't know for so long."

"I don't want to sound crass, but any conversations about the dying process or death that we could air? I think folks would be interested."

"Well, O.K. I don't think it's crass. I'll gather some thoughts together and see what John might like to add. He's very communicative these days. It's been really nice."

"Yes? How nice? Just kidding."

Becky laughed. "You'd better be. Enough of that. Anyway, I think folks are probably going to be more concerned about going to heaven or hell than dying. They usually go for what they are frightened of instead of what we are presenting."

"True. But we can try. Call you back at show time." Karla rang off and Becky turned to her bookshelf, selecting the few new books on death and dying.

Becky had been hesitant to ask John to do this, but he suggested it himself. In fact he wanted to go on the air. "I may as well share the journey as much as I can. I've taken people into the theoretical cosmos according to John Sherman. Now let's approach the next expression in living the same way. I want to teach to the end. This time it's more than just theory. Now it's up close and personal."

"Friends, the topic tonight is death and dying. We have Dr. Becky Temple here and a surprise guest we'll identify just as John. John is on the phone from his room at hospice and has agreed to comment when he can."

"So, Dr. Temple, how do you approach the subject of death? Why don't we talk about it more than we do?"

"We know that everybody dies. We know it is unavoidable to leave this lifetime at some point. People would rather talk about things they feel they have some control over. When they walk into a dying person's room they are likely to talk about things that are going on outside of that room as if the dying person would be inspired to leave the dying and return to his or her life. The church teaches about heaven and yet instills fear of death at the same time by threatening hell as a punishment. The artist, Dante, depicts hell as eternal agony in horrible images. It's no wonder people shy away from the subject."

"Go ahead caller."

"Does it seem to you that there isn't much focus on the practical challenges of dying? Instead it's the hereafter and all its terrors. I'm more interested in a description of how we can approach death sensibly, gracefully."

"Good point. John if you're still on the line, jump in anytime."

"Yes, Karla, I'm still here. I've been as guilty as anyone of avoiding the reality of my life as I know it here on planet earth. I've been like the man of steel, resolutely turning to the study of humanity's future on the earth and other planets, but not beyond the physical in human death. When I became ill I went to the medical profession only when I couldn't function any more. Then it was too late for them to help me, if they even could have. I kept it from my son and friends until I collapsed and nearly died alone. But something caused me to call for help as I was passing out. Very late I've discovered how valuable friends and family are, and how they can soften the harsh reality of losing your life. I guess I would say approach death with all your life participants involved. We can teach those who aren't dying by letting them be part of it vicariously. As we teach, we make the experience meaningful step by step to ourselves as well."

Becky was close to tears. "Dr. Becky, what can you add?" She jumped a little and shook off the rising emotion.

"We're often afraid to stress our loved ones by confronting them with our condition, but often they already know something's up and they're already stressed not knowing what it is. They are waiting behind the closed door to be let in. I think there's a sense of relief at the possibility of being there and maybe even being able to help in some way."

"Come on back in caller."

"Should we ignore the heaven and hell stuff? It is so ingrained in our thinking that even non-believers, which I am, refer to it."

"Dr. Becky?" Karla was wondering at her short hesitations.

"I refuse to take on the heaven and hell stuff as my belief, but I certainly wouldn't ignore the possibility that someone else is very much of that thinking. I don't hesitate to gently share my ideas with them as an alternative to their fears. They may be open to it or not. I just follow their lead, ask questions, and try to understand where they are."

Becky asked if John was still on the line. Karla replied, "It seems we've been temporarily disconnected. We'll try to reconnect."

Becky felt a shiver run through her. Playing for time she asked, "Caller, do you have an experience you'd like to share?"

"Yeah, as a matter of fact I do. I was twelve when my grandma died. I was right there in the room and she told me all about it. She said she saw angels all around her bed and there was nothing to be afraid of. It was natural. She took my hand, kissed it, and went to sleep…forever I guess. Do you think she really saw angels?"

"You have her word for it. I wouldn't second-guess her. Many people report seeing light, flowers, beings, and angels. They mention feeling warm, welcomed, loved and safe."

"Have you heard of anyone seeing hell or darkness?" asked Karla.

"Actually, I've never heard of that happening except in the movies. My experience is limited but I've read several books with testimonies about near-death experiences. It's always the same feeling. Maybe different visuals, but never anything fearful."

Karla interrupted. "John, you are back with us." Becky gave a small sigh of relief.

"Yup. My I.V. tube got tangled. Cut us off, but I was listening to you on my radio. I'm sort of in the pre-angel part. Not quite there yet. I would like to see something that tells me in ways I can understand that I go on consciously. That I participate consciously, that I still have a part to play in something. I want to know that everything doesn't just stop. Guess I want to be sure I still have some choices. I believe the physical mind goes dark, but the universal mind is still functioning and is free of physical constraints. I want to know what will matter to me in that new place and what I'll know, what I don't, or can't know now. As you can tell I'm a bit apprehensive and am clinging to my own hypothesis about what it will be like. The human mind doesn't know how to let go and be nothing. It has to have its framework to hang stuff on, stay busy, or it will fly apart."

"John, it's Becky. Have you had out-of-body experiences or anything that might be a clue?"

"Good to hear your voice, Doc T." Becky thought she blushed and was glad no one could see her. Doc T was a very recent designation John created. Was it his way of indicating equality with him or something more?

"I suppose I've had what you'd call out-of-body experiences, but I still think they were essentially constructed by my own human mind set. The question being, was I experiencing what I wanted it to be or was it beyond my fantasies. I really don't know. As I mentioned I was clinging to my own hypothesis and I'm not sure we ever get outside of that while we're here."

"John, do you think then that we can't explore the next experience in living other than by actually doing it? There's no mystical glimpse ahead of time of the next plane?"

There was a short silence and then John's voice, a little weaker, came through.

"As I recall, Jesus said something about going to prepare a place, but the disciples weren't ready to follow him. Were they not ready to understand or actually die and go there? He didn't say, but he seemed to know something more when he mentioned the 'many mansions' which I interpret to mean many dimensions of being. That could have been his best guess or his experience. It sounds like a bit of doubt may have come up in the garden when he said '...let this cup pass from me.' Can't say as I'd blame him. I've probably said it several times an hour since I got this diagnosis. I can swing from acceptance to rebellion, courage to doubt, and outrage to begging in less than thirty seconds."

"John, what has surprised you about the dying process?" Becky was regaining her balance and poise.

"Oh, I've been surprised at the unpredictability of how I feel from one minute to the next and my inability to control it. I've been surprised that the pain lessens with people I care about around me. It's harder to handle pain when you're alone. For me the dying brings on an intense process whether I'm asleep or awake. I wonder if it is really me or the 'divine processor' at work."

John's voice was beginning to fade and Karla said goodbye to him so he could ring off and rest.

"Go ahead, Caller."

"Thank you. I'm an elderly lady of ninety-two. I've gathered a lot of comfort from hearing this program tonight. Am I to understand that you think death is good and there is nothing to be afraid of?"

"You sound like a very young ninety-two."

"Oh, I am. I'm pretty spry, but the unpredictability the gentleman spoke of is real. My heart stopped one day. Just stopped flat and I dropped right to the sidewalk on my face. Had to get stitches. But my heart started again immediately, no damage done to it. My granddaughter had me get some medication so that wouldn't happen again. She threatened to get me a full-face helmet to keep me from damaging myself. It was a surprise to find myself on the ground and not even remembering falling."

"Bless you! In answer to your questions, I have found that more people fear there might be pain before death than the actual death itself. I don't think death is good or bad. It is part of our living process. The physical body wears out and we can't do our work on the planet with a worn-out body. We need a new body, one that would afford us a greater freedom in growing. Jesus returned in a higher form that Mary Magdalene didn't recognize. She recognized his voice, however."

"Yes, I noticed you commented on my voice too. I wonder if we sound the same on either side for some reason. Or did Jesus realize he needed to make himself recognizable to her and that was the quickest way?"

"Great question. I think that may have the answer we are looking for. We want to be recognizable in some way to ourselves and others. I've started to think if we can determine what and how we want to be in a lifetime here, maybe we can do that in the next as well. We can go on co-creating with God our own way. As John said, we'd like to continue to have choices."

"I quite agree. I always wanted to be a lively one to the end. Maybe there's no end and I'll continue to be lively on into the next 'mansion.'"

"I hope so. Will you let us know?"

"I'll do my best, you can bet on it. Thanks again. Got lots to think about and plan for. Goodbye."

Becky was back in John's room the next morning. He was asleep and looked very gray and tired. She took his hand. His eyelids fluttered but they didn't open.

"John?"

"Yeah, I'm here. I just can't come out and play right now. Too tired."

"Did you hear the end of the show?"

"Yup. Loved the elderly lady." His eyes remained closed and his voice sounded far away.

Becky noticed his oxygen wasn't hooked up. "Where's your oxygen?"

"Don't want it. I'm going. Had enough."

Becky went out to the nurses' station. The nurse said, "He doesn't want any unnecessary assistance. He's content to go. We keep the pain medication going, but nothing else."

"Does Jim know?"

"Yes. He was here all night. They made the decision together. He should be back in a few minutes. He's washing up and changing clothes down the hall."

Becky called Georgina and Chaim. "He's going. Maybe we should all be here."

They all sat around John's bed. Becky, Georgina, Chaim, Nathan, and Jim simply kept a quiet vigil. They spoke from time to time, but found the silent company most comforting.

After a while, Chaim began to chant a Jewish prayer. Georgina picked up on it and chanted with him. Becky started a meditation with Jim and Nathan adding to it as they went. Becky held one of John's hands while Jim held the other. He would open his eyes from time to time, look around at each one, and close them again. At one point he squeezed Becky's hand and then Jim's and was gone with a peaceful sigh.

The nurse came in quietly to check his vital signs and stopped the I.V. "Stay as long as you like." She went back out to the desk to make the necessary calls.

The same small band of people went up into the hills to a quiet meadow overlooking a valley, where they could remember John together. Jim brought John's ashes to scatter at the top of the hill. Becky need not have worried about the service, because it was beautifully shared by all and love carried the day.

Mom and Pop's was crowded and full of laughter. It was a welcome relief to join the merriment, have their favorite pizza, and talk about the future.

"Jim, what will change for you now that he is gone." Becky reached over and touched his hand.

"I didn't think anything would change because I didn't think he was a legitimate part of my life. But now I realize that he isn't there to blame for my circumstances. Not that I did much of that, but evidently some part of me did because I feel the loss. Also, I can no longer wait for him to finally be a close, warm father in my life. There was always the fantasy that someday he would, even though I knew it was a very long shot."

Nathan was reaching for the pizza the waiter was bringing to the table. "I have a little sense of what you are saying. My father is off in another world and not available even to communicate. I don't really know how I am attached to him since it's been a long time even seeing him. But he's still here, so to speak, and I'm not sure what I would feel."

Becky's guilty feelings came roaring back full force as she listened to Nathan. She hadn't thought about his father for a long time. Why couldn't she have chosen a man who would be able to be the father the children should have had?

"Mom. Mom. Where are you? You look disturbed."

"Oh, I hadn't thought about your dad for years. I guess I just went spinning back into those times. I still have regrets about marrying him and that you didn't have a real father."

"How could you have known, Mom? You can't be to blame. He has some responsibility too."

"I suppose there were signs, but I was young and didn't know what they were or what to do with them."

Nathan touched Becky's hand. "There are a bunch of signs I haven't read either as you well know. How many relationships did you watch me go through to disaster? I'm just lucky they wouldn't marry me. Please don't feel guilty. I'm fine. So's Lissa."

"It was momentary. I guess that stuff never really disappears. We just learn to manage the memories when they are triggered."

Chaim reached for his soft drink. "We have to manage memories that aren't there as well as memories that are there. I don't think we're ever free. My father has been angry and emotionally abusive all my life. It's been a struggle every day, especially when I was a kid and thought it was all my fault. I don't even remember the beginnings of it. That's what I meant by memories that aren't there."

Georgina picked up her soft drink and held it high. "A toast! To the overcomers of childhood memories and childhood guilt. May we continue to grow, enjoy life, and celebrate ourselves and each other a little more every day."

"Hear! Hear!"

The conversation turned to the projects they all had been planning. Georgina revealed a musical she was writing about Laura's life entitled "Laurasong."

"I've just about completed the music and lyrics. Laura is going to play herself in certain parts. There are several producers interested in it and I've asked Steven to be our agent. He jumped at the chance. I can't wait for you all to hear it."

"Well how about tonight? Let's finish up here and go to your studio. You can play some of it for us. I know some of the music. Let's have a preview!" Becky was ready to sing again and Georgina was delighted to share some of her work. Chaim didn't beg off this time. They all needed to be together for a while longer.

Twenty

The word had come that Georgina's musical was accepted by a producer in an off-Broadway theater. Steven was beside himself. He began immediately working on the legalities and arrangements.

"What do we do now?" Becky was just as excited. She and Georgina had put together Laura's story with a cosmic flavor using some of John's work.

"Write! Finish the last part! Pack! Call Steven. He'll know what else to do." Georgina was at the piano changing some words, tweaking chords, revising endings. Discarded paper was all over the floor around her piano. Music scores, scripts, and stage directions were stacked in boxes ready to go.

Most excited of all was Laura. She had grown into a beautiful teen and was taking acting lessons from a local retired drama teacher. Nick and Doris had written the stories of her early life and their struggles. A local writer had put them into a play form, recreating the characters and experiences. It was a huge community project that had been going on steadily for many months.

"I didn't realize John was even paying attention when we spoke of Laura's challenges in the Monday evening class." Becky was gathering up the waste paper and stuffing it into a recycling bag.

"He was working with Nick and Doris to determine how he could help, and he just decided to fund the musical as much as he could. I told him it might not fly very far, but he didn't seem to care." Georgina was talking with a pencil in her teeth, fingers flying over the keys.

Becky stepped back in time once again. She had that all too familiar feeling of "Because I'm a fool I'm left out of the loop." All the closeness she felt with John as he was dying evaporated in that moment. Why didn't she know about this other side of him? Had she been so concerned with her own feelings of inadequacy and judgment of him that she couldn't see it?

"Becky! What's the matter? You suddenly look ill. Are you O.K.?" Georgina was pulling her into a chair.

"Yes, I think so. It's just an old problem that cropped up. It seems that I've been so judgmental of him, and here is this whole side of him I didn't know about. Was I too self-absorbed to see it?"

"Becky, this caring side of him didn't show up until he knew he was dying. He could risk reaching out because he knew he wouldn't have to follow through on any relationships. I know he got close with you at the end, but he wouldn't have to act on his feelings, so it was safe. Understand?"

Becky took a sip of soda. "Hmm. Well I guess it was safe for me as well to let him do that. I knew I wouldn't be obligated either."

"You're way too hard on yourself, Beck. You are always open to love and willing to risk letting someone in. More often than not you give others more of your trust than they have earned or deserved. Better you are a little too open than too closed, I guess. I'm the one that was ready to kill him several times. Well, not actually, but you know what I mean."

"Yup, I understand what you are saying. What I'm having trouble figuring out is what hits me in the gut so hard that I nearly pass out. I think one word is at the bottom of it all. Fool. Exposure of my hidden shame or my impostor-ship on this planet. I don't know how to dig out that old lie buried deep inside. It's one of those memories that isn't there, as John said. It still comes roaring up unbidden through my feelings. No words or triggers I can get a hold of. It just grabs me and shakes me good. It's probably the taproot of a lot of things if I could just get to it."

"Shame is in the story of Adam and Eve. They were naked and ashamed. Do we sometimes get stripped to our nakedness and shamed when we are just kids? Probably many times. I don't mean physically naked, but emotionally. The Lord asked, 'Who made you ashamed? Did you eat of the tree I forbade?'"

"I guess we learn to eat of the tree of shame so early and never get over it. That's probably why God forbade it. Because we spend a lifetime getting over it. Hence the whole process of the Old Testament." Becky's color was coming back. "Phew, I feel better. Thanks, Dr. Georgi."

"Great. Grab a deep breath and sing through some of this for me. I think I'm almost done."

Becky sat in her living room with pen, paper and a tape recorder. She began to meditate on the questions she wanted to ask her higher self. She had a little experience with this kind of meditation now and the interesting answers that came through her. When she was completely quiet and centered she began:

"How do I still the ego self-talk?" She waited completely relaxed. Then she spoke into the tape recorder.

"Allow me to still it for you. Don't struggle. Simply ask. It is done."

After a few minutes she asked again. "What is my deepest purpose?"

"Your deepest purpose is to align yourself with all co-creators, co-workers with God, to know yourself fully and completely as a god-being and to know all other co-creators as yourself. Oneness."

It all sounded so simple. Was she already knowing this? Was it already within her and just now coming out? She continued.

"What do I teach?"

"Teach what is in your heart. Trust that. Allow it to guide you. Speak from the heart. I will speak through you and the purpose is accomplished."

Becky was feeling a little more confidence. She had certainly been doing that and it was a relief that she seemed to be on the right track. She took a deep breath and focused on the idea of co-creatorship.

"Is my co-creative teaching correct and how do I do more of it?"

"Keep searching AS a co-creator, the scriptures. Keep developing. Follow your heart. Read, see, and live as your god-self and it develops. Be patient. Be patient."

Be patient. How does one be patient when releasing the pain of old ways. The possibilities were so thrilling and she wanted to rush toward them.

"I want to free myself of old stuff." A great sense of compassion came over her.

"I know you do. I know you truly want to be free. Learn to let it go. Not to push it away, not to beat on it. Not to take violent action against it. Learn to simply let go. It does not exist."

It does not exist. Of course. She hadn't thought of all this stuff in terms of non-existence. It was only her thoughts and reactions to memories, not reality.

"I want to manifest my higher nature."

"Yes, and you are. Simply believe that it is so. Love your universe. Love your life. Love each little thing you do. Love each moment of the day. Do not allow your vibration to drop below this level. When the vibration becomes agitated or disturbed, stop. Let go. Understand through your god-self. Rise up and continue on. You are a teacher. You are a healer. You are a Christ. And most of all you are loved."

Becky stopped, caught her breath, and turned off the tape recorder. She sat quietly in deep amazement. Was it God speaking? Was it her own higher nature? She wanted to be sure. She felt so much love and peace in this moment. She wanted to sit there as long as possible, holding the state as long as it would last.

Becky, Georgina, and Chaim met at Mom & Pop's for dinner. Becky had transcribed her meditation tape and brought the transcription with her. "Chaim, do you believe God talks...I mean actually, in words? English?"

"Well, if you believe the Moses story, not only does God speak, but chisels it in stone tablets." He smiled, hands open questioningly.

"I'm not exactly Moses, and the tablets were in the form of a cassette tape." She explained to them what she had experienced.

"I asked my higher nature, or god-self, to speak through me and answer some questions. This is what happened. I know it wasn't me because I never would have been that gentle with myself. Such a compassionate feeling came over me that it was like a higher, more loving consciousness coming through."

Georgina furrowed her brow. "But is it your voice on the tape?"

"Oh yes. Definitely. It wasn't an entity taking over or anything. I've read about some of those conversations and they gave me the creeps. This didn't give me the creeps. It was very soothing and comfortable. The answers were right on target. There were answers that fit so well, it was like I already knew them and just had too much stuff in the way to bring them to the surface."

"Would you care to share some of it with us? Or is it too personal?"

"Oh, I transcribed it so I could keep it with me. I just like to read through it over and over throughout the day. I'd love to share it." Becky began reading the first question and answer.

"Tell me what self-talk is." Chaim was in his thoughtful mode with his hands folded under his chin.

"It's the chatter that goes on all the time in the mind. It gives dire warnings, fear messages, criticizes like parent talk. It's often unpleasant and ultimately damaging to self-esteem and every day functioning. It can even make you ill."

"Oh God, do I have a lot of that! It sounds like my father's voice and it yells at me all the time. I'm not good enough, I wreck everything, shame, shame!" Chaim reached for his iced tea and twirled the spoon in it.

Georgina reached for the dinner salads as the waiter picked them carefully off his extended arm. "What are you going to do with the answer?"

"Just ask every time I'm aware of the chatter, as it says."

"I'd be asking every few minutes!" Chaim shook out his napkin.

"If that's what it takes, I'll do it. I have an idea that it will start to take hold in the subconscious mind and become automatic eventually. We have to regroove those habit patterns."

"That sounds more hopeful. I'll have to try it. See if I can at least turn off my father's voice. I have been battling it by getting angry and verbally combative. I was probably giving it more energy. No wonder it gets louder. I'll have to try a different tack. Have you started this yet, Beck?"

"Immediately. It took a while to stop putting energy into the request for it to stop, sort of daring Higher Power to keep its promise. I finally got over that and now I ask quietly to have it removed. It's much easier and works better."

"What do you say?" asked Georgina.

"When I notice I'm into an internal conversation, I just say, 'Please stop this now.' Verbalizing this pulls me back to the here and now, and it stops."

"For how long?"

"Well, I guess until my mind drifts into idle you might say. Staying conscious all the time is something we're not used to. Except for grade school when the teachers yelled at us to pay attention, we really have no training in staying focused."

"Maybe that's why people complain they can't meditate. The chatter gets in the way. I've got my whole Italian family in my head. It's enough just to focus on singing. They all sing, you know. Badly, but they sing. I hear all their raucous comments and wonder if I'm ridiculous as well. It's a struggle. I'm not sure Higher Self can handle my whole family, but I'll certainly give it a chance."

They finished dinner sharing their self-talk with lots of laughter. Becky was feeling jubilant. "Somehow talking about it seems to lighten the load. With all of us trying it, maybe we've got collective power. The task doesn't seem so daunting and serious. It's even fun."

"Yes, well I guess fun is a new concept for me when it is used regarding my personal stuff. I guess I haven't been what I'd consider a fun guy."

"Chaim, you are easy to be around. You are gentle, affirming, encouraging. Whatever fears or terrors I've had, you just smoothed them away so many times. You've been a good friend and teacher."

"I guess I was unaware, Becky. You never looked like you had any of that. Did I make you uncomfortable somehow?"

"No. Actually, I did it to myself. Just like what we were discussing tonight. The critical self-talk kept me worrying about how I came across to you, whether I was stepping on your toes, and sometimes feeling foolish. None of it coming from you. That's what I'm saying. You could always say just the thing to make it all disappear."

"I never saw it. I guess I was so wrapped up in my own stuff. I thought you were so self-assured and friendly. I trusted you immediately. I was so grateful for your welcome and willingness to help me out anytime I asked."

"Georgi always knew what I was doing to myself and kept me from getting too crazy."

"I guess if we each knew what went on in the other's heads, we'd be amazed. My brother is a recovering alcoholic and he always said, 'don't compare your insides to someone else's outsides. I guess it's something he heard in a meeting."

"I've heard that too, Georgi. We assume because someone puts on a good show, they must be just super together. Often they're not." Chaim scooted his chair back and picked up his check.

They left quietly, agreeing to look at the rest of Becky's questions and answers at a later time. They each had a lot to think over.

Lissa delivered her second daughter, Rachel Arlaina Moireen Davies. "Well, you managed to get the grandmothers' names in, sort of." Becky was amused.

"We altered them a little. The kids will be living with their first names Sarah and Rachel, and the middle names will be there as a heritage. I think Mark's mother wishes she had let us use her name, so we wouldn't create a hybrid. Your mother loved hers. She may just adopt it for herself."

"Yes, she called and said she intended to legally change hers just to leave reminders of the past behind. I'm always amazed at the things she decides to do. It's always just about the time I think she wouldn't change a thing, she does it. She idolized you, Lissa."

"She speaks that way of you too, Mom. I think we are her lifeline and now her springboard. She has been reading your work, you know. I sent her copies of "The Way Home" stuff. She loves it. It is giving her a lift."

Becky was silent for a minute.

"Mom?"

"Yes, Lissa, I'm here. I was just thinking I could at last give something back to my mother for all the years. I was the skinny kid with the drippy nose and scuffed knees. The one who just didn't get it in school. I always felt so out of step. She put up with a lot with me. Tell me what she says about it."

Lissa filled her in on the conversations with her grandmother while tears brimmed in Becky's eyes. It was sadness and gratitude all mixed up together.

"Mom, she's really O.K. She doesn't see you the way you've seen yourself for so long. You're her inspiration, her princess tomboy, her last baby that she cherishes."

Steven called a meeting of everyone in "The Way Home" organization. He set it up to take place in the spring.

Arline came from Hawaii to care for Lissa's children there at a summer house on the property that they had rebuilt as an added space. Mark said he wouldn't miss it, which pleased Lissa. Ginger was concluding a training in Florida and would be arriving shortly. It was a family reunion along with the work time. Everyone had become family. Steven pampered Arline, now Arlaina, seeing to her every need and whim. Karla and Sandy hadn't seen her for so many years and were delighted that she came.

Becky sat for long spells holding Rachel and watching her sleep. Sarah was beside her "reading" from a book. She was just describing the pictures, but she called it reading.

"Gramma Becky, can I hold Rachel?"

Becky helped Sarah onto her lap, holding the baby to one side while she got settled. Then she carefully moved the baby onto Sarah's lap while she held them both safe and secure. All Becky could think of was how thankful she was for it all. Her family, her friends, and all that she had come through and learned. The miracle was that they just loved her with no special qualifications except that she was theirs. Home was manifest on earth for a moment.

Chaim sent his regrets. He was on his way back to Israel, perhaps for good. His father had passed on and the family of origin urged him to go home. They gave him his inheritance, so he could sustain himself as he integrated back into the Israeli society and established a research department for a new university there.

Jim and Nathan had become business partners since John's death, and had several enterprises in the works including the John Sherman Memorial Library. The Way Home had given everyone so many ideas to try and the results were promising.

The organization had grown. It became more prosperous and sophisticated. Becky saw that she needed a real home, a much larger space to accommodate the whole group, a quiet location in the hills of Connecticut close to Johnston Crossing. She searched for the perfect place and found one just coming on the market. The literature said it had many potential bedrooms, large areas for parties, and overlooked a valley.

She, Georgina, and Nathan went to see it immediately. They walked around it in amazement. There were high beamed ceilings, large windows, old barn wood floors and a large deck. Georgina was waving her hands and spinning around. "How will we fill these huge spaces?"

"Fear not, friend! We will have people coming and going, accommodations, privacy for each of us, work spaces, relaxing areas inside and on the deck. The potential is endless! Just like our work." Becky smiled at the words, our work.

Steven dealt with the realtor, closed the deal and their move began. They brought furniture from their present homes and slowly it started to take shape.

Months and even years were flying by. Everyone was working at top speed. New organizing and planning were taking place. Training circles were created all over the country now and Alexei had taken the ideas back to Moscow for his people to translate and implement.

Steven's partner, Loren, took over publications and distribution of training manuals. There was so much excitement as new people discovered them and wanted to become participants.

Along with the business end of things, Becky and Georgina were preparing an extended visioning time in several segments. The visioning was to last two days with brainstorming sessions and prayer.

"I would like everyone to write down ideas. Don't worry whether they will work or if they can be done. Just write whatever you think up. Then we'll put them all on the table, share them with each other briefly and then leave them there as we start a meditation. We're going to ask Spirit to bring into consciousness the right choices, the right conditions, and the right unfolding of them."

Jim was a little puzzled. "Well, how will we connect what is on the table with what is coming in meditation? How do we know there will be a correlation?"

"Actually, Jim, we don't. But we won't be thinking up things intellectually. We put ideas on paper to empty the intellect and then we go to a higher vision for confirmation, expansion, or something entirely above and beyond. It is a way of offering everything up and freeing ourselves to receive."

"Awesome!" Jim drew a sheet of paper to him and began to write. Everyone else around the huge lodge table did the same.

Ginger slipped in quietly and joined the activity. She knew what to do because she had shared the idea with Lissa on one of their trips together and they had tried it out.

Georgina closed the session with a chant she learned from Chaim. She had several in her repertoire that he had taught her. They would begin extensive visioning the next day.

They spent the first part of the morning in silence, and then began to speak as they were moved. Becky began, "I'm seeing that I need to retire from teaching, or just be an adjunct teacher. I'm not sure when that will be, but it is the first time I've envisioned myself retiring from the college."

Georgina continued. "I have more musicals to write. Laura's is well on its way to success and more ideas are coming. I wonder if a spiritual opera is possible? Something less demanding and formal than oratorio perhaps with a story line. I can hear the music. I'm not sure about the story yet."

"This sounds silly, but there's a sort of garden of Eden forming in my mind. Its purpose is to showcase an ecosystem with buildings that are waste free, harmonious, with healing and educational facilities. People from all over the world come to see it and take the ideas back to their communities and countries. It spreads all over the world." Jim had a really peaceful, glowing smile on his face for the first time since they had known him.

Nathan and Lissa began at the same time and she giggled. "Nathan, maybe we have the same vision. I'm traveling from place to place to support the work, just to keep people energized and involved."

"Not too surprising, Lissa. We do that a lot. It may be a brother and sister act. I'm going into places of conflict, however, to do peacemaking. I don't know a lot about that yet, but I've been taking some courses in the latest ideas."

Becky was jolted out of her reverie when she heard the word conflict from Nathan. She tried not to let her mind wander into "what if" and "oh, no." She had to trust that higher way, knowing he would be guided and secure. It was a bigger task to trust everything to spirit than she had imagined at first. She could easily trust for herself, but her children were another matter.

Steven was seeing a retreat center out of which more ideas flowed out into the world. Loren was seeing books of poetry and short inspirational stories going out from him.

The days went quickly as they ate pizza and spaghetti, while putting their visions on easel sheets and tacking them to a cork strips on the wall. They drew and painted their visions until a cohesive plan began to gel.

Karla had found a source of grants and funding for various areas and Sandy was working on ways to expand the accounting and record keeping. Computer programs were becoming more user friendly and she listed some that might work for them.

Karla was thinking of an all-night show called "Spiritual Company" in which they could present many spiritual subjects and music for those who were working at night or simply didn't sleep well.

After dinner Becky suggested they envision where they would all be in their last decade of their lives. She guided them through a meditation that brought them to that place in their lives and each one began to write.

A vision unfolded in Becky's mind.

Twenty-One

Karla was by the railing overlooking the distant tree tops into the valley. "It's good to sit on the veranda again. The winter seemed longer this year. I guess my old bones are creakier and I was wishing for the warmth more fervently."

Becky was pouring coffee. "I suppose for that reason we'd be smart to move to Florida or Arizona, but I just can't leave the tranquility of this place, and the privacy. I don't think I could stand the traffic and bustle of those places. I'll just take a few more aspirin or whatever, and survive the winters."

"I like watching the wildlife. They still roam free and the landscape is somewhat unspoiled so far. For all the spirituality we've studied, taught, and written about, it all comes back to the land and the peace it gives, doesn't it, Beck?"

"I remember Goethe wrote that Faust was sitting on the shore of Maine at the end of his life reclaiming the land from the sea. I feel like we're reclaiming the land of truth from the sea of confusion and chaos. I feel like we've come through the journey of human ignorance, pain, and searching, to the place of new beginnings. The birds still lay eggs here and they hatch into more birds. The forest nurtures its seedlings. The simple cycle of birth to birth still under scores all of our struggles to understand, and of going 'to and fro upon the earth.'"

"Don't forget our date on the radio tonight late. I'll be broadcasting through the local station again. Too much trouble to get into the city on a Friday evening. We've gotten the contract completed so we can start tonight." Karla sat down to work on some pieces of her quilt that she carried in her bag. Her prize-winning quilts had become almost as well-known as her innovative radio shows.

Becky brought out some snacks from the kitchen. "By the way, I did get in touch with the seniors' community and they would love to have Georgina start a therapeutic music program. We'll be video-taping it for a promotional packet and the management is evaluating the benefits by poling the residents. We may even have some testimonial shots if the residents give us permission. It is coming together nicely. People seem really enthusiastic."

"Where is Georgina, anyhow? Has she been away?"

"Just down to Hartford at a music conservatory working on one of her musicals. It is easier to use their equipment than to install a lot of expensive stuff up here. Although, it is tempting to create a better studio here. Who knows, we may be able to get a grant of some sort to do it. She got back last night. She's resting at home, or so she says. She's probably gathering music for the high school production she is consulting on. Knowing her, the music teacher will have a light load because Georgina will run with the ball. She still just loves working with students and thinks up all sorts of things for them to try."

Karla was fitting pieces of cloth together. "Steve and Loren are on their way from the airport. They were so sure they couldn't bear to leave San Francisco, but that's changing fast. Especially since they have money now to build their dream house and travel. The prices in California were eating them alive. They've commissioned me to make a quilt for them, so I've just started to lay out some ideas and colors."

A Jeep came roaring up the driveway and slid to a stop in front of the carport, a cloud of blue smoke trailing behind it. "Oh, God, it's them and their newest find, a smoking jeep." Karla set her quilt pieces on the table and went down the stairs to the lower deck.

"Look what we just couldn't resist! Isn't it great? Got it for a song." Steven was ecstatic. Loren just sat and smiled, shaking his head.

"Shoulda sung louder," hollered Karla in reply. "What's the blue smoke? Stage effects?"

"Oh, that. Just a little engine work needed. Burns a little oil. But it climbs the mountain roads just great. Taking it to the garage tomorrow."

"Have some coffee? Tea? Food?" Becky uncovered a few more dishes as they arrived at the top of the stairs.

"Oh, yeah! Haven't eaten since leaving for the airport. Wouldn't touch the stuff on the planes. Not even the pretzels." Loren was reaching for the celery.

"First class and you get pretzels?" Karla filled her coffee cup again.

"There was other food, but note I said, 'not even the pretzels.' I don't trust any of it."

Steven was unpacking his laptop. "Look here at what we've got. Final plans for the guest house down the road." Pictures and drawings popped up on the screen as he battered the keys furiously. "This picture is a place almost like the one we are building. Ours probably costs a third of what this one set some friends back."

"Is your stuff coming? Are you actually moving into the basement, or the garage? Do you need to store some stuff here? I can make room." Becky was studying the screen.

"We think it will all fit into the garage we just completed, but we're not sure. Thanks for the offer. We may need a little more room for a bit."

"Yes, especially since you bought that pool table we hadn't figured on! I thought we'd have to suspend it from the garage ceiling until the spa is finished." Loren was gesturing at the ceiling.

"Our gathering of the World Family of Peace folks is all set for next weekend. They are staying at a hotel in Springfield and we are bussing them back and forth. We have a scenic cruiser available to us before the tour season starts. We're equipping it with meditation music, bottled water and fresh fruit." Becky looked very pleased with her idea.

Karla pulled out her sewing again, "We have a broadcast set up especially for them to set forth their plans for the coming year and their conferences in Israel, Jordan, and Germany. It's ground breaking stuff. I'm really impressed. The new people in their organization seem to have come onto the planet with plans for greater spirituality and the next level of being. It's almost a new language. I'll need it explained to me in more detail. I can't even quote what they've told me so far."

Becky picked up a sheaf of papers from her stack of projects. "It is a study of the second and third levels of DNA that we haven't yet utilized. We need to advance in awareness before it will kick in. They seem to have some experience with how to do that. Some lab experiments and reports. I can't wait to hear the details."

"Do you think we're too late, too old, or too loaded with old stuff to get on board?" Karla was serious and Becky looked a little surprised.

"Uh, well, I guess I've never thought of us as too old or too far gone to fathom something new. I've always assumed that we would grow along with our discoveries and rise to the next and the next. The question is will they think we're over the hill?" They all laughed.

Georgina was coming up the steps and overheard them. Her Porsche was so quiet they didn't hear her drive in. "I think we're much higher beings than we give ourselves credit for. We came here to the planet to do a job so these youngin's could catch on and we took them as far as they could go leaning on us. Now they need to think for themselves, and we get to observe and see how they are doing."

"Brilliant!" Karla was enthusiastic about this idea. "I think we brought as much with us onto the planet as the traffic could bear, and we'll bring more in the next lifetime if they do their job and progress well."

"Well said." Steven and Loren said together and high fived each other, nearly upsetting the food tray. "Just like moving from San Francisco, there was only so much we could bring without hiring a second truck. We opted to be selective, the pool table notwithstanding."

"Alexei has been sending emails by the bushel, Becky. And he always wants to know how you are." Steven smirked.

"Right. Did you tell him I like his wife better than him? It's hard to tell if that ego trip is purely Russian, or if it is a wall to protect him from seeing himself. Anyway he gets a bit tedious. Somehow, he doesn't get it. He wants to use our material on other people, not himself."

"It's both." Georgina was sampling the dips. "That is the Russian male for sure. And it is hard for another culture to understand our approach. The older ones think looking at yourself is a big waste of time. They don't see any point to it. They think people can't change. That's why they are so set in their ways. Interestingly enough, they accept that in each other. They overlook personality completely. We take offense and they don't."

Loren joined Georgina at the snack tray. "What do you think is the future of what we are doing? Have we wasted our time trying to save the world?"

No one else seemed ready to answer and after Becky thought for a while she began, "The United States has been the beginning and proponent of individuality and personal freedom. The Greek culture had glimmers of it, but for a couple of centuries we have been the vanguard, leading the world in industrialization, technology, business, media, you name it. In trying to bring the other cultures of the world along with us, we've almost run ourselves aground, and stopped our own advancement.

"Our spiritual teaching has always been for the individual. Spiritual advancement is a personal matter, that which takes place within us. It has never been a group effort. No one can advance another person. We can teach and offer information, but ultimately each person has to walk the path for themselves.

"The early church couldn't control the population if they were all on individual paths, so they set up the collective. The population was largely illiterate, so they created symbols and rituals for them. No one had to think for themselves. Jesus was about the individual spiritual path. He didn't talk about defeating or converting the Romans, although some of the Romans were converted to his teaching. He spoke about things that each person could take within and change their own lives for the better.

"We have no idea how revolutionary 'love thy neighbor as thy self' was. They didn't love their neighbors. They defended themselves against their neighbors. And for centuries, people never got the last three words of that quotation, 'as thy self.' Loving themselves wasn't even a concept. They thought it was self-aggrandizement, when actually it meant that you have to love yourself before you can love anyone else.

"If I thought our job was to save the collective instead of teaching the individual, I'd have quit a long time ago because I don't think it works that way. I'm not sure God meant us to change the school, but rather to educate the students in it. This planetary experience was meant to be a school. Like a school you either pass or you repeat the grade. You either advance or you keep repeating the experiences until you do.

"So, for every individual regardless of culture or station in life who has benefited from what we've worked so hard to share, it has been worth it. I think we have truly carried on the work of Jesus in reviving the individual spiritual path. We have taken the teaching out of the realm of folklore, such tales as Jason and the Golden Fleece, and brought it back into actual life experiences. I think we have touched the consciousness of those who were ready, and it will be carried on by those people to others who have evolved. The golden fleece is within us."

"So…you feel it's been worth it?" Loren was absorbed in writing on a legal pad.

"Absolutely. What better life could I have led than to delve deeply into the spiritual pathways and learn so much. It has changed my life in so many wonderful ways that I can't count them all. I could be out there in a mundane job wondering if my life was going anywhere, or just climbing the corporate ladder somewhere. Even if my whole understanding of this is nothing more than a fantasy, it still has been worth living it. Our lives are a result of our thinking regardless of where we are, so one fantasy is as good as another. It depends upon what makes you happy, fulfills your longings, gives you hope, and makes your life work for you. This works for me and helps lots of others make their lives work, too. I love it with all my being."

The sun was setting and the land was darkening. The light sensitive switch turned the yard lights on, but the veranda remained unlit. As Karla sat back in her chair sipping coffee she began to add, "I was on that corporate ladder at the university and I couldn't see anything I wanted at the top. There was wrangling, politics, headaches, and so many were disillusioned. I really didn't know where to turn, until I learned to turn inward. I tried Buddhism and chanting. It helped me shut the chatter of my mind off, but it wasn't the whole story. I needed to be able to make conscious choices, but didn't know what else to choose. I went to the radio program to get ideas from others. Lots of great ideas came from that, but the best ones were yours, Beck. Everything came together and made sense, and my intellectual mind could relax because it wasn't going to be shut out. Just redirected in a satisfying way."

Steven was leaning against the railing watching the valley disappear in the darkness. "San Francisco was a crazy quilt of spirituality, fantasy, charms, and gimmicks. It was hard to figure out what was worth paying attention to and what wasn't. It seemed that each one had part of the puzzle, but not the whole thing. Loren and I explored fortune telling, psychic healing, crystals, spiritualism or speaking to the dead, and all sorts of weird stuff. When I heard you on the radio, all I could think of was Eureka! I've found it! I just knew it was right. I just had to be part of it. I nearly drove Loren crazy because he was fed up with the other stuff. He didn't want to explore one more thing. I thought he'd leave me, but thank God he didn't."

Loren reached over and took his hand. "I was tired and disgusted, but not crazy. It just took me a while to find the energy to try one more time to understand. I wouldn't have left you, my love, but I sure thought I might have to take a vacation alone somewhere and clear my head. It all started to make sense, as you all have said. It came together easily. I didn't have to stretch my mind into all sorts of contortions to accommodate it. It was as if I already knew these things, just hadn't articulated them. It all just fit and I was so grateful. Still am. Deeply grateful to us all."

Becky invited them all inside. She sat down at her computer. "Let me read to you something I have been working on called 'Choosing the Next Life Design:

"Are there choices to be made in the next dimension of being? What choices can we possibly make for a world we do not yet know? Are they even ours to make?

"Pierre Teilhard de Chardin said that we are on the leading edge of our own spiritual evolution. We are not pushed by our biology, but beckoned and invited by the Creator, the Omega, the Ultimate Absolute of Creation.

"How did we know what to create in this present dimension? Where have our ideas come from? How are they implemented?

"Divine Ideas are an inheritance from God. They flow to us, so to speak, constantly. They are bytes of God's wisdom that we can apprehend with the human mind, comprehend, and bring into our life experience for our highest good.

"If our Creator/Sustainer has supplied us so richly in this dimension, we will not be deserted in the next as we continue on! Jesus said he was going "to prepare a place for us" in the next experience in living. That higher consciousness within each of us has what it takes. At that time he said we, as humanity, weren't prepared to follow him, but we would eventually be, if we believed in and practiced the things he told us about it. The Apostle Paul took it a little further when he said, 'Grow up into the head of Christ.'

"Strange, but maybe the easiest place to start making these decisions is with what we don't want in the next dimension. We usually know better what we don't want in our lives than what we do want! I have thought of paper work, credit cards, pollution, starvation, isolation, hatred, sickness, poverty and stupidity, for openers! When we look at our "don't wants," we can perhaps turn to the flip side of them for a clue. Intelligence, abundance, clarity, fulfillment, health...it works both ways. We can begin to put our ideals into spiritual terms.

"This is why I have always been a Star Trek fan. That advanced thinking put us well along the road to thinking beyond our present realities. We have the equivalent of the silver screen in our minds, and a projector, a faculty called imagination. We can project new images upon the screen of our minds, leaving out what we don't want, and freeing ourselves to progress in what we do want and beyond.

1. How will you enter the new realm?

I think I would like to ascend in consciousness to where I can have a transformed body of light rather than be born an infant and take thirty years to mature. Since the Book of Corinthians says we are transformed from glory into glory, or dimension to dimension, I see myself becoming lighter, brighter, and able to shift my vibrational level at will. I will appear and disappear instead of being born and dying!

2. How will you communicate?

I can see us as beings who merge thinking patterns and who co-create new patterns together. There need be no secrets because we have ascended out of the need for pain and darkness. We have ascended into the realm of love and acceptance, and readily lavish it upon each other.

We will share ideas instead of opinions. If there are struggles, it will be to see the greater and greater picture. We will be to open to greater and greater wisdom. Each struggle culminates in success. Breakthroughs will dawn simultaneously upon the thought patterns of everyone who is ready.

3. What about having children?

We will co-create a divine child the same way we bring forth any other Divine Idea. We will create a beautiful place for another soul to inhabit, give it the best that we are and have. We will love and nurture it carefully through each stage of its development. We will be honored to care for a godling emerging into our midst.

4. What about sex?

Rather than procreation, two souls choose to continue to co-create together, continuing to weave their ideas together in ever more wonderful patterns.

5. What about government?

As ascended beings, we are individually and wholly responsible for the expression of Spiritual Principle as our governing force. When one completely governs from the Christ Principle within, everything works out harmoniously for the highest good of all. Other than the perfect governing principle of spirit, what else would we need except perhaps a melody or melodies that we could all soul-sing together.

6. What about God?

God is, always has been, and always will be the First Cause, Creative Principle. God is the Grand Impersonal made personal through us.

"Here we get into what we have called the abstract. In the present dimension we have wanted everything to be concrete, in form, dense, touchable, inert and solid. This illusion makes us feel comfortable and safe in our three-dimensional world and thinking.

"Eventually, we find ourselves no longer satisfied by this illusion and look for something with more potential. We look for a way out of limitation and a way to advance somehow. There was a salamander on the window ledge of my mother's car. I tried to shoo it off, but it kept running toward the mirror mounted on the door. Over and over it ran into the mirror, the illusion of freedom, only to be thwarted again and again. Finally, I placed a book I was carrying in front of the mirror, and the salamander scampered down the door to freedom!

"In our fourth dimensional way of being, we no longer hide in the illusion of form, but discover our safety in the unformed. The absolute. The invisible.

"In the past we have created God in our human image and likeness. We gave God gender, voice, emotion, opinion, victory, rage, vengeance, jealousy, and parenthood. Now we must recreate God as our self-image changes and the Christ emerges. Seeing the invisible at last, the Christ Pattern as our reality, we know the body, intellect and emotions as a temporary vehicle. We more easily conceptualize the invisible God, the Principle, the First Cause. The abstract is no longer remote, but a very intimate and real-life force within us as us. We know where home is and now we know the way home!

"We innately know where home is because God is always within us. There is a still small 'voice' that speaks to us continually and we must remember how to listen. It is often referred to as following our bliss. Bliss is a little explosion of joy, like silent fireworks in the night sky. It happens when we are totally on track. It is usually a split second happening because our intellect quickly takes hold and classifies it as an emotional experience or fantasy of not much value.

"We are beginning to discover the difference between feeling and emotion. The feeling nature draws our attention toward the invisible, the eternal. Emotion draws us toward the physical and quickly burns us out. The "voice" of God is a feeling, an intuition, a shift, an expansion, an empowerment, a lifting! The feeling nature is a spiritual receiver. Emotion is a physical experience.

"In the garden Easter morning, Jesus said to Mary Magdalene, 'Why do you weep?' In other words, why are you having a physical experience instead of a spiritual one? I have taught you to be a healer, teacher, transformer, and when I reveal to you the greatest achievement of all, you drop back into the physical/emotional state! 'Go, find the disciples and tell them I have risen!' Go to all the faculties within you and tell them you are now a new being in Christ.

"And so, dear friend, we launch ourselves into the next stage of existence. The Book of Revelation called it 'the New Jerusalem.' Jesus called it 'many mansions.' The Book of Corinthians calls it 'changing from glory into glory.' Language as we know it is limited in its ability to express the higher experiences. We try to put divine revelation into words and explanations that always sound a little crazy. But keep talking! A new language is already emerging. We are creating the words, the mental technology, and the spiritual super highway that carries us inward and upward.

"God ideated creation and man is the man-ifestor of God in form. Man is the chooser, spearhead, and co-creative partner with God. Man, in Sanskrit, means hand. We are the hand of God stretching forth through eternity into creation so that God can experience as well as Be."

The room got quiet as Karla reached for her headset and dialed the phone. "Show time, Beck."

Becky picked up her headset and joined her. "Show time, Karla!"

"Welcome to our program, friends. As the Vision Continues we want to take you into living in the fourth dimension, a spiritual credo and devotional experience.

"Tonight, we are introducing a colleague who sees into the other dimension that we all have been seeking. Her path has amazing parallels to ours and she helps us take the steps, opening the windows to the beyond. Here is Rev. Jeanette Herrington on the air with us from San Francisco, California, to share her discoveries. Welcome Jeanette!"

"Thank you, Karla and Becky. It is a joy to be with you!

"We are eager to hear your story!" Becky had her note pad and pen ready.

"It began long before I was aware. A friend introduced me to spiritual teachings years ago, and declared that she would never try to live them. She only liked to read and argue about them. In my ministerial training I was curious that many people read the books about the Spiritual Truth Principles, but did not comprehend that they needed to live them. To me the teachings are a precious roadmap to learn how to live the spiritual life.

"I read books and more books about it. There were books in my kitchen, my living room, the bathroom, the car, and my place of work. Truly a wonderland was opening to me that I was thrilled to explore.

"In the three-dimensional or physical level, being the victim of life meant battling through circumstances with wit, resources and fortitude. I was a single mother, holding down two or three jobs, raising two sons, finishing my college degrees, and deciding upon a career. The question kept coming to me, 'Is this all there is?'"

Karla was on the edge of her seat. "How did you answer that question? How can people stop being victims of circumstance? What do you think causes the change to something else?"

"That something else is to see yourself as the hero of your life. It was a sudden realization! Lights coming on! A teacher said we are not born to be the victim of life but the hero of our lives. It was the first time I ever heard that! My thinking flipped over like a pancake! I began to see myself as a hero and everything changed."

Becky looked up from her notes. "I saw that change in myself and it happened just as you said. The lights kept coming on, and each time I took another step in my spiritual understanding."

"Right, Becky. You see, that is a spiritual truth that already lives within us and when we discover it, it takes on a life of its own like a yeast leavening everything. While in my ministerial training I expressed a frustration to a teacher that more people didn't discover this and begin to live it. He said, 'You have to realize that most people live in the third dimension and touch the fourth occasionally. You live in the fourth dimension most of the time and touch the third occasionally.'"

"Did you not know this about yourself?" Karla was engrossed.

"No, not really. He saw in me what I did not see or even understand at that time. I was humbled. I did not know how this happened or when. Now that I look back upon my journey there were many guides such as this person who pointed out that I was on a path and I did not yet realize the true nature of it."

Becky mused, "I have often wondered how people see us as we stand in front of a classroom or seminar. What are they seeing? How many of me are standing there? Probably as many as there are people attending."

Karla was jolted when the phone light flickered. "Hello caller! Welcome! What is your question or comment?"

"I have been listening to this program for a long time. I guess my question is 'When do we get there?' It seems to be a long path and some folks might give up. We are a generation of instant gratification. We want to see results!"

"Great question! Jeanette?"

"When I began to realize what this path was about, really see it unfolding, it sped along taking me with it. Time is a human construct. It is how we measure our life experiences. If we are bored it seems to stretch out, and when we are excited it flies by. It is three-dimensional. But in God or Spirit, there is no time. There is no past, no future, only the now."

"Go ahead, caller."

"But we do have a past and we do plan for the future. The now moment seems so fleeting."

"We are always in the now moment. There is nowhere else we can be. What we call the past is now moments that are gone, and the future does not exist except in our imaginations. The only reality, the only place we can live is in the now moment. Tomorrow is not guaranteed. Only now."

"So, when we live in the past as many people do, or live only for the future, we are missing something."

"Yes, we are missing the only opportunity we have to create, to learn and to grow. To be really alive!"

"But where do I start?"

"Where are you right now? What is around you? What are your thoughts just now? Meditate on these things. Take some time each day to do this and you will find that you focus on what is now more and more. It becomes your way of being with no effort."

"Thank you, Jeanette, Becky, and callers. That is all for today. Tune in again when Rev. Jeanette will share more fascinating discoveries with us! Good night from me, Karla, from Becky and the Vision Continues!"

Twenty-Two

Becky and Karla moved their broadcast to the local radio station where the advancing technology and availability of new equipment would better support their efforts. Jeanette had come in from San Francisco to stay at Becky's so they could coordinate the material and plan the direction of the broadcast. They took Jeanette to the Patrician Grille for dinner. Karla was eager to continue. "Please, tell me about your steps from being a clerical worker to entering the spiritual life."

"The clerical worker time in my life was the dark ages. I knew nothing about any other options. After exposure to people with troubles and my own as well, I learned more about it and wanted to help people. I decided that I wanted to be a counselor and I counseled for a few semesters at the university I attended. I had begun to study spirituality, but in that setting I couldn't talk to clients about their spirituality. I had to be free to share the spiritual Truth with those who asked for help and guidance."

Karla was thinking about their next program. "I think folks would like to know what kept driving you onward. Perhaps they have that same urge and don't know what it is about."

"I became an ordained minister and was called to my first church. I still had one foot in the psychological world I was graduating from and the other foot on the spiritual path I was trying to follow."

Their food orders arrived and the fragrances reminded them how hungry they were. The conversation was momentarily suspended as they dug into their dinners, but not for long.

"Trying to follow? Were there challenges that kept you back?"

Jeanette took a deep breath. "The mistakes I made were the result of not staying on the spiritual path. There were wonderful Alcoholics Anonymous people in that first church. They were struggling to follow the spiritual path set out by AA because their very lives depended upon it. They lifted me up when I stumbled, dusted me off, and set my feet back upon the path. I don't know what I would have done without them and all they taught me about their twelve steps.

Approaching the table the waiter heard the mention of AA. "AA saved my life," she offered.

Becky smiled and asked her more about it while the dishes and drinks were placed on the table.

"Excuse me, I didn't mean to eaves drop or interrupt. The last step is for us to go forth and share it with others. It keeps us on the path so we don't backslide. Will there be anything else?"

"We are good for now," answered Karla for all three of them. "Thanks for your input. We appreciate it."

"Please continue, Jeanette," begged Becky as she reached for her glass of wine.

"After seven years I went to a second church. There were a lot of angry dysfunctional folks there who prided themselves in giving their minister a really difficult time with constant criticism and backbiting. For everything they did, I simply taught Principle as it applied without naming their actions. I soon began to realize that standing on Principle was keeping me safe. In Psalm 91 it says, 'A thousand may fall at your side, ten thousand at your right hand; but it shall not come near you.' I found it easy to rise above their angers and fears, and did not return their attacks. I was truly claiming the fourth dimension of living as my own, and feeling such relief!"

They ate in silence for a while, each one savoring what they had heard.

Steven and Loren were busy creating their nest as they liked to refer to it. Becky, Georgina, Karla and anyone else who arrived were conscripted into moving boxes, furniture, putting hanging lamps together, painting and sweeping out sawdust. Packages were delivered daily and left by their mailboxes. Georgina couldn't wait to see what was in them. She was "ooing and aahing" over the decorative items.

All was fitting in beautifully except the pool table. "We may have to build a separate room for it. We can't just plunk it into the middle of the room like the proverbial elephant." Loren was sure they didn't really need a pool table, but here it was.

"Well, I was a fairly good player in college and thought it would be relaxing and maybe I could even improve my game with practice. Maybe you could learn to play too!"

Loren shook his head. "Maybe."

Georgina sat down with Becky on their deck for a late evening glass of wine. "I have something to share with you," Georgina began.

"Great! What?"

"While I have been at the University I met a classmate from the past, Anthony. We have been working together on music and lyrics, and we are maybe even falling in love."

"Lovely! Is this sudden?"

"Well, yes and no. We dated in college, but he went to Europe and I went to work here. We lost touch for a long time. It has been wonderful to have someone working with me on my production, someone like you who really cares."

"Interesting! Will we be meeting him…eventually?"

"He keeps the ball rolling at the conservatory when I am here, and I don't know how things will eventually play out. It is just nice to have him there being supportive, interested in my work, and even caring about me."

"You know, I'm here for you always. I am looking forward to updates! You deserve lots of love in your life, Georgi. We have soloed together for a long time."

"Oh, I plan to continue to do that. I'm not taking any eggs out of this basket! I just wanted to tell you."

"We've shared everything all these years and it is the best part of our relationship. We would not have gotten this far without supporting each other through everything. May it continue!"

The radio program grew in listeners and callers. Karla was glad they moved the program into the station, rather than calling in from home. The station put on a few more staff people to increase the efficiency of handling all the demands. Becky asked Sandy to join them to keep their notes and information in order. Sandy was thrilled.

"Thank you! I am so delighted to help. I have never been in a radio station before. Tell me what you need and I will bring supplies, office folders and such. I don't have to talk, do I?"

Becky laughed. "No, you don't need to talk on the radio. Here is a short list of what I think you will need, and there is a small room adjacent to the broadcasting room that you can use, where you can hear and see everything."

When Becky and Jeanette arrived at the station, Karla and Sandy were already making sure everything was in place.

The station manager handed Becky a folder. "What is this?"

"It is a list of questions that people send in. Some call the station and leave them on the answering machine. I don't know how you want to handle this…"

Sandy slipped in beside Becky and reached for the folder. "Thanks. I will categorize them while Karla decides what to do with them. We want to include everybody who is interested and we'll find a way to respond."

Becky's eyebrows went up. What a nice surprise to see Sandy confidently picking the responsibility right away! "Thanks for running with the ball, Sandy! We can't respond to all of them on the air, but we can create a way to include them."

Jeanette sat down at the microphone with Becky and Karla, arranging a few notes in front of her.

"One minute to air time." Karla potted up the mics, checked the levels, and got ready to hit the "on the air" button.

"Good evening listeners! This is another segment in the presentations by Rev. Jeanette Herrington. What do you have for us this evening, Jeanette?"

"Good evening! Happy to be here again! Pierre Teilhard de Chardin wrote that we rise out of the two-dimensional state by crossing the line of complexity consciousness. This is the step into the three-dimensional consciousness. That is the point where humanity is aware of itself and its surroundings as being separate from itself.

"Ideas start forming in the mind and humanity begins to think of ways to improve its conditions, such as tools, housing instead of caves, stored food and a variety of clothing. This frees the intellect to develop higher skills such as the desire for education and perhaps eventually contemplating the meaning of life."

"Where is God in this, Jeanette? Wasn't there some kind of god worshipped in the earliest of times?"

"Yes. People made gods of what they feared such as the thunder, volcanos, and other threatening things they didn't understand. They developed worship rituals that they hoped would appease the gods.

"Teilhard wrote that the Alpha, the beginning was our biology pushing us forward physically. The Omega, that which we would call God, was beckoning us upward. We were beckoned by the creator to continue developing upward consciously, spiritually, in a very fast rise. He draws physical development as a horizontal line until humanity crosses into complexity consciousness, and then the developmental line curves sharply upward."

"Are we speaking of the upward curve as an entry into fourth dimensional living?"

"Yes, definitely. But the fourth dimension is our choice, different from the biological level where development is physical evolution. Many may choose not to advance spiritually, like the Apostle Paul who fell off his horse on the road to Damascus. He was going to persecute the followers of Jesus, and encountered a spiritual vision of Jesus saying, 'Saul, Saul, why do you persecute me?' Then he was physically blinded, and his sight was restored when a follower came to him and opened his inner sight."

"Hello, caller. Go ahead."

"Who is this Pierre somebody? What is the name of his book?"

"Thanks for asking. His book is entitled *The Phenomenon of Man*. It is still in print and is very popular. He was a Jesuit Father and a noted paleontologist. He was interested in the synthesis of the material/physical with the world of mind and spirit. It is quite scientific.

"I became aware that spiritual teachings had to be lifted to higher practice. This was my next adventure in understanding fourth dimensional living. There are many tools available but some of them are merely gimmicks, taught in classes and seminars to people who wish to improve their lives and circumstances, but not spiritually based. They are mostly third-dimensional efforts that eventually bore and exhaust the intellectual mind. People soon give them up."

Yes, caller?"

Hi, Jane here. I have been in those seminars. I thought they were pretty helpful. Are you saying they aren't?"

"Thanks for the chance to clarify this, Jane. They are really good for getting a handle on your personal life and making it better, and they are the stepping stones needed as you move into spiritual work. When they have accomplished their purpose, the mind asks for something more. That something more is spirituality."

"Thank you, too. I have a pretty good handle on my life now that I have done all their recommended work. My relationships are good and my sense of self-esteem is in place. I have been wondering what comes next. Now I understand how this fits together. Do you have classes or groups that I can attend?"

"Yes, Jane. We will put Sandy on the line with you off the air and she can tell you more about them."

Karla switched off all the microphones except hers. "Thanks folks! We'll be back next week! Join us then and be blessed! Good night."

The Patrician Grille was busier than usual, but Becky found their usual booth. It was just vacated and the waiter was clearing the dishes and wiping the table. He smiled when he saw her with Karla and Jeanette.

"We have a terrific special called the Fourth Dimension Sensation!"

"Really? What is in it?"

"Just kidding. It is your usual. I was listening to the program in the kitchen."

They all laughed and the waiter invited them to sit down. "Is there somewhere I can learn more about this?"

Karla took a menu from him. "Yes, there is! Give me your phone number and I will have Sandy, our administrator, call you with information."

"Is that Sandy Stratford by chance?"

Becky's eyebrows went up. "Yes!"

"I met her at the office supply store! She was carrying so much stuff and dropped it in the parking lot. I helped her get it into her car and we had coffee together!"

Jeanette began as she sampled her dinner, "I need to go back to San Francisco in a week. We could pose a few more questions and I can leave you with my new meditation devotional booklet."

Becky hesitated a moment. She had not thought of Jeanette leaving, but of course she would have to eventually. "It has been wonderful to have you here and please plan to come back any time!"

"OK, one more program will be great and I am eager to have a look at your devotional booklet!" Karla was taking a few notes for the next week. "What is it called?"

"A Spiritual Credo for Living in the Fourth Dimension."

Twenty-Three

"Hello Callers! Becky and I are back with the last segment of the interview with Rev. Jeanette Herrington. We have been talking about the Fourth Dimension as our next step in living our spiritual growth. Jeanette?"

"Hello everyone! It has been a wonderful journey with you these last several weeks. I will be returning to San Francisco to continue my work there. The question I want to address this evening is 'How do I do this? How do we step into this wonderful spiritual path and continue upward?'

"The key is that we don't do it. We open in mind and heart to recognize our Original Nature and Truth comes forth from within. In the physical world the wisdom is, the harder we work the more we will accomplish. The opposite is true in the spiritual world. In the Fourth Dimension we travel through this Higher Mind, God Mind, where there are no physical dimensions, no distances, to discover the ideas that are pathways to the nature of the Fourth Dimension and of Pure Being.

"Elizabeth Barrett Browning, in Sonnets from the Portuguese, wrote the famous poem that starts 'How do I love thee? Let me count the ways. I love thee to the depth, breadth, and height my soul can reach when feeling out of sight for ends of Being and Ideal Grace.' ... feeling out of sight for ends of Being and Ideal Grace caught my attention years ago. She was reaching into the fourth dimension in her mind with a sense of eternal love."

"Hello Caller. Go ahead. What is your question or comment?"

"Hi! How can we live with no physical dimensions? I can't even imagine it!"

"Thank you, caller. You are so right that we cannot imagine it. We are always using the earthly mind that cannot go beyond the physical world. We have believed that the only mind we have is the physical/ego mind. But we have a much greater capacity than we have previously thought.

"We have the Christ mind, access to God mind. Jesus, who is called the Christ, said, 'I am in the Father, you are in me, and I am in you.' He was always interfaced with God Mind and indicated that we should be too. The Apostle Paul is quoted to say, 'Christ in you, your hope of Glory…we are to grow up into the head of Christ.' These are indications that we have a much greater conscious capacity."

"Go ahead caller." Becky was leaning into her microphone with intense interest.

"OK, if we expand into this Christ Mind, what impact does it have on the earthly plane? What can we do with it?"

"Our greatest example today is the Dalai Lama who knows no fear, only love, joy and peace. In living in this fourth dimension he has terrified the entire Chinese government. They want to control or eliminate him. But how do you control someone who has no fear? How do you instill hate for someone who has only love? How to you squelch joy and peace with the powerlessness of darkness? You can light one small candle and no matter how large the room of darkness, it cannot put out the light. The light always puts out darkness. We have to trust that the influence is not us at the human level, but the power of Christ Mind coming through us, but as us, that does the work."

"This is big! Really big! Wow, I can hardly get my mind around it, but I am determined to try! Thanks for all the inspiration tonight, Rev. Herrington!"

"Thank you, caller! As we bring this program to a close, I want to thank Jeanette, Becky and all our callers for a fascinating and exciting experience. Jeanette is leaving with us her devotional booklet which will be available through the station for $10 per copy. Call in on our secure line to give Sandy your name, address, and credit card number, and a copy will be mailed to you. Good night, and blessings to you all." Karla switched off the microphones, heaved a sigh, and reached for a bottle of water.

Back at Becky's place Steven, Loren, Sandy, Georgina, and Karla gathered to set up the shelves for the boxes of booklets along with their seminar brochures, and correspondence. Sandy was cataloging everything, numbering shelves and boxes.

Becky and Georgina were asked by the college to come back to teach some classes on their material to their students. Georgina poured some wine into several glasses. "You know, Beck, we have been on a whirlwind for years now and it feels kind of good to go back into the college atmosphere and connect with our beginnings again."

"I think you are right, even if it is just for a little while. Our offices are still there, and the mess we left them in. But I am sure we will have a different experience because we are different."

"Now that the internet is growing and becoming a great information and communication tool, maybe we can create a website. Maybe we can be in touch with Chaim again."

"Maybe my musical will even be on it! I am told the possibilities are endless!"

"Now about those booklets...let's read through one..."

THE DEVOTIONAL

A SPIRITUAL CREDO

FOR MEDITATION ON LIVING IN THE FOURTH DIMENSION

YOU ARE ENTERING THROUGH THE GATE TO THE SACRED PLACE.

YOU MUST ANSWER THE SACRED QUESTION TO BE ADMITTED. BE HUMBLE AND BE NOT AFRAID.

PSALM 15

"WHO SHALL BE WORTHY TO ENTER INTO THIS SACRED PLACE?

HE WHO WALKS BLAMELESSLY AND DOES WHAT IS RIGHT,

AND SPEAKS TRUTH FROM THE HEART..."

Open the Gates to the Holy Place

Question: *Who shall be worthy to journey into this Holiness?*

Answer: *One who seeks higher understanding. In quiet blessing I wait.*

Welcome to the Gateway of the Breath of God

"God caused a wind to pass over the earth...God formed man from the dust from the ground and breathed into his nostrils the breath of life; and man became a living being." (Genesis 2:7) The word breath is from the root word "bheu" meaning to be, to exist and the future form, that is to be.

The eternal breath of life is the Holy Spirit in which we move and have our being. To breathe is movement, to be alive. Breath is that without which we cannot live in the physical more than a few minutes. It is the only constant intake the body does on its own. We must act to eat and drink, but the body continually breathes in and out, awake and asleep, and whether or not we are aware of it. The breath of God in-flowing through you is the mover. The breath of God moves into your silence and out into expression as your life. It is your choice to entreat the Divine or block it out, but not whether it exists. It is there awaiting the open door of your consciousness.

God-breathed, referring to the *divine inspiration (inbreathing)* of Scripture as written in Second Timothy 3:16, indicates Divine origin. Through the invitation of human consciousness, the Divine was inbreathed into Scripture to inspire what is written. The Divine is that which is not manifest. Nothing happens in the physical world except from the inbreathing of the Divine into human consciousness and then into the manifest form as man understands and decrees it.

From the Gospel of Thomas, Saying 50, "Jesus said, if they say to you, 'Where do you come from?' Say to them, 'We have come from the light, from the place where light came into being by itself, established itself and appeared in their image.' If they say to you, 'Is it you?' say, 'We are its children and we are the chosen of the living Father.' If they ask you, 'What is the evidence of your father in you?' say to them, 'It is motion and rest.'"

We breathe in the Divine and breathe out the Divine into manifestation. We are the inlet and the outlet of God. We breathe in the inspiration of God and breathe it out into expression as we in the form that we choose. Humanity is the chooser of what the form will be.

"The sun is the outer self, the inner Self is Breath. Hence the motion of the inner Self is inferred from the motion of the outer self...Breath is the life of all beings." (from Upanishad vi.1)

In Ecclesiastes 3:14 "...whatever God does endures forever; nothing can be added to it, nor anything taken from it...that which is, already has been; that which is to be, already has been..." The Absolute, the single dimension that has no width, breadth, height nor depth, simply Is. It is not easy for the limited human mind, which is our mental instrument that carries us through the physical existence, to even begin to comprehend eternity. The fish does not comprehend the ocean, but lives in it.

"Peace be with you. As the Father has sent me, even so I send you. And when he had said this, he breathed on them, and said to them, 'Receive the Holy Spirit." (John 20:21)

How shall we live in this dimension?

The disciples went out to do the work that Jesus did on the physical plane. Each one of them was martyred or murdered, according to information found in Catholic research. Does this mean we will also meet the same violent fate? Life on planet earth is subject to many physical challenges. Everything in physical form is subject to entropy or death in some manner. We do not live eternally on the physical plane. We live eternally in Spirit.

Jesus moved through dimensions at will. He eluded the grasps of a mob trying to kill him, seeking to throw him from a cliff. He turned and went away among them. In changing his vibrational level he became invisible to them. He showed up in a physical form on the road to Emmaus and on the shore of the sea of Galilee. He said that he was from above. He was living in what we call the fourth dimension and seemingly was free of the limitations of earthly life.

In the fourth dimension we live in the spiritual realm, not subject to death. Our concern is not how we will physically die, but how we will spiritually live. We move through dimensions of thought by teaching our own consciousness spiritual Truth. We rise and open to the Breath of the Divine. The apostle Paul called it building the spiritual body for our eternal ongoing. We rise and move on the breath of God.

Open the Gates to the Holy Place

Question: *Who shall be worthy to journey into this Holiness?*

Answer: *One who hears the Celestial Music*

Welcome to the Gateway Celestial Music

The beginning of music was a simple one-line melody. The earliest fragment of written music found in the Greek theater is written as only melody, with no harmony or chords. It may have been written by one who heard celestial music as an inner urging and brought it down into a written music score.

From Wikipedia, "The Seikilos epitaph is the oldest surviving complete musical composition, including musical notation, from anywhere in the world. The epitaph has been dated variously from around 200 BC to around AD 100, but the first century AD is the most probable guess. The song, the melody of which is recorded, alongside its lyrics, in the ancient Greek musical notation, was found engraved on a tombstone (a stele) from the Hellenistic town Tralles near Aydin, Turkey, not far from Ephesus. The Seikilos epitaph melody is the earliest musical notation found in a tomb. Translated into modern musical notation, the tune is something like this:"

The orient heard music in quarter tones. European composers heard it in whole and half tones such as we find in the piano-forte octave.

Celestial music is described as "A perfectly harmonious music thought by Pythagoras and later classical and medieval philosophers to be produced by the movement of celestial bodies but to be inaudible on the earth. The quality of life on Earth reflects the tenor of celestial sounds which are physically imperceptible to the human ear.

"The Music of the Spheres incorporates the metaphysical principle that mathematical relationships express qualities or 'tones' of energy which manifest in numbers, visual angles, shapes and sounds – all connected within a pattern of proportion. Pythagoras first identified that the pitch of a musical note is in proportion to the length of the string that produces it, and that intervals between harmonious sound frequencies form simple numerical ratios. In a theory known as the Harmony of the Spheres, Pythagoras proposed that the Sun, Moon and planets all emit their own unique hum (orbital resonance) based on their orbital revolution." *Excerpted from Wikipedia*

The sound of the earth according to eastern understanding is "OM." It is chanted by many monks and heard in powerful resonating tones in eastern monasteries.

How shall we live in this dimension?

This celestial music is within us and all around us. We may be able to sense it as a low resonating tone, feel it as a vibration or other "sound" by deep quiet silent listening within. We do not struggle to hear it with the physical sense of hearing. It is a huge vibration of the lowest tone as to underscore all creation.

Open the Gates to the Holy Place

Question: *Who shall be worthy to journey into this Holiness?*

Answer: *One who sees and delights in joy.*

Welcome to the Gateway to Cosmic Joy!

Metaphysical Bible interpretation is the training manual for spiritually interpreting your own life. That is its purpose. Just as we see more deeply into the messages given by the events in the Bible, we see more deeply into our own lives. Rather than interpreting an outer event, we look inward to see what was going on in our minds at that moment. Outer events are the evidence of a spent force. The force is within us and we will be the instant, conscious creator of our lives when we immediately see and direct the force before and behind the appearances.

Cosmic Joy is a constant state of delight that blesses all events in our lives. We cannot always control outer events or prevent them, but we can look upon them with delight that they can be transformed. A painful event can be transformed to blessing, and a happy event can be lifted to be part of our spiritual or eternal body.

We can see down a bumpy road one bump at a time, or we can rise higher and see the whole highway of life without bumps and blocks. The bumps you learn from are already in the past. What lies ahead is an open road and we are the conscious vehicle of God. The cosmic creator we call God rolled out the whole creation in a cosmic instant perfect and complete. We are that perfect and complete creation manifesting now.

This is not easy to discern with the limited human mind in a time-space world. Just knowing that we are spiritual beings, living in a spiritual realm and simply looking upon the time-space world is the open door to the cosmic. A Course in Miracles says that God takes that step for us when we are ready. Until then let joy fill your days as you enjoy your life travels on all levels. In John 15:11, Jesus said, "These things I have spoken to you, that my joy may be in you, and that your joy may be full."

How shall we live in this dimension?

We shall ask to understand and experience joy throughout our whole being, to permeate our minds and hearts. To ask is to claim the joy which is already ours, awaiting our recognition of it. No longer do we allow negative thoughts and feelings to dominate our experience of life and being. Through joy we reach the Christos, the clear Christ pattern of our being that has no shadow, but only light.

Open the Gates to the Holy Place

Question: *Who shall be worthy to journey into this Holiness?*

Answer: *One who seeks their spiritual path. I am open to this blessing that awaits me. I step into it in peace and love.*

Welcome to the Gateway to Creating Our Perceptual World

What is our perceptual world? What is it for?

We live in a physical world where what we physically see is what we believe our actual reality to be. How we choose to see it creates our perceptual world. Everyone has an individual perceptual world. Just as no one reports the same details when witnessing an accident, no one sees the same world as anyone else.

Individual perceptions create our experiences from our thoughts and feelings about them. Those thoughts and feelings live in our memories in subconscious mind and color everything we see. It is the condition of living a physical lifetime, that we can never live outside our own perceptions. I cannot see you as someone else does. They cannot see you as I do, even though we agree upon certain aspects such as color, size, shape, and sound.

This is the understanding that A Course in Miracles expresses when it says, "there is no one out there." Of course there are people around us, but our individual perception of them is ours alone. In that sense there is no one out there as we perceive them, even though they are physically there.

We have command of our personal world because we can change how we see it. We can create a happy world full of joy and peace. Or we can create one of pain and unhappiness. Many people do not realize they have this choice. They believe that what they physically see is the only reality, so they can only judge according to the physical mind. They are not aware that they can change their experience of an event without the event itself changing.

Until we leave this physical world our job is to make our experiences as wonderful as we can. The Christ consciousness, true happiness, is the highest spirituality we can attain. The Apostle Paul said, "I strive toward the upward call of God in Christ Jesus." (Philippians 4:13)

How shall we live in this dimension?

We shall remember who we are as spiritual beings. We shall store up reminders in our consciousness that spring forth when we momentarily forget. We shall create our perceptions through spiritual eyes or spiritual mind. We shall remember that perceptions are only images on the screen of human mind. We will not live from lower human ego mind trying to look up to discern Higher Mind. We will live from Higher Mind looking upon our world, but not identifying it as ourselves. We shall choose images of beauty, and choose the perceptions that make us happy, joyful and at peace.

What shall be the purpose?

Our purpose is to co-create with God, as God, as us. We are here in the physical world, born into a physical body, knowing nothing about the world. We grow through physical and psychological stages into adulthood where we become ready to be admitted to planet earth school. Our classrooms are perceptions that we choose to conjure up as the physical world impacts our bodies and minds. Our thoughts create physical forms to fulfill our physical needs. More importantly we begin to create the spiritual body that will be our eternal vehicle.

Open the Gates to the Holy Place

Question: *Who shall be worthy to journey into this Holiness?*

Answer: *One who sees the Divine pattern.*

Welcome to the Gateway of the Divine Pattern

In 1970 I read something by Ernest Holmes, founder of Science of Mind, where he said that someday we would be thinking in patterns. I could find nothing more in his writings about that, but the idea stuck in my mind. Now entering the spiritual realm, we become able to see larger and larger patterns and dimensions of the Creator.

"In the field of economics, Kondratiev waves are proposed cycle-like phenomena in the modern world ... The Soviet economist Nikolai Kondratiev was the first to bring these observations to international attention." (Wikipedia)

Kondratieff discovered the 80-year wave pattern of human conscious existence, the pattern of the ups and downs of the economies, wars, and general living. Popular wars, those easily financed, occurred at the top of the wave and unpopular wars occurred at the bottom of the economic wave. In his time this pattern was not previously discovered because the life span of humanity was approximately fifty years, and the wave would not complete itself in one person's lifetime. Everything is subject to this wave including churches and businesses.

Communism believes that we are all different and must be herded together and formed into one identical unit, everyone being the same. A Russian friend said, "Yes, we have it upside down!" We are all diverse, each unique, but one and identical in spirit. We come from the One, flung out into diverse as unique expressions, and we return to the One from which we were never truly separated.

It took many centuries on the earth for early scientists to discover that our earth traveled in an orbit around the sun. Orbits were circling patterns created by the pull of gravity from a celestial body. Centrifugal and centripetal forces, flinging out and drawing in, kept the bodies moving in the curvilinear or orbital pattern.

Patterns in the Fourth Dimension are concerned with that which is not physical, but spiritual. The Apostle Paul saw a pattern beyond the physical, built into the holy writ of humanity. He wrote, "If there is a physical body, then there is a spiritual body." (1 Corinthians 15:44)

It is often pictured by some that everything emanates from the physical body, which creates the emotional body, then the psychic body, etc. But these patterns are like prisms, all coming from and pointing to the Center, also referred to as the Still Point. God is the Still Point and we are flung out from and revolve around the still point. The whirling dervishes whirl their bodies while keeping their minds on the Still Point. This center point does not turn, only the outer turns.

Another pattern is a spiral. It is thought that as we rise in consciousness we move upward in a spiral that returns us to the same experiences in each round, but at a higher level of understanding upon each return.

How shall we live in this dimension?

We shall maintain the understanding that the physical world is not the beginning of understanding but the mirror of our growing consciousness. The physical world is created from human thoughts and ideas, and is the spent force of an idea that was expressed and has died. Everything in form is subject to entropy. Everything in physical form is decaying and eventually returns to its atomic stage.

We look beyond this decaying physical expression to the spiritual source which does not decay or die. We see beyond the patterns of physical existence to the creative force of Spirit. We function in our lives according to the creative force as co-creators with Spirit. We are co-creators with God, as God, as us.

Open the Gates to the Holy Place

Question: *Who shall be worthy to journey into this Holiness?*

Answer: *One who sees only the spiritual universe in all things. I enter seeking light.*

Welcome to the Gateway of Being Drawn to the Light

We are drawn irresistibly into the Light, the Omega. From infancy on we are drawn to the Light and miss it when it is absent from our world. A child will ask for a light to be on in the bedroom at night. There is an innate fear of the dark and what it might contain. Folks spend a lot of money on outdoor lights to light up the night and to create a modicum of safety around their homes. We love bonfires, campfires, and fire places. They are thought of as providing peace of mind, warmth and friendship. We feel safe in the light.

In mythology, the god Prometheus brought fire to humanity so that it might have heat and light. Without light there could be no life. The Pharaoh Akhenaten believed in one god and he thought that god was the sun disk. He called the god Aten.

Nona Brooks was the founder of Divine Science. She and her sister were quite ill and decided to attend a class given by a spiritual teacher. The teacher taught about light in each class. Nona decided to begin meditations on light to see what would happen. Her mind would eventually fill with light until it seemed that the whole room was full of light as well. When she felt "a sufficiency of light" she knew the healing had taken place. Her prayer work for others was always about a sufficiency of light.

Hebrew Testament Exodus 34:30, and 2 Corinthians 3:7b "the Israelites could not look at Moses' face because of its brightness…" Moses spent much time on the mountain with God and did not cover his face, but he wore a veil over his face when speaking to the people because they were frightened of the light.

From the Gospel of Thomas, Saying 50, "Jesus said, if they say to you, 'Where do you come from?' Say to them, 'We have come from the light, from the place where light came into being by itself, established itself and appeared in their image.' If they say to you, 'Is it you?' say, 'We are its children and we are the chosen of the living Father.' If they ask you, 'What is the evidence of your father in you?' say to them, 'It is motion and rest.'"

Definitions of glory from the Dictionary of all Scriptures and Myths, Gaskill; "The Divine sacerdotal and kingly glory which proceeds from the Absolute…The Divine Ray of consciousness and life…"

"Glorifying of God – the perfecting of the soul, which then returns to the Absolute…the purpose of Self-expression, which being completed, corresponds to the Glorifying of God."

In John Chapter 17 is the glorification prayer by Jesus. In Chapter 17:5 "And now, Father, glorify thou me in thy own presence with the glory which I had with three before the world was made."

Jesus awaits the restoration of his pre-incarnation glory or light.

From an ancient Byzantine Prayer, "Serene Light that shines in the ground of my being, you draw me to yourself…" The references to divine light are everywhere. We come from the light, we live in the light, we are made of light, we are drawn to the light, and we return to the light.

How shall we live in this dimension?

New Testament, 2 Corinthians 3:18, "And we all, with unveiled face, beholding the glory of God are being changed into his likeness from one degree of glory to another, for this comes from the Lord who is the Spirit." How will we change from glory to glory? We shall be changed.

All thoughts of the physical world are shadow, images of our thoughts that stand in the light and create shadow or the illusion of reality. Our reality is the light, not the shadow. We answer the call of beckoning glory as we allow our minds to be drawn to the light. We begin to sense where the light is coming from. It comes from Higher Mind or as in the book of James, the Father of Lights.

James 1:17 "Every good thing given and every perfect gift is from above, coming down from the Father of lights, with whom there is no variation or shifting shadow."

Open the Gates to the Holy Place

Question: *Who shall be worthy to journey into this Holiness?*

Answer: *One who seeks the riches of the spiritual kingdom.*

Welcome to the Gateway of the Atomic Beginning

The Corpus Hypercubus painting by Dali broke out of three dimensions and created an image in a dimension we cannot see….he was able to enter the fourth dimension with the help of astronomers and mystics as well as mathematicians. He believed that geometry, atomism and science could be a route to eternal salvation.

Focusing on the atom, I talk to my body, to my car, to everything in form praising it and giving thanks that all is in perfect order. We understand that Myrtle Fillmore, co-founder of Unity, spoke to her body daily in affirmative terms to heal the error thinking that caused its illness. But why talk to a car and pat it on the hood when I approach it and leave it? When the universe responds to us, it responds at the atomic level. Everything begins at the atomic level and forms are created according to the rate and character of the vibration of the atoms. We determine the rate and character of the vibration by the content of our thinking.

Scientists made the amazing discovery years ago that when viewing a molecular structure directly through a microscope, it changes configuration according to the influence of each person looking at it. When viewed indirectly through a series of mirrors, the structure returns to its original configuration, which then looks the same to all viewers using the mirrors. The difference is in the direct focus of the consciousness and energy system of the viewer.

In other words, we influence the configuration of all we look upon. We influence the atomic level by our predominant thinking. The universe responds to our individual thought patterns and configures Substance to bring us a match of what is in our minds. The universe responds because atoms are made up of God Substance, that which substands or stands under everything in form. The word substance comes from the Latin *substare* which means "to stand under." God is standing under and responds to us according to how we think, not according to "what God thinks we should have," as many believe. We create in our experience the thoughts we hold predominantly in our minds.

The definition of faith is in Hebrews 11:1. "Now faith is the Substance of things hoped for, the evidence of things not seen." This is a truly mystical passage that speaks of evidence or the reality of things not yet seen, God Substance. Verse 3 states, "By faith we understand that the world was created by the Word of God, so that what is seen was made out of things which do not appear."

How shall we live in this dimension?

We don't have to make God alive. We must cause ourselves to live in the awareness of the invisible. We live, move, and have our being within God and God is within us, as us. The key action is to bring Spirit alive in our mental experience and express it in our world every day.

This is simple, but the human mind is full of doubt. We must untangle our doubts and fears from our minds and remove them. Jesus said, "Whosoever...shall not doubt in his heart, but believes that what he says comes to pass, he shall have it." (Mark 11:23) Any doubt will stop its flow into your life.

Open the Gates to the Holy Place

Question: *Who shall be worthy to journey into this Holiness?*

Answer: *One who speaks spiritual Truth to one's own mind.*

Welcome to the Gateway of True Freedom

Freedom from error thinking is to always remember who you are. You are the Christ of God, the only begotten, one with God. Many have found freedom under the direst of circumstances, under repressive governments, prisons and dungeons. They found freedom in the world they created within their own minds. Many are imprisoned by worries and fears, even though they live a prosperous life, free to do whatever they choose. Freedom is determined by the way we think and not by outer circumstances.

The five senses are for living in the physical world. The intellect is always going in circles trying to figure things out according to the information coming from them. We are entangled in the senses of the body and the physical world because we have been taught that they are reality. We live in society of social rules and civil laws. We also live subject to laws of the planet and nature. We need shelter and food, and must find them for ourselves. These are the conditions of living a lifetime on the planet earth. To insure these things are provided, humanity banded together into tribes. The tribes eventually established cities where manufacturing and trade could thrive, and provide for physical needs on a larger scale.

From birth we find ourselves enmeshed into these conditions. Freedom is to know ourselves as spiritual beings having the things of earth, but not being possessed by them. Jesus said, "My kingdom is not of this earth." Our kingdom is not of this earth and as soon as we realize that and reach toward the upward call of God as the Apostle Paul said, we find true freedom in mind and spirit. To evolve we must lift our thoughts to a higher plane, where we meet the true reality of our spiritual nature.

Ephesians 6:16 states, "Having done all just stand. Stand, therefore, having girded your loins with Truth." We free ourselves of all entanglements and stand in joy and contentment. We stop our worries about social interaction, whether we are liked or approved, and no longer struggle for success in the economic world. Struggles and strivings to be loved are based in fear. Letting go of them we discover love and success are already ours. Jesus alluded to this by saying, "Pray believing you have already received." Everything is already ours in Spirit and will come forth to manifest in our experience when we let go of fear.

How shall we live in this dimension?

Living free is realization, making the Truth of our being real in our consciousness, knowing that only God is real and "all else is a lie." We embrace everything with love and spiritual understanding. We look upon all circumstances and events around us from Higher Mind, God Mind, and bless all we see. "God is the Mind with which I think." (A Course in Miracles). Jesus did not use personal mind, but God Mind. He was always interfaced with God, turned Godward in his thinking. We release personal or ego mind, and interface with God, thinking spiritual thoughts and seeing only through the eyes of Spirit. We do not have to struggle to do this. We have only to turn Godward and freedom is ours.

Open the Gates to the Holy Place

Question: *Who shall be worthy to journey into this Holiness?*

Answer: *One who is open to higher realms of being.*

Welcome to the Gateway of Christ

Jesus didn't ask for more. He was more. He was and is all, as are we. We look at our physical surroundings and discern what may be lacking. Then we ask for more to fill in the lack. But the consciousness of lack produces more lack because that is what we are seeing. People have learned to do this because of the words of Jesus where he said "Ask whatsoever you will and your Father will give it to you." (John 16:23)

Living in the three-dimensional consciousness we assume this means ask for material goods, anything in the physical realm including healing of the body. This gives way to the belief that there is some magical prayer formula for getting God to favor us with material things. But when those things don't come, this compounds the error, thinking God must be displeased. There is plenty about God's "displeasure" written in the Bible to support this error thought.

Living in the Fourth Dimension we understand that it means to ask for what is already ours in Spirit to come forth. It means "Give us this day" our spiritual bread, our spiritual understanding. While it is true that we must have physical sustenance living in the physical realm, how we manifest it is through our knowing that all originates in Mind. The ego or temporal mind has the ability to focus upon material things and amass them, but those things are temporary. Those who amass much are always guarding them, keeping possession of them, and worrying that they will be taken away by thieves or economic downturns.

From Matthew 6:29 "Do not lay up for yourselves treasures on earth, where moth and rust consume and where thieves break in and steal, but lay up for yourselves treasures in heaven where neither moth nor rust consumes and where thieves do not break in and steal. For where your treasure is, there will your heart be also."

This is an either/or situation. Treasures in heaven means knowing that God Mind is where everything is in potential. Our heart, the center of our whole being, will be there in the midst of creative potential. When Jesus said he had overcome the world, he meant he had overcome the temptation to make the material world his focus. He knew who he was and that he was One with God, his Father.

In Jesus' culture the son spoke for the father, and Jesus claimed to speak for God as his Father. The people called his words blasphemous and wanted to kill him, because they didn't understand the spiritual realm that Jesus was speaking from in his teachings. This is what he meant when he said, "I am from above, you are from below." I understand from spiritual mind, you understand from human mind.

How shall we live in this dimension?

Fourth-dimensional thinking is from God Mind, three-dimensional thinking is from the ego mind. In God Mind we claim what is already given. The word "ask" means claim, not beg and beseech.

We shall claim spiritualization of understanding, faith, wisdom, love, strength, order, will, purity, zeal, imagination, power, and life. These are the twelve spiritual principalities within us that serve our Christ nature. We contemplate each one of them as we seek to understand their place in our spiritual development.

We understand our spiritual nature in all its aspects as Jesus understood his Christ nature. Jesus claimed the kingdom of God which was already his, and ours. We shall claim it and give thanks for it.

Open the Gates to the Holy Place

Question: *Who shall be worthy to journey into this Holiness?*

Answer: *One who stands in the light of the Ground of Being*

Welcome to the gateway of the Ground of Being

Translation of an ancient Byzantine prayer:
Serene Light that shines in the ground of my being
You draw me to yourself
Past the snares of the senses
Out of the mazes of the mind
I am free of symbols, words
To discern that which is symbolized

"Being is Absolute Existence in its perfect and unqualified state; the essence of existence." American Heritage Dictionary.

Paul Tillich was a German American Christian existentialist philosopher and theologian who is widely regarded as one of the most influential theologians of the twentieth century. He was critical of the view of God as a type of being or presence. He felt that, if God were a being, God could not then properly be called the source of all being (due to the question of what, in turn, created God). As an alternative, he suggested that God be understood as the "Ground of Being-Itself".

Tillich felt that, since one cannot deny that there is being (where we and our world exist), there is therefore a Power of Being. He saw God as the ground upon which all beings exist. As such, God precedes "being itself" and God is manifested in the structure of beings.

Another attempt to explain this is in the term Holy Ground. "Holy Ground is a symbol of the spiritual nature of the soul, which is the foundation of manifest existence." From The Dictionary of all Scriptures and Myths; Gaskell

There is something that sub-stands all creation. Even though we use these terms to attempt to explain it, it is still unknowable by the human mind which is limited by the boundaries of language. We think of it in physical terms as a foundation like a building foundation. Charles Fillmore, co-founder of Unity, speaks of it as the ether. "The spiritual substance in which we live, move, and have our being and out of which can be made whatever we desire…One with spiritual understanding knows that the ether exists as an emanation of Mind…" (meaning God Mind)

How shall we live in this dimension?

We shall live by faith and more than faith, a sense of knowing. This knowing is the mystical connection with the Ground of Being, or God. And we are content with knowing without putting words to how we know or where this knowing comes from. It is inherent within our being.

"…free of symbols, words, to discern that which is symbolized."

Open the Gates to the Holy Place

Question: *Who shall be worthy to journey into this Holiness?*

Answer: *One who is returning to our First Home.*

Welcome to the Gateway of Where Home Is

We innately know where home is because God is always within us. There is a still small voice that speaks to us continually and we must remember how to listen. It is often referred to as following our bliss. Bliss is a little explosion of joy, like silent fireworks in the night sky. It happens when we are totally on track. It is usually a split-second event because our intellect quickly takes hold and classifies it as an emotional experience or fantasy of not much value.

We are beginning to discover the difference between feeling and emotion. The feeling nature draws our attention toward the invisible, the eternal. Emotion draws us toward the physical and quickly burns us out. The "voice" of God is a feeling, an intuition, a shift, an expansion, an empowerment, a lifting. The feeling nature is a spiritual receiver. Emotion is a physical experience.

In the garden Easter morning, Jesus said to Mary Magdalene, "Why do you weep?" Why are you having a physical experience instead of a spiritual one? I have taught you to be a healer, teacher, transformer, and when I reveal to you the greatest achievement of all, you drop back into the physical/emotional state! "Go, find the disciples and tell them I have risen!" Go to all of your inner faculties and tell them you are now a new being in Christ.

Star Trek - In the transporter room of our inner being, we will dematerialize our limitations and travel unhindered to whatever dimension calls us to explore it. We will truly "go where no one has gone before" because it is not in human form that we go there, but in the essence and expansiveness of our spirituality.

In the consciousness of god-likeness we are offered eternal life, not to be confused with sitting on a cloud playing a harp, but actively exploring God. In Malachi 3:10 it is written, "Put me to the test..." We are invited to test and explore the very dimension of God.

The quote goes on, "...and see if I will not open the windows of heaven..." You will see and co-create heaven everywhere. "...And pour out for you a blessing so great you will not be able to contain it!" You will love this experience with such a vast love that you will have to constantly give it away. This vast love is home.

And so, dear friend, we launch ourselves into the next stage of existence. Revelation called it "the New Jerusalem." Jesus called it "many mansions," or dimensions. The Book of Corinthians calls it "changing from glory into glory." Language as we know it is limited in its ability to express the higher experiences. We try to put Divine revelation into words and explanations. A new language is already emerging. We are creating the words, the mental technology, and the spiritual super highway that carries us inward and upward.

We create the Divine Design of our own being as we go along. You could say that God is fascinated to experience the design through us, as us. God ideated creation and man is the man-ifestor of the Divine Idea in form. Man, in Sanskrit, means hand. Man is the chooser, spearhead, and co-creative partner with God.

We are the hand of God stretching forth through eternity into creation so that God can experience as well as BE. We are always spiritually rooted in our First Home, God Mind, where the light never fails and creation goes on eternally.

How shall we live in this dimension?

We shall remember that all is created in mind with new mental technology. Our usual way of thinking does not take us beyond our present existence. The intellect has its limitations, but our power of imagination has no limits. Our true home is in the realization that we live in God and that can never change. We are at home wherever we are because we are always in God and God is in us.

Open the Gates to the Holy Place

Question: *Who shall be worthy to journey into this Holiness?*

Answer: *One who seeks the keys to the kingdom.*

Welcome to the Gateway of the Keys to the Kingdom

We come into life with a key. At some time in our development we find the door that the key opens and behind that door is a whole universe of Truth.

"...we will all completely awaken together. We will all be changed 'In the twinkling of an eye.' So we are all trying to open those spiritual eyes and get them twinkling together. Once awake we can begin work as co-creators with God, our true vocation." The Divine Design, Lunde.

There are keys that open preliminary doors if we will acknowledge them. My first key was a message from the pulpit that I was created to be the hero of my life, not the victim of it. I could stop thinking of myself as a victim of circumstances and see myself as a hero having experiences that I can turn into blessings. It changed my thinking like a train switching onto a new track.

Another key: I learned that I had what Maurice Nicol called the observer self. There was a higher dimension of awareness that lifted me out of the intellectual into the spiritual. I didn't realize it was a doorway to the spiritual yet, but I was fascinated and continued to contemplate and explore it.

Another key: I lived in my own perceptual world, my own film upon which I could create the movie of my life. I was completely in charge of the kingdom of my own being and I could create the highest and best of my dream by focusing my thoughts.

Another key: To be aware that the usual prayers we are taught, are just intellectual exercises hoping to get the attention and favor of a supposed deity. Focusing my mind on and aligning my thinking with my inner spiritual nature became my prayer. I remember my mother asking me if I prayed to myself. Well yes, but not the physical or psychological self. My prayer was intended to acknowledge my spiritual nature.

The key I was ultimately seeking was "Christ in me, my assurance of Glory" to paraphrase the Apostle Paul. I realized that the Christ, the Christos, is a clear pattern of divinity that informs each one of us. It has no shadow, no darkness, no error. It is the clear Divine being, the image and likeness of the Creator that we are to express. Our task is to live as that inner Divine being and not as the ego centered being of the physical world.

How shall we live in this dimension?

We shall awaken to the signs and clues of our divinity. They are everywhere and anywhere on our life path. The more we become aware of them, the clearer our vision, eventually seeing life as symbols of spiritual events. In this way we learn to spiritually interpret our own lives.

This is about living now, in a larger world than we now see. It is about being involved in a celestial tapestry of our own conscious choosing and yet Divine. It is understanding who, what, and why we are spiritually at any given moment. It is about understanding our greater purpose, our higher nature, and how it all fits together in divine order.

Open the Gates to the Holy Place

Question: *Who shall be worthy to journey into this Holiness?*

Answer: *One who speaks Spiritual Truth to one's own mind.*

Welcome to the Gateway of Lost in God

Myrtle Fillmore claimed she was "Lost in God." She was the co-founder of Unity School of Christianity and Silent Unity. It began with Silent Unity and Myrtle's belief in affirmative prayer. Charles Fillmore was concerned with the day to day business, their three sons had their part in the building of Unity as well. But Myrtle was the prayer worker, the one who constantly explored her relationship to God, her oneness with God. She healed herself of a deadly disease by affirming the spiritual truth of her body, that God created her whole and perfect in every way. She taught this to thousands through her prayers and letters. She considered herself to be lost in God as she prayed, not in or of the physical world. Her son said she was far more comfortable in the spiritual world than she ever was in the physical world.

The last thing we want is to be lost, so we struggle to keep control of everything. Giving everything up to God is scary because most people believe that God's will for them is something they do not want and that it will be imposed upon them. This is not true. Being lost in God is being untethered from the worries and concerns of the day and to rest on the sustaining breath of God. It is a time of joy, healing, and communion with God.

There is no fear or struggle living in the Fourth dimension. We spiritually interpret events rather than emotionally react to them. We rise into a place of blessing where we affirm wholeness for everything we look upon. When we stay in this place of blessing there is no need to go out of it regardless of what appears or happens in the physical world. To step out of it would put one in a place of judgment, vulnerability, fear and all the negative aspects of fear. Once we begin to live in the fourth dimension we never want to leave it. It becomes the only way to live and fully express God. We still function responsibly in the physical world, but our perspective is from a higher understanding where there is only peace.

How shall we live in this dimension?

"I Sought for God" is a poem by James Dillet Freeman, *Prayer The Master Key.*

"Then out of that perfection of mind, a voice said, "Let go of your mind, for myself and yourself must grow to be one.' …Then I gave up myself. Me and mine were no more. That which is more than I stood barefoot, naked, bodiless, mindless, selfless. But where I had been, God was."

We shall choose to experience life from that higher place where all is peace. We become comfortable in the spiritual realm. Whenever a habitual thought of struggle or fear arises, we turn to the spiritual thoughts until they become our habit. Our power resides in the peaceful place and we return to it time and again until we do not leave it for the lower vibrations of ego mind. The ego mind wants to grumble, get bored, think about difficulties and conjures up stories of fear and lack. But instead we do our daily tasks keeping our mind in the spiritual realm of joy.

Joy is the feeling of the spiritual nature. Jesus had joy and came that we might have his joy in us. We learn about that joy in us, how to live in it and find our fulfillment there. We enjoy or infuse our thinking and actions with joy. We rejoice or express gladness. Rejoice in God.

Open the Gates to the Holy Place

Question: *Who shall be worthy to journey into this Holiness?*

Answer: *One who seeks only the Spiritual universe.*

Welcome to the Gateway of Only God

There are many beautiful images that fill books and support error beliefs. Some of them are of angels, guides, entities, and fantasy. There are many books on each and often fill the whole consciousness of one who desires a spiritual path. There is nothing harmful in them so long as we understand they are kinds of thoughts in consciousness. Angels are not floating around in the air coming to us and going away. It is easy to be distracted from our spiritual path by focusing upon them. There is artwork showing angels hovering over children on a bridge ostensibly to protect them. If we believe angels protect us, then when we are injured or in trouble, what then? Did they just fly away to help someone else and leave us vulnerable?

Are there good and bad entities? Many believe so. Race consciousness is filled with every human thought, good or evil. When looking around the world we can see that there is much evil or negativity that seems so powerful. When we begin to believe in entities, we open ourselves to the contents of race mind and invite those influences into our consciousness and experiences. If our thinking is not centered and untrained we can be confused by whatever messages come through. Those who channel entities will advise us not to do that without an experienced trainer. They know the dangers of turning the control of our minds over to something "else." This entity energy can hypnotize us the same as a hypnotist do.

The hypnotist will release the mind, but this other influence from race conscious mind will not. Ouija boards and automatic writing are not to be toyed with. They are serious doorways to race mind which should not be opened by someone believing that these are a spiritual path. They are not.

In a book entitled "The Spear of Destiny" by Ravenscroft, the author surmised that Hitler had opened himself to those evil influences at a broken and vulnerable time in his life. The author said he opened himself to the whole principality of Lucifer. It took him over and did evil in the world through him. So these things are not to be taken lightly. The focus upon the loving God is the only safe course of thought.

That dark principality does not have its existence in God but in human consciousness. God is light, humanity creates its own darkness and it is all stored in race mind. In the beginning God created or ideated, and rested on the seventh day. Humanity takes up creation from then on and our entire human world is made up of everyone's thoughts and perceptions.

The important thing to know is that everything that is not a focus on God is a distraction from our spiritual development. People pray to the angel Michael and other limited images. While it is true that angels are mentioned in the Bible, Jesus did not mention them. Biblical writers wrote about angels to indicate a blessing or a higher state of being. Jesus' entire interface was with God Mind, nothing less.

How shall we live in this dimension?

We shall guard our thinking from all that is not Spiritual Truth, all that is not God, and all that would take control of our thinking and entrap us in error thought. We will not turn to "readings" or forecasts of our future as a guide for our decisions. We will turn within in prayer and trust that we are filled with wisdom, courage, and strength to live our lives from our own spiritual plane, free from any lower influence.

Open the Gates to the Holy Place

Question: *Who shall be worthy to stand in this Holiness?*

Answer: *One who seeks to be pure in heart.*

**"Blessed are the pure in heart, for they shall see God."
(Matthew 5:8).**

Being pure in heart involves having a singleness of heart toward God. The Greek word for "heart" is *kardeeah*. This can be applied to the physical heart, but it also refers to the spiritual center of life. It is where thoughts, desires, sense of purpose, will, understanding, and character reside. A pure heart has no hypocrisy, no guile, no hidden motives. ...an *internal* purity of soul.

Our heart, the deepest and most powerful vibration of our being, is focused and functions in purity with no shadow or trepidation. The pure heart is transparent. The Christos or the clear crystal pattern, is the creation of the Presence and Power of the Most High. The Christ pattern in us is our glory, our Eternal Light.

In Psalm 24:3, "Who shall ascend the hill of the Lord? And who shall stand in his holy place? He who has clean hands and a pure heart, who does not lift up his soul to what is false..." We can only ascend the hill, rise in consciousness, when we are not burdened down with error thinking, self-blame and self-castigation. Many believe the more than hate themselves, the more God will love them. They confess a myriad of "sins" and weep copiously as a sign of repentance. We can only love God as we love ourselves because we are God in action as us. Repentance means to turn our thinking around and return to the Truth of our innocence.

To be pure in heart means to no longer blame ourselves, but to bless ourselves as sacred beings. We are born in original blessing, and innocence is the Christ pattern within us which is pure and without shadow.

How shall we live in this dimension?

We shall no longer blame ourselves for perceived failings. This kind of thinking only creates for us a world of guilt and frustration. We will release error thoughts as they come up and replace them with affirmations of Spiritual Truth. We continue to be diligent in clearing our consciousness of error thinking, and treat ourselves as the sacred beings that we are.

Psalm 51:10, "Create in me a pure heart, O God, and renew a steadfast spirit within me." A Course in Miracles reflects this in stating that God takes the final step for us. The power is there to lift us up when we continue the cleansing of consciousness. It is written that the Apostle Paul said, "I die daily." We die to the error thinking constantly. And to quote the Apostle Paul, "Forgetting what lies behind, and straining forward...I press on toward the goal for the prize of the upward call of God in Christ Jesus."

Open the Gates to the Holy Place

Question: *Who shall be worthy to journey into this Holiness?*

Answer: *One who sees rightly, sees God.*

Welcome to the gateway of Seeing Rightly

Jesus said he saw what the Father was doing and he did likewise. When the disciples asked Jesus to show them the Father, he replied, "When you have seen me you have seen the Father."

In Mark 4:11, when they asked why he taught in parables and figures, he replied that it was given to the disciples to perceive the deeper truth in the teachings. The masses could not see directly, so he spoke to them in stories.

We have been taught to look outward with the eyes at only what is physically obvious and no further. An example is the Apostle Paul when he was blinded on the road to Damascus. Before that he saw only with eyes of hatred and murder. After his sight was restored he changed from Saul to Paul, and began to see the spiritual nature and eternal life in all people. He coined the phrase "Christ in you, your hope of glory."

When we look within to see what God is doing within us, we perceive with spiritual knowing. We see the spiritual nature coming into bloom within us it expresses effortlessly in our experience.

Psalm 91:8 states, "You will only look with your eyes and see the recompense of the wicked." We will see rightly, but not be subject to the challenges that are caused by error thinking. In the Book of Revelation 4:1-2, the voice said to St John the Divine, "come up here, and at once I was in the Spirit…" From then on he was shown and carried over the difficulties that error thinking brings on. He looked upon them but did not experience them.

How shall we live in this dimension?

We shall obey the command to rise in consciousness and to look from above at all things. Dr. Frederick Keeler said our only job is to "look upon and to bless." Ego mind wants to fix things it judges as wrong. We will not lower our consciousness to fix things. Christ mind sees only perfection, which then draws all unto it. Jesus said, If I be lifted up I draw all unto me." And so we shall be lifted up.

Open the Gates to the Holy Place

Question: *Who shall be worthy to journey into this Holiness?*

Answer: *One who knows the Silence*

Welcome to the Gateway of Silence and Light

"The silence to a metaphysician means something more than merely being still and closing the eyes. Silence is prayer. The silent part is merely the way you pray or the attitude. I notice this get-together meeting has acquired in the last year an increased ability to go into the silence and pray with power. You might wonder how I know that. Through many years of prayer and prayer means meditation, and it means the use of your mind interiorly.

"Now most of us use our minds and express ourselves exteriorly, without, but as you develop this inner consciousness you will find you can express your mind interiorly through the power of your thoughts, and through the development of these inner mind forces you can come in touch with other minds and can detect what they are doing in their mental realms, what the power is…when we get together and all agree on a certain mental attitude, we tune in and begin to find that we can change the atmosphere…and if there is someone in the group that is not really getting hold of what we call the silence, one who is trained in this work of using his inner forces can tell it instantly…So let us take for our silent thought: 'I AM THE LIGHT'

"You must become a quickened soul to handle the light. Light represents intelligence, the knowing quality in you…If we are always listening, we never amount to much, we must be generators. There is a dynamic quality in every one of us and using that dynamic power we have better understanding, better light. That is what we are all striving for, to get into the light and our generator, your thought is generating 'Christ thought. Let us begin to say, "Let there be light!"' (Charles Fillmore, Co-Founder of Unity)

Charles Fillmore sat in the silence for hours at a time. His granddaughter said that when as a child she was ill, he would come and sit by her bedside in silence throughout the night. In the morning her illness would be gone. Her school mates asked her if they ever called a doctor. She replied, "No, we just call my grandfather."

The silence is where we clear away all the outer influences, so we can discern the power of Truth coming forth in us. Jean Auel, author of The Clan of the Cave Bear and other books, wrote fiction about humanity in its earliest stages, when population of the earth was very sparse. Language was a series of hand motions and grunts. There was silence except for the murmurs and animal calls of nature. This is a huge contrast with today's world where one can hardly find a place of silence except in deep underground caves or man-made structures where there is sound proofing. We cannot depend upon outer silence in our environment, but we can depend upon inner silence to do our spiritual listening.

How shall we live in this dimension?

We shall "Be still and know that I am God." Sometimes we just use the words "be still and know." Knowing is not reasoning, but being in the state. We quiet the inner chatter as much as possible in order to be still. The human mind is set up to constantly think, chatter, figure stuff out, worry, and be fearful. It truly never becomes completely quiet, but we can turn our attention away from it.

Centering Prayer is a method of being in the silence for a period of time and using one word as a reminder to return to God when the chatter wants our attention. Choose a word that does not remind you of other things. I chose the Hebrew word Ahava because it means love, but the different language does not trigger anything else in my mind. You shall find your word that returns you to silence and God.

Open the Gates to the Holy Place

Question: *Who shall be worthy to journey into this Holiness?*

Answer: *One who goes into the courts of the Lord and goes no more out.*

Welcome to the Gateway of Staying the Course

The greatest temptation is to allow the mind to wander in to areas that are limiting and do not serve your spiritual growth. Someone said, "Where you mind goes, your behind goes." Our actions always follow our thoughts and emotions. We are accustomed to constantly allowing our minds to be distracted by outer things. The outer world has been our primary influence since birth.

Now as we become aware that we are first spiritual beings, we seek to live in that spiritual consciousness even more completely than we have lived in the physical world. We discover the tremendous power of God within us as we align with that fourth-dimension consciousness and vibration. We cannot align with it just sometimes, or intermittently, and receive a reliable flow. We know when a car is sputtering and running rough, the power is not there to carry it forward. When the car runs smoothly, all the power is available for our use.

In James 1:17, "In God there is no turning, no shadow." God as Principle is constant. There is no change or weakening in Principle. Principles of health, abundance, wisdom, and life never change. We turn from them when we deviate from perfection through our error thinking.

Our job is to train the mind to stay on course. We allow conversations among others to lull us into their conscious state. Their conversations are mostly about problems, being victims, and judging others. We also need to be aware when our inner self talk is chattering. What is it saying? Usually it is going over the past, problems and general useless stuff. We learn to catch this chatter immediately and refocus the mind on productive spiritual thinking as we create a fourth dimensional consciousness.

How shall we live in this dimension?

We shall train the mind to stay on course. These Epistles of Paul and his scribes are about staying the course. His churches constantly wandered off course because there was such a powerful influence of different cultures and beliefs. He wrote to them and visited them. When he realized that Jesus was not returning in the foreseeable future, he began to teach them to grow in spirit instead of waiting for an outer event.

Ephesians 4:23 "...be renewed in the spirit of your minds, and put on the new nature, created after the likeness of God in true righteousness and holiness.

Philippians 4:8 "...whatever is true, whatever is honorable, whatever is just, whatever is pure, whatever is lovely, whatever is gracious, if there be any excellence, if there is anything worthy of praise, think about these things."

Colossians 2:16 "...let no one pass judgment on you...let no one disqualify you insisting upon self-abasement and worship of angels..."

Colossians 3:12 "Put on then, as God's chosen ones, holy and beloved, compassion, kindness, meekness (be teachable) and patience."

Open the Gates to the Holy Place

Question: *Who shall be worthy to journey into this Holiness?*

Answer: *One who sees only Wholeness.*

Welcome to the Gateway of Wholeness

There is no need for healing at the spiritual level. Everything is created from a Divine Idea of the Creator, which has no flaws, no shadow, no darkness. If the body were not spiritually perfect, healing could not take place. That which needs healing is a flaw in our thinking that causes malformations in the body and affairs. But the perfect pattern is always there to draw us back to our original perfection.

When people asked Jesus to heal them, he didn't see the illness or deformity, he saw their innate perfection and with his powerful vision of the Truth of their being, brought forth their perfection to manifest in their bodies. He said we could do the same and even greater things than he did.

Metaphysicians have been proving that all is mind. Phineas Parkhurst Quimby, first metaphysician in the United States, helped people heal themselves by drawing their attention away from their problem to focus instead upon a story he was telling them. He learned about the mind from Mesmer, who created mesmerizing or hypnosis. Mary Baker Eddy was a patient of Quimby's and carried on a spiritual work of her own.

All cells in our bodies are programmed to reproduce themselves identically. There is no illness or aging in the cells. Only thought can interfere with their reproduction and change them. Believing in "time and space will make us old, makes our cells slow down. We need spiritual energy for our cells. I am free from the limitations of time and space." (Charles Fillmore, Co-founder of Unity)

This is Charles Fillmore's lesson about letting the mind wander into illness:

"Letting go of sense consciousness and realizing that every cell and atom in our body temples are renewed and that we are eternally youthful. That doesn't mean the beauty of being sixteen, it means spiritual youth.

"The very cells of our bodies are loaded with qualities that, released, would bring us into a new vibration or a new body-energy."

How shall we live in this dimension?

We shall live in the dimension of mind, the key. The Truth is we are already whole and free of error. Mind is the only connection to God, Spirit, the Divine Cosmic Creator. There is no anthropomorphic god in the sky judging us and dabbling in our life experiences. There is only our perfect alignment in mind with Higher Mind, God Mind, that brings forth the perfection of creation into our experience.

We shall remember that our youth, our health, and wisdom are already within us. We are created whole and complete with everything we need to co-create a lifetime on planet Earth and the spiritual body for eternity.

Amen

It seemed like forever had gone by when Becky and Georgina finished the booklet. They sat together in silence for a long time not even sure what day it was. Everyone else was gone and the place was quiet. It was dark outside.

"I think we have come home at last or as close as we can be to it," whispered Becky.

"I think we have, and it feels wonderful," returned Georgina.

"Let's go back to the college and get things ready for our students. It should be a fabulous year and I can't wait to meet them!"

"I need to be sure they tuned the piano. I can't play celestial music out of tune!"

Mom and Pop's was still open and they were hungry. The booth in the back was waiting for them. Everything seemed comfortable and normal, and yet everything was somehow different.

☎ 2922666   **PIZZA EXPRESS** ЛЕНИНГРАД   ☎ 2922666   **PIZZA EXPRESS** ЛЕНИНГРАД

Доставка: 10.00—02.00	Toimitus: 10.00—02.00	Delivery: 10.00—02.00

Заказчик:
Nimi:
Name:

Адрес:
Osoite:
Adress: *Литейный пр. 42   Zunde*

Номер телефона:
Puhelin:
Telephone:

Замечания:
Huom:
Notes:

Заказ	Tilaus	Order

10 Vegetariana
10 special
30 кока
20 sprite
3 Mineral water

Время
Klo
Time _____

19.10.91

Fim 1216,0

us $ 294-64
214.64

Напитки Валюта:
Valuutta:
Currency:

Кредитные карточки:
Luottokortti:
Credit cards:

Столовые приборы:
Ruokailuvälineet:
Knife & fork:

Ресторан: ул. Подольская д. 23   Ravintola: Podolskaya 23   Restaurant: Podolskaja 23
Открыт: 10.00—23.00   Auki: 10—23   Open: 10—23

Если Вы не довольны обслуживанием, сообщите нам по телефону 292-02-17 с 14.00 до 17.00.

Jos et olut tyytyväinen saamaasi palveluun, ota yhteys ravintolapäällikköön 19—19, 292 0217.

To express your wishes, please call us 292-02-17 from 6 p.m. to 7 p.m. Monday—Friday

Printed in the United States
By Bookmasters